RENEWALS 458-4574,
DATE DUE

WITHDRAWN
UTSA Libraries

CRITICAL
Confrontations

CRITICAL
Confrontations

LITERARY THEORIES IN DIALOGUE

Meili Steele

UNIVERSITY OF SOUTH CAROLINA PRESS

© 1997 University of South Carolina

Published in Columbia, South Carolina, by the
University of South Carolina Press

Manufactured in the United States of America

01 00 99 98 97   5 4 3 2 1

Library of Congress Cataloging-in-Publication Data

Steele, Meili, 1949–
   Critical confrontations : literary theories in
dialogue / Meili Steele.
      p. cm.
   Includes bibliographical references (p.) and index.
   ISBN 1–57003–141–X (cloth). — ISBN 1–57003–161–4 (paper)
   1. Criticism. 2. Critical theory. I. Title.
PN98.S6S74 1997
801'.95'09045—dc20   96–25249

Library
University of Texas
at San Antonio

Contents

CRITICAL
Confrontations

Introduction

The thesis of this book is that the dominant paradigms of contemporary critical theory block out rather than enable the analysis of gender, race, and difference that lies at the heart of today's cultural reflection. The key problem of contemporary theory is that it has developed elaborate schemes for examining the marginalization and oppression of cultural voices, but it has not offered theories to empower these voices or ethical/political ideals to guide multicultural conversation. Frustrated with disempowering theories, the marginalized have abandoned the strictures of poststructuralism to speak about their experience and traditions so that we see the flourishing of what Eve Sedgwick calls the phenomenon of minicanons.[1] The critical terrain is thus divided into the poststructuralist camp, which exposes the operations of discursive power that work behind the back of the subject, and those who defend the self-understanding and value of cultural traditions.[2] What has been missing is a defense of the idea of tradition as a theoretical problematic and a recuperation of democratic ideals. The result has been the growth of alternative traditions without a satisfying theoretical and political articulation of what a tradition-based view of language looks like and how such a view could get along with theories that are designed to cut against the grain of traditions, such as poststructuralism.[3] The goal of this book is to broaden the interpretive space of critical theory so that tradition-based views of language can talk to antihumanistic theories in the context of democratic ethical/political ideals.[4]

In addition, I hope that this book will serve an important pedagogical function not served by the numerous "introductions to theory" that are now available. There certainly are many books that attempt to explain and apply critical theory, and they fall into two general types—the Raman Selden type and the Terry Eagleton type.[5] The Selden type gives a descriptive encyclopedia entry on each critical school and then an application to a poem or story. The author does not articulate his view or create a space for comparison or assessment. The reader is given no way to examine the conflicting claims of different paradigms, such as structuralism and hermeneutics, or explore how they might talk to each other. We simply move from one approach to the next, and the student is given the impression that he/she can use theories as if they had no consequences for the user.

The Eagleton type tells a story from a definite point of view, in which we get a page or two of exposition and then a critique from the perspective of the author, which is Marxist in Eagleton's case. My book is like the Eagletonian survey in that there is elementary exposition of the key ideas from a definite theoretical position that permits assessment. However, unlike Eagleton, I am writing a story of interpretation from inside the position I am defending. Eagleton takes a Marxist position, but he never discusses the problems in the history of Marxists.[6] The result is that he brings in a vague notion of social liberation to assess the worth of a particular theory. In this way, he avoids putting his own cards on the table, avoids filling out the interpretive view from which he tells the story. My hope for this book is that the reader will emerge with an understanding of what the major interpretive problematics are, what the challenges to these positions have been, what the strengths and weaknesses of these different theories are, and how these theories can dialogue with each other to meet our current demands for democratic interpretation. Moreover, I want to foreground the consequences of these theories for the self-understanding of the reader.

To realize these goals, I will have a much narrower focus than a survey book. No one can hope to survey the diversity of theories that exist. Even a book that tried to cover only one critical concern, such as feminist theories or postcolonial theories, would be difficult to write. Instead, I will be covering basic critical paradigms and telling a progressive story about them.

In chapter 1, I begin this story in two steps. First, there is a backward look, in which I lay out the influential interpretive paradigms that preceded current debates. I begin with a brief discussion of the Enlightenment (especially Kant), since its conflicted legacy has been one of the crucial concerns of contemporary theory. I then move to modern examples of this legacy, contrasting the interpretive assumptions that inform the debate between the New Critics and E. D. Hirsch with the assumptions that inform the hermeneutics of Martin Heidegger and Hans-Georg Gadamer. These philosophers open an important understanding of the relationships among language, history, and interpretation, an understanding that overthrows the scientific paradigm of knowledge, which continues to impoverish culture and theory today. A critical theory that merely deconstructs New Criticism without offering an alternative philosophical horizon leaves students inarticulate about the relationship of language to knowledge. This is not to say that the hermeneutic views are without problems but that the treatment of hermeneutics found in most theory books either ignores or dismisses it.[7] In the second part of the chapter, I take a forward look, in which I assess the strengths and weaknesses of Gadamer's view in light of our current theoretical interests. I pursue this forward look through a reading of Susan Glaspell's "A Jury of Her Peers," a story that dramatizes the needs of contemporary cultural interpretation.

Chapter 2 examines two challenges to tradition-based interpretation: structuralism (Saussure, Barthes, and others) and social theory (Jürgen Habermas).

Both of these approaches insist that we need an explanation (structural and causal, respectively) to supplement our interpretation of texts. In the first half of the chapter, I introduce the structuralist project, principally through the work of Saussure, and then look at two philosophers who respond to it in very different ways: Paul Ricoeur, who grafts it onto his hermeneutics, and Mikhail Bakhtin, who rejects it. Since Bakhtin's work offers the most sophisticated philosophy of language for the consideration of literary texts, I enrich my exposition of his ideas with a Bakhtinian reading of Ralph Ellison's "Flying Home." In the second half of the chapter, I look at the challenge to tradition-based dialogue proposed by the social theory of Habermas. I then offer an answer to Habermas by drawing on Bakhtin's theory and Glaspell's story.

Chapter 3 addresses poststructuralist views of language. My account shows both their power to expose the hidden oppression in humanistic and hermeneutic accounts of language and their omission of the new self-understanding that must emerge from any critique. I begin with Jacques Derrida's development of Heidegger and structuralism and show how his critique of language can used to enrich our understanding of Toni Morrison's *Playing in the Dark*. In the second half of the chapter, I analyze the debate between Jean-François Lyotard and Habermas over the nature of language and the genealogical critique of Michel Foucault. I conclude with a brief summation of the argument to this point. This will prepare the way for chapters 4 and 5, which address arguments among feminist and postcolonial theorists.

Chapter 4 opens with a mapping of the liberal, gynocentric, and constructivist positions in feminist theories. I then critique and appropriate aspects of each of these positions through a reading of the work of Nancy Fraser, bell hooks, Seyla Benhabib, and Jessica Benjamin. Their works exemplify the kind of interpretive moves required to fill the needs of feminist theory today. They offer women the possibility of solidarity without essentialism, a way to recuperate as well as to critique Enlightenment political ideals, and a capacity to tell stories of agency to accompany stories of oppression. I highlight the advantage of their work by showing the failure of "strategic essentialism" before concluding the chapter with an analysis of Marie Cardinal's novel *The Words to Say It*, in which the theoretical conclusions of the chapter are brought to bear on the controversial story of a woman's emergence from madness during the course of her psychoanalytic treatment.

Chapter 5 looks at interpretation and global politics through a contrast between Edward Said's politics of exile and Cornel West's politics of rootedness. In the first half of the chapter, I focus on Said's highly acclaimed *Culture and Imperialism*, which performs what he calls a "contrapuntal" interpretation, in which stories of imperialism are juxtaposed against stories of resistance. The stories of imperialism expose the ways that narratives and values that inform the great traditions of British, French, and American cultures have been complicitous with imperialism. The stories of resistance take up the work of such thinkers as Aimé Césaire, Frantz Fanon, and C. L. R. James, thinkers who transcend any narrow and reactive nationalism for a politics of liberation. Such a politics recognizes that the stories of the world overlap and that cultural hybridity is a resource. The problem is that Said refuses to recuperate the traditions and values he wants to advance, to give himself a theoretical as well as ethical/political location. "Tradition" and "culture" appear only in stories of exposure but never in stories of retrieval.

West provides a theoretical contrast to Said, even though the two share many of the same political goals. For West, critics need to attend to the traditions in which they are rooted and from which they draw their nurturance. To deprive people of their traditions in theory or practice is particularly damaging for those who have been marginalized and dominated by the reigning cultures. Moreover, rootedness does not necessarily lead to the political pathologies of ethnocentrism or nationalism, which is Said's great fear; rather, our positioning in cultural traditions is the position from which we think of ourselves in a democratic community. The claims of traditions are mediated by the democratic norms that shape multicultural dialogue.

This book does not assume a prior knowledge of theory. However, it does have a progressive structure that builds on what comes before. It advances and then circles back in order to remind the reader of connections and to make comparisons. My goal is to create a space for metatheoretical dialogue among the different theories. Needless to say, I am forced to be selective in the works I discuss by each author. In the notes, I refer the reader to full-scale treatments of each figure.

1

The Background to Contemporary Interpretation

TWO CONFLICTING PARADIGMS

In order to understand the arguments in contemporary theory, we need some "background." The problem is that the way one constructs this background depends on the position one takes in the arguments. My way around this circle will be to state my reasons for my construction and to introduce other ways of reading the past as we encounter them. I will locate the background in two places: in the argument between New Critics and the historical intentionalist E. D. Hirsch, and in the radically new understanding of interpretation proposed by Martin Heidegger and Gadamer. What unites Hirsch and the New Critics and separates them from Heidegger and Gadamer is a shared understanding of the Enlightenment's scientific paradigm for knowledge.[1] In fact, the question of how to understand this legacy informs all the thinkers that I will discuss in the book, and I will return to it in subsequent chapters. My exposition of the well-known dispute between Hirsch and the New Critics will be short, simple, and schematic. I will sacrifice the nuances and complexities of this American debate to the mapping of the fundamental assumptions in their methods, assumptions that I will then contrast with those of Heidegger and Gadamer. These philosophers show how the Enlightenment tradition of inquiry, which still dominates American culture, has prevented us from understanding how we are first and foremost beings in and through language, not the objects of scientific explanation. Scientific practices are secondary to, get their sense from, the more primordial linguistic self-understandings of a culture. This view will be a thread that we follow all the way through the book as it undergoes challenges from various fronts. In the second half of the chapter, I will apply Gadamer's hermeneutics to Susan Glaspell's "A Jury of Her Peers." This application will reveal some of the complications and controversies surrounding Gadamer's work and flush out the concerns of those who are suspicious of hermeneutics. I selected this work precisely because it is the kind of text that Gadamer's critics might use, for it is not in "the tradition," and it thematizes the issue of power.

5

New Criticism

New Criticism is an excellent example of the conflicted legacy of the Enlightenment in the twentieth century. The five characteristics of New Criticism pertinent to hermeneutics are the following: (1) the distinction between literary and scientific knowledge; (2) the distinction between literary language and ordinary language; (3) the definition of the form and being of the work of art; (4) New Criticism's understanding of history; and (5) the connection between the claim about the nature of the work and the normative claim about a good work.

New Critics struggle to establish the autonomy of literary knowledge and value, but they remain prisoners of the presuppositions of the preeminent Enlightenment philosopher, Immanuel Kant. In his three critiques, Kant sought to mark out separate spheres for reason in science, ethics, and aesthetics.[2] To do this, he developed his famous transcendental mode of argument, which seeks to establish the logical conditions that make claims possible in each of these three spheres. In looking to our subjective reason as the source of validation, Kant breaks with premodern views, from Plato to the Enlightenment, that seek to ground philosophies of our position in the universe by reference to external conditions—the order of the universe, tradition, myth, and religion.[3] For Plato and Aristotle, for example, truth is not narrowly focused on the prediction and manipulation of the world but on our attunement to the order of the universe, an order that offers a telos for us and all things. A good life is a life that is true to the order of things inside and outside us. Thus truth, goodness, and beauty are not separate or subjective. The Renaissance idea of the world as a text written by God continues, in Christian form, this connection between truth and the telos of humanity. With Enlightenment, truth is separated from any teleological view of the world or humanity's position in it. The truth about nature is revealed through scientific causality, which is mechanical and impersonal. Speculation about the first or final causes of the world is a religious and not a scientific matter. As Kant says, "I found it necessary to deny knowledge in order to make room for faith" (1965, 29). When we want truth, we go to scientists, not poets or religious leaders.

Moral reason requires an entirely separate point of view on humanity's place in the universe, a point of view that removes us from the scientific world of causality and offers us freedom: "When we think of ourselves as free, we transfer ourselves [from the world of phenomena] into the intelligible world [supersensible world] as members and recognize the autonomy of the will together with its consequence—morality" (Kant 1964, 121). Morality can rely on no external source such as the church; instead, it is deduced from necessary and universal conditions established by reason.[4] Morality is separated from desire and the narratives of everyday life and made to fit the form of impersonal maxims, which Kant called the "categorical imperative."

Aesthetics requires its own sphere, one that is concerned with neither truth nor morality but beauty. Aesthetic judgments are disinterested and based on pleasure. This pleasure does not refer to an object but to the harmonious play of our mental faculties. Beauty refers to the internal order of the object, not its function, so that an aesthetic object has its own mode of being that separates it from the utilitarian considerations that inform our relationship to other human constructs.

Many philosophers and critics who followed Kant—such as the Romantics in England and Germany and important hermeneutical thinkers such as Wilhelm Dilthey—rejected the idea that art (the humanities) made no claim to knowledge, but they did so not by taking on the assumptions that underwrite scientific inquiry but by establishing a separate domain for literary truth that left science alone. This distinction was institutionalized in the opposition between the human sciences (*Geisteswissenschaften*) and the natural sciences (*Naturwissenschaften*). We see the anguish of this split in departments of social science such as psychology and political science. Some researchers in these departments treat human behavior with explanatory methods modeled on natural sciences, while others insist that the "data" of social science cannot avoid the hermeneutical point that humans are self-interpreting linguistic beings.[5]

The New Critics found themselves caught in this opposition. They preserved much of the Kantian structure by isolating "literary knowledge" from scientific knowledge and by consigning literary truth to the internal world of the subject. As Cleanth Brooks and Austin Warren say, "Scientific precision can be brought to bear only on certain kinds of materials. . . . Poetry . . . also represents the specialization of language for the purpose of precision; but it aims at treating kinds of materials differently from science" (xxxvii). These materials—"attitudes, feelings and interpretation"—have the status of eternal truths. They are universals of human nature just as scientific laws are. The New Critics thus move the province of literary truth to the subjective realm of human nature.[6]

The New Critics do not oppose literary truth simply to the experimental truth of science but also to the truth of everyday conversation. They base their claim for the distinctiveness of literature not on the nature of language in general but on literary language, which they oppose to "ordinary" linguistic usage. Literary values such as truth and beauty, among others, unlike scientific value or the value of conversation, are inseparable from the language in which they are stated. This is what Cleanth Brooks calls the "heresy of paraphrase."[7] Literature's special status legitimizes the development of a special vocabulary for describing the properties of poems and the establishment of standards of interpretation. The appropriate response to such grand beings as poems is not to reduce them to authorial intentions in the way that we do in ordinary communication. As William K. Wimsatt and Monroe Beardsley say in their classic essay "The Intentional Fallacy," "Poetry differs from practical messages, which are successful if and only if we correctly infer the intention" (5). Here we see how the distinctiveness of literature as language and knowledge is connected to the idea of intention. Wimsatt and Beardsley do not so much want to attack intention as they want to set aside the practice of determining the intention from biographical information, a practice that, in their view, ignores the literariness of literature and literary truthfulness.

The New Critics' ideas about the autonomy of the work and its formal integrity draw on the Kantian legacy as well. The closure of the literary work is a formal and semantic principle of self-determination. The work establishes its own purpose or telos.[8] This does not simply mean that no text is reducible to utilitarian function; rather, the claim is that the work has a being/meaning separate from other linguistic and nonlinguistic products.

The New Critics' claim about literariness is often cited as evidence that they read ahistorically—that is, not only is the author's intention irrelevant, but so are the historical circumstances at the time of writing. Instead, as Gerald Graff says, we should see them as working "within the view of history held at their time. This view reduced history to background and saw only an extrinsic connection between history and literature. The New Critics followed the historians in thinking of literary history as at best a body of preliminary information that, however indispensable, could be set aside once the would-be explicator had done a minimal amount of homework" (1987, 183). Literary history became largely an internal matter of the works themselves. Indeed, René Wellek and Austin Warren's highly influential *Theory of Literature* divides literary study according to the distinction between intrinsic and extrinsic approaches.[9] Cleanth Brooks says, "Even where we know a great deal about the author's personality and ideas, we rarely know as much as the poem itself can tell us about itself" (cited in Graff 1987, 190). Here we see again how New Criticism's commitment to literature's ontological distinctiveness informs its view of history. Moreover, New Critics are not interested in thematizing their historical distance from a work. They do not say whether they are offering a historical interpretation or a modern interpretation. Instead, they focus on the internal structure of the story, emphasizing the internal cohesion of its parts, the universality of its themes, and the unparaphrasability of its language. The result is what Gadamer calls "aesthetic consciousness," which helps create the impoverished interpretive culture of the museum, in which we ignore the specifics of the original context and the work's truth for the present in order to preserve a "pure" work of art.[10]

The poetics of New Criticism is also bound up with the issue of value. Tying a text to a historical context would undermine its universality and hence its value. Brooks says that criticism had "to be distinguished from scholarship of the history of ideas, for the obvious reason that the historian of ideas may find just as much to explain in a poor and unsuccessful poem as a good poem. . . . for a round up of sources will never tell us what a poet has done with them" (1962, 106–7). Keeping poetry distinct from other writing meant that poets of ideas—Milton, Wordsworth, Blake—went down in value, while poets who worked with images and symbols went up in value—for example, T. S. Eliot's demotion of Milton and his elevation of the Metaphysicals. New Criticism was not self-conscious about this relationship between theoretical claims and their normative ones—that is, the New Critics do not discuss the relationship of their claims about the nature of poetry ("this is what poetry is") to their claims about what good poetry is. Contemporary theorists, who are so conscious of the inseparability of fact and value, still run normative and ontological claims together in an unsatisfactory way, as we will see.

Hirsch

In his two major works, *Validity in Interpretation* and *The Aims of Interpretation*, Hirsch responds to the New Critical idea that the work of literature has distinctive properties that set it off from other forms of discourse and detach it from the author's intention. Hirsch fears relativism coming not only from New Criticism but from Gadamer's hermeneutics, which in Hirsch's view confuses readers' responses to a work with its meaning. Hirsch seeks to establish a means of validating interpretation, and the touchstone for validity is the author's meaning. Meaning for Hirsch is something that the author wills in choosing a language to represent meaning: "The interpreter's primary task is to reproduce in himself the author's 'logic,' his attitudes, his cultural givens, in short his world. . . . [T]he ultimate verificative principle is very simple—the imaginative reconstruction of the speaking subject" (1967, 242). If Hirsch works to deny the distinctiveness of literary language, he also works against the "linguistic turn" initiated by Heidegger and Ludwig Wittgenstein that now dominates contemporary theory, in which language articulates being. For Hirsch, "Meaning is an affair of consciousness, not words" (4). Hirsch sides with the phenomenology of Edmund Husserl against Heidegger and Gadamer. For Husserl and Hirsch, the intentional structure of consciousness is deeper than language.

In Hirsch's view, the author's meaning must be unchanging if there is to be any objectivity (1967, 214), and the interpreter must leap over time and culture to rediscover this meaning. Hirsch wants to dispel the claims of "the skeptical historicist [who] infers too much from the fact that present-day experiences, categories, and modes of thought are not the same as those of the past. He [this historicist] concludes that we can only understand a text in *our* own terms, but this is a contradictory statement since verbal meaning has to be construed in its own terms if it is to be construed at all" (135).

Hirsch stakes out positions on the three dimensions of hermeneutics—understanding, explanation, and application—that reinforce these views. David Hoy describes the distinction between "understanding" and "explanation" in traditional hermeneutic theory: "The former notion refers to the construction of the text's meaning in its own terms, while the latter refers to the explanation of the meaning, perhaps in terms different from those in the text, but more familiar to the interpreter and his audience" (1978, 14).[11] The third dimension, "application," is the way the text under consideration speaks to the present.

Hirsch argues for keeping these three dimensions distinct: "[T]here is clearly a sense in which we can neither evaluate a text nor determine what it means 'to us, today' until we have correctly apprehended what it means" (1967, 209). "Understanding," what he calls "meaning," is what the author meant to say. "Explanation" (what he calls "interpretation") still aims at this common core of meaning established by understanding: "We could not possibly recast a text's meanings in different terms unless we had already understood the text in its own" (134). "Application," what he calls "significance," is a distinct affair. Hirsch gives a restricted definition of "significance" (application), for it is crucial to his project to isolate this subjective and variable element from the objective and stable component. He names this variable element "judgment" and "criticism" and says that the object of these is not the work's "meaning" but its "significance"—that is, "any perceived relationship between construed verbal meaning and something else" (140). "Significance" may be the meaning's "relation to ourselves, to history, to the author's personality" (143). If we stage *Measure for Measure* as a play about the issues of gender and power, we should not confuse this "significance" of the work with Shakespeare's meaning. Hirsch's argument is directed at Gadamer, as he says in his review of Gadamer's major work, *Truth and Method*: "The fundamental distinction overlooked by Gadamer is that between the meaning of a text and the significance of that meaning for the present situation" (255). Before discussing Gadamer, however, it would be beneficial to consider the philosopher who challenged and transformed the scientific paradigm within which Hirsch and the New Critics work: Heidegger.

Heidegger

Heidegger's *Being and Time* is concerned not with literary texts but with revising the ways that we think about ourselves and the world, and he attacks the Kantian division of modes inquiry that informs much of the history of philosophy and literary theory through Hirsch and the New Critics. One of Heidegger's central claims is that "understanding" is not just one kind of knowing—for example, as opposed to explaining or making aesthetic judgments.[12] Rather, understanding is the power to grasp one's own possibilities for being within the context of the everyday world in which one exists. Understanding is not something possessed but a constituent element of our being-in-the-world. All scientific culture is derivative of this primordial sense of understanding that makes us who we are.

Heidegger's aim is to change the epistemological paradigm of science that dominates modern life. In this view, subject stands over against objects and seeks to gain knowledge by methodological investigation of the properties of these objects. For Heidegger, the scientific attempt to step back and examine an object severs it from its living context, which we already understand before attempting to isolate an object. Mind and world are not ontologically separate, and there is no space of reflection into which we can step back and examine the mind. Heidegger abandons the old vocabulary of "subject" and inaugurates his own notion, *Dasein:* "Self and world belong together in the single entity Dasein. Self and world are not two beings, like subject and object;. . . Self and world are the basic determination of Dasein, the unity of the structure of being-in-world" (1962, 297). According to this view of understanding, the subject does not use its categories to dissect an object; rather, subject and object emerge together within the horizon of cultural practices that make up our preunderstandings. We cannot step outside these practices. Our understanding is situated in history. Our being is in time. For Heidegger, the future is privileged over the past and the present, for we are "thrown" into the world; we are "ahead of ourselves" since we are projected toward our possibilities.[13]

Heidegger does not deny the value of scientific practices but rather makes them less fundamental than our everyday interaction, not vice versa: "The kind of dealing which is closest to us is . . . not a bare perceptual cognition, but rather that kind of concern which manipulates things and puts them to use" (1962, 95). Heidegger gives the example of hammering in a workshop. The carpenter does not see an object with certain properties (as an object of perception and knowledge); rather, the hammer is part of the project of carpentry: "The less we just stare at the hammer-thing, and the more we seize hold of it and use it, the more primordial does our relationship to it become, and the more unveiledly is it encountered as that which it is—as equipment" (98). Only when the hammer breaks does the carpenter step back and examine it.

What this means is that our understanding of the world does not get in touch with raw data outside our human practices; rather, it is shot through with our preunderstandings. Heidegger proposes a hermeneutic circle to replace the epistemological paradigm in which the subject analyzes an ontologically distinct object: "Any interpretation which is to contribute understanding, must already have understood what is to be interpreted. This is a fact that has always been remarked, even if only in the areas of derivative ways of understanding. . . . In a scientific proof, we may not presuppose what it is our task to provide grounds for. But if interpretation must already operate in that which is understood, and if it must draw its nurture from this, how is it to bring any scientific results to maturity without moving in a circle, especially if, moreover, the understanding which is presupposed still operates without our common information about man and the world? Yet according to the most elementary rules of logic, this circle is *circulus vitiosus*" (1962, 194). (This circle is often expressed in terms of the following paradox: to understand the parts, one needs a knowledge of the whole; to understand the whole, one needs a knowledge of the parts.) However, it is vicious only if the ideal of knowledge is scientific objectivity. If we are aware of Heidegger's new way of thinking of ourselves, the question becomes how to come to terms with our practices in a fruitful way, not how to escape from them in order to grab hold of the truth: "But if we see this circle as a vicious one and look out for ways of avoiding it, even if we just 'sense' it as an inevitable imperfection, then the act of understanding has been misunderstood from the ground up. . . . What is decisive is not to get out of the circle but to come into it in the right way" (194–95).

Heidegger's remark applies to both New Critics and Hirsch, for they both try to continue the epistemological fight to make claims to knowledge stand outside the hermeneutic circle. For Hirsch, the critic can and should abstract himself/herself from the historical practices of the moment and go back to find a distinct verbal object that is isolatable. The New Critics' acceptance of this scientific paradigm appears in their conception of the poem as aesthetic object, in their acceptance of the isolation of literature from claims to truth, and in their abstraction of the text and the reader's activity from historical traditions.

Heidegger's argument in *Being and Time* against the scientific paradigm retains the transcendental dimension of philosophy initiated by Kant, in which the conditions of the possibility for things are sought. However, Heidegger wants to investigate the nature of Being and our being in the world rather than the necessary presuppositions of science. While Kant works in a tradition that throws our everyday experience into doubt and that deduces what must be the case if we are to know what we know, Heidegger gives us back our daily existence, so to speak, by seeking out not the necessary categories of understanding but the basic structures of Dasein, what he calls "existentials."[14]

Heidegger argues that his understanding of Being is "more primordial" than the understanding offered by preceding philosophers. In doing so, he makes a "transcendental argument," an argument made famous by Kant. Such arguments, in the words of Charles Taylor, "start from some feature of our experience which they claim to be indubitable and beyond cavil. They then move to a stronger conclusion, one concerning the nature of the subject or his position in the world. They make this move by a regressive argument, to the effect that this stronger conclusion must be so if the indubitable fact about experience is to be possible (and being so, it must be possible)" (1978–79, 151). This kind of argument claims that preceding thinkers have been so massively off course in their conceptions of the fundamentals about the nature of the subject, language, interpretation, Being, and related concepts that it is pointless to argue within their vocabularies. Instead, we need a new vocabulary to redescribe ourselves. Kant called his own radical redescription a "Copernican Revolution." This kind of argument is important for our study because all the figures examined in the first three chapters make such a claim.

Unlike Kant, however, Heidegger does not conduct a deductive logical argument designed to correct and further scientific practices of the time. Instead, he tries to persuade us that the existing vocabulary of science and daily life leaves out or obscures basic features that are opened up by the new vocabulary he is offering—for example, Dasein. The integrity of his argument depends on the use of a vocabulary that breaks with a way of talking that provided the standards for what constitutes an argument. This rather technical analysis is important for understanding the way debates in contemporary theory take place and for grasping the motivation for their obscure vocabularies. One of the reasons contemporary theory is so difficult to read is that many critical theorists have followed Heidegger's style of argument, in which a new vocabulary for talking about the most basic features of texts or existence is introduced—for example, Jacques Derrida's "différance." The result is that theorists have so many different ways of talking that they cannot point to "this" or "that" issue and have an argument. Since their differences are about entire packages of beliefs, they do not share enough assumptions to make a common object of argument come into view. Many philosophers maintain that Heidegger, as well as some other thinkers we will study, such as Derrida, are making not philosophical arguments but speculative, poetic statements.[15]

Because Heidegger is making a transcendental claim about Dasein, he produces a universal portrait of humanity. As Hubert Dreyfus says, Heidegger's "demonstration is 'transcendental' since it does not discuss what it means to be a human being in a specific culture or historical period but attempts to lay out the characteristics of self-interpreting being which apply to all times and places" (70). Needless to say, the fact that Heidegger's discussion of Dasein is not inflected by considerations of gender, race, class, history, or age has not gone unnoticed. Moreover, Heidegger's privileging of our preunderstandings, of our deep embedding in practices and tradition, and his later, more radical critique of modernity have led to an enormous controversy over the relationship between his philosophy and his personal connection with Nazism.[16] Although I will not get into the Heidegger controversy specifically, I will deal with the connection between ontology and politics, which surfaces both in the Gadamer-Habermas debate (chapter 2) and in poststructuralism (chapter 3).

Gadamer

In *Truth and Method,* Gadamer develops themes from *Being and Time.* Gadamer, like Heidegger, seeks to break down the scientific stranglehold that reduces truth to what can be methodologically demonstrated, so he is quick to announce that his work does not propose a method or theory of interpretation: "The purpose of my investigation is not to offer a general theory of interpretation and a differential account of its method . . . but to discover what is common to all modes of understanding" (1994, xxxi). But if Gadamer is not offering a theory, he is offering a philosophy. As he says, Kant asked, "What are the conditions of our knowledge, by virtue of which modern science is possible, and how far does it extend? Thus the following investigation also asks a philosophic question. But it does not ask it only of the so-called human sciences . . . but of all human experience of the world and human living. It asks (to put it in Kantian terms): How is understanding possible" (xxix). Here we see Gadamer following Heidegger's appropriation of the transcendental argument. That is, Gadamer thinks he, like Heidegger, is asking *the* primordial question:

"My real concern was and is philosophic: not what we do or what we ought to do, but what happens to us over and above our wanting and doing" (xxviii).[17]

Whereas Heidegger talks about our embeddedness in terms of practices, Gadamer speaks about the ways we inhabit traditions that cannot be set aside in order to look nakedly at the world or ourselves: "Understanding is to be thought of less as a subjective act than as participating in an event of tradition, a process of transmission in which past and present are constantly mediated" (1994, 290). Thus, he asks, "What consequences for understanding follow from the fact that *belonging* to a tradition is a condition of hermeneutics?" (291, my emphasis). The subject and the world are always already in traditions. Drawing on Heidegger's discussion of the "fore-structures of understanding" (that is, preunderstandings), Gadamer attacks the Enlightenment's opposition of reason (as scientific procedure or universal faculties of the mind) to the prejudice of traditions by speaking of the "prejudice against prejudice" (271–300). Prejudices are constitutive of our being: "Thus the meaning of 'belonging'—i.e., the element of tradition in our historical-hermeneutical activity—is fulfilled in the commonality of fundamental, enabling prejudices" (295).

Gadamer's embedding of the subject in tradition informs his account of the hermeneutic circle, for the agency of understanding comes both from "us" and from tradition: "The circle, then, is not formal in nature. It is neither subjective nor objective, but describes understanding as the interplay of the movement of tradition and the movement of the interpreter. The anticipation of meaning that governs our understanding of the text is not an act of subjectivity, but proceeds from the commonality that binds us to the tradition. . . . Tradition is not simply a permanent precondition; rather, we produce it ourselves, inasmuch as we understand, participate in the evolution of tradition and hence further determine it ourselves. Thus, the circle of understanding is not a 'methodological' circle, but describes an element of the ontological structure of understanding" (1994, 293). The hermeneutical circle is not an account of what we should do but what we *inevitably* do because of who we are.

Gadamer insists that the tradition is not an absolute authority or a monolith. Tradition includes criticism: "Hermeneutical consciousness is aware that its bond to this subject matter does not consist in some self-evident, unquestioned unanimity, as is the case with the unbroken stream of tradition. Hermeneutic work is based on a polarity of familiarity and strangeness" (295). In a subsequent text, Gadamer confronts his critics directly: "It is a grave misunderstanding to assume that emphasis on the essential factor of tradition which enters all understanding implies an uncritical acceptance of tradition and sociopolitical conservatism. . . . In truth the confrontation of our historic tradition is always a critical challenge of this tradition. . . . Every experience is such a confrontation" (1987, 108). Nonetheless, it is clear that Gadamer's holistic idea of tradition ontologically precludes any radical critique since it assumes that we are constituted and held together by a common language and texts. (He speaks of "commonality" in his definition of the hermeneutic circle above.)

In this shared being is the presumption of the development of a certain canon that is for the most part nurturing. Such a view ignores the differences among conflicting traditions, texts, and subjects as well as the question of power. As Richard Bernstein, one of Gadamer's most sympathetic interpreters, says, "Gadamer's philosophical hermeneutics is virtually silent on the complex issues concerning domination and power" (1983, 156). Glaspell's story, discussed later in this chapter, poses these issues in a concrete and productive way.

Gadamer sets his sights on a form of historical consciousness that "posit[s] the past as a closed matter that can be totally described . . . and posit[s] the present as having complete mastery and the last word over the past" (Hoy 1978, 63). He replaces this notion with that of "historically effective consciousness" (*Wirkungsgeschichtliche Bewusstein*), which is an authentic awareness. Historically effective consciousness is open, not locked into the certainty of its own superiority, for it assumes that the tradition still has something to teach us. Understanding is not what the reader pulls out about the text but a dialogue, in which both sides, the work and the reader, make claims and pose questions: "The task of hermeneutics [is] entering into dialogue with the text" (Gadamer 1994, 368). The interpreter does not seek the worldview of the author but the question that motivates the text. The Hirschian effort to separate meaning and significance truncates a work's productivity and truth: "The real meaning of the text, as it speaks to the interpreter, does not depend on the contingencies of the author and his original audience. . . . Not just occasionally, but always, the meaning of the text goes beyond its author. That is why understanding is not merely reproductive but always a productive activity as well. . . . [W]e understand in a *different way, if we understand at all*" (Gadamer 1994, 296–97). The dialogue of text and reader requires an "art of questioning" (368), not a scientific method.

Gadamer supplements his account of interpretation as dialogue with the idea of play, which he calls "the clue to ontological explanation" that discloses "the ontology of the work of art and its hermeneutical significance" (1994, 101). Play, like dialogue, redefines the hermeneutic activity of reader and text in a vocabulary that avoids Cartesian assumptions about an interpreter operating on a separate object. He characterizes these assumptions as follows: "The work of art is not an object that stands over against a subject for itself. Instead the work of art has its true being in the fact that it becomes an experience that changes the person experiencing it" (102). The text is not an object but "what 'takes place' in the event of performance" (147). Gadamer redefines play so that we do not think of text and reader as separate and disconnected elements in interpretation: "Play clearly represents an order in which the to-and-fro motion of play follows of itself. . . . The structure of play absorbs the player into itself and thus frees him from the burden of taking the initiative, which constitutes the actual strain of existence" (104–5). In the fluid, exploratory boundaries of the event of interpretation, "the players are not the subjects of play; instead play merely reaches presentation through the players" (103).[18]

15

Gadamer seeks to replace the vocabulary of subject versus object with a holistic one that makes the search for objectivity and the specter of subjectivism disappear. There is no pure seeing of the past without reference to the present, but the present is understood only through the intentions, ways of seeing, preconceptions of the past. We cannot go back and recover Shakespeare's intentions because his work comes to us through the tradition of interpretation that precedes us. The past is not like a pile of facts but an interlocutor whose otherness is as important as his/her similarity. Hence "temporal distance is not something that must be overcome. This was, rather, the naive assumption of historicism, namely that we must transpose ourselves into the spirit of the age, think with its ideas and thoughts, not our own, and thus advance towards historical objectivity. In fact the important thing is to recognize the temporal distance as a positive and productive condition enabling understanding. It is not a yawning abyss but is filled with the continuity of custom and tradition, in the light of which all that is handed down presents itself to us" (1994, 297). The history of reception of texts shows how every age reinterprets texts in order to understand itself (296).

Yet Gadamer does not simply collapse the difference between the historical position of the work and the historical position of the interpreter. Instead, he speaks about the "horizon" of each in order to characterize their situatedness. He defines "horizon" as "the range of vision that includes everything that can be seen from a particular vantage point" (1994, 302). Yet he warns that we should not think of a horizon as a prison and take the visual metaphor too literally: "The historical movement of human life consists in the fact that it is never absolutely bound to any one standpoint, and hence can never have a truly closed horizon. . . . Thus the horizon of the past, out of which all human life lives and which exists in the form of tradition, is always in motion. The surrounding horizon is not set in motion by historical consciousness. But in it this motion becomes aware of itself" (304). This hermeneutic motion brings the horizons of text and interpreter into fusion. The horizon of the interpreter can be expanded to include the horizon of the past: "When our historical consciousness transposes itself into historical horizons, this does not entail passing into alien worlds unconnected in any way with our own; instead, they together constitute one great horizon that moves from within and beyond the frontiers of the present, embraces the historical depths of our self-consciousness" (304). But "fusion" does not mean "reconciliation": "Every encounter with tradition that takes place within historical consciousness involves the experience of tension between the text and present. The hermeneutic task consists in not covering up this tension by attempting a naive assimilation but in consciously bringing it out" (306).

Gadamer revises the traditional distinctions among understanding, explanation, and application. Application does not take place after understanding and explanation; rather, all three work together: "Understanding is here always application" (1994, 309). The simplest way into the question of application is to think about biblical interpretation, in which readers use stories or passages from the Bible to offer guidance on contemporary problems—for example, divorce, drugs, and so on. The Bible is thus read not merely as a document of historical interest but as a source of wisdom for the present. In literary criticism, interpreters make implicit reference to this dimension whenever they ask us to pay attention to a text, not just when they give a modern staging of Shakespeare. Application is rarely discussed in literary theory, and literary theorists' inexperience with this notion accounts for some of the misdirected venom in such controversies as the canon debate. On the one hand, we have those who follow Hirsch and the New Critics. These writers abstract the issue of the canon from our present concerns and from the values and assumptions behind their own judgments. On the other hand, we have those who attack the epistemological, ethical, and political agendas of such thinking by merely exposing its false objectivism and political conservatism. These critiques do not sketch an alternative problematic for thinking about the question of value or even clarifying the values informing their own arguments.[19]

Gadamer is not advocating that we simply modernize all texts and make them like us. The interpreter is situated in the present in a way that makes impossible a leap into the horizon of the text in order to "understand" the text purely in its own terms. We inevitably "interpret" or rephrase it in our own. This does not mean that we simply "project" our meanings. Words such as "projection" illustrate precisely the kind of subject-object thinking that Gadamer wants to critique: "The interpreter dealing with a traditionary text tries to apply it to himself. But this does not mean that the text is given for him as something universal, that he understands it per se, and then afterwards uses it for particular applications. Rather, the interpreter seeks no more than to understand this universal, the text; i.e., to understand what this piece of tradition says, what constitutes the text's meaning and significance. In order to understand that, he must not seek to disregard himself and his particular hermeneutical situation. He must relate the text to this situation if he wants to understand it all" (1994, 324). The epistemological interpretive practice is an impoverished way of understanding our relationship to the texts of the past, a practice that overlooks the way the impetus for interpretation comes to us as listeners, not from our will-to-know: "Understanding begins . . . when something addresses us" (299). In *Truth and Method*, Gadamer gives an example of his own through his reading of Aristotle, in which he shows how Aristotle's understanding of practical reason (*phronesis*) provides an important critique of the narrow notions of reason that modern philosophers have provided.

The last feature of Gadamer's philosophy of interpretation that I will touch on is his view of language. For him, language is the historical medium in which we live, not an instrument that we use. We have no access to ourselves or the world without it: "Experience is not wordless to begin with, subsequently becoming an object of reflection by being named. . . . Rather, experience itself seeks and finds words that express it" (1994, 417). Gadamer wants to displace not only the perceptual basis of Husserlian phenomenology but the long tradition that makes the mirror rather than the dialogue the focus of philosophy.[20] Gadamer's take on understanding does not ask how we organize our perceptions of the physical world, a view that makes our language and culture impediments to naked confrontation with the real; rather, he says that all our understandings of ourselves and the world are mediated by language and tradition: *"Being that can be understood is language"* (474, Gadamer's emphasis). Gadamer does not put us in a prison house of language, for this worry about linguistic solipsism is produced by the assumption that we are set over against a world of objects from which language screens us: "Not only is the world 'world' only insofar as it comes into language, but language, too, has its real being only in the fact that the world is re-presented within it" (443).

Gadamer follows Heidegger in replacing philosophy's reductive concern with the isolated proposition or word with a holistic understanding of language: "Every word breaks forth as if from a centre and is related to a whole, through which alone it is a word. Every word causes the whole language to which it belongs to resonate and the whole worldview which lies behind it to appear" (1994, 458).[21] Language, for Gadamer, is not an object of linguistic analysis but an event of understanding: "What constitutes the hermeneutical event proper is not language as language, whether as grammar or as lexicon; it consists in the coming into language of what has been said in the tradition: an event that is at once appropriation and interpretation" (463). Because of our linguisticality, we cannot understand ourselves in the same way that we try to understand the rotation of the planets because language makes human beings "self-interpreting animals," in Charles Taylor's phrase.[22] Explanations of our behavior cannot overlook the self-understandings of the explainers or of those for whom an explanation is sought. Thus the languages through which we understand human relationships take a logical priority over the explanations of science.

Gadamer's view of language helps him respond to the charge of relativism. The idea of relativism comes from the notion that a God's-eye view of a text (or history) is possible. Once the possibility of a such a view drops out, we are forced back on the resources of our traditions to support our arguments. These claims are neither totally private nor random, for the holistic context that is the condition of their intelligibility insures that we share a great deal with those who disagree with us. We share a language and a community of inquiry. What disappears is the notion of the external world or self that is uncontaminated by language. Gadamer offers a reunderstanding of the idea of reference, not a denial of it.[23] His principal goals are to offer a new problematic for understanding language, history, and subjectivity and to retell the story of modern philosophy from this perspective.

Since this linguistic turn is now a received wisdom of contemporary critical theory, I will not develop Gadamer's ideas on language any further here but rather wait until the discussion of his debate with Habermas and Derrida. No one that we will discuss urges going back to a pre-Heideggerian view. What is very much at issue, however, is the nature of language and the role of material forces in shaping this language. We are now ready to put Gadamer's ideas to work.

I take as my example Susan Glaspell's "A Jury of Her Peers" for two reasons. First, the two major characters in the story dramatize the issues in hermeneutics discussed in this chapter. Second, the text asks questions that Gadamer's hermeneutics cannot satisfactorily answer. In posing these questions, Glaspell's story forces a major revision but not an abandonment of hermeneutics, the kind of revision that is necessary if hermeneutics is to inform contemporary critical theory.

The story begins when Mrs. Hale is called from her work in the kitchen to join her husband, Mr. Peters (the sheriff), and his wife. Mrs. Hale, the center of focalization for the third-person narrative, learns that Mr. Wright, the husband of an old friend, has been killed. The sheriff suspects Mrs. Hale's friend Minnie has killed her husband. The group proceeds to the Wrights' home, where it splits up. The men go out to the barn to look for evidence that can establish a motive for Minnie, while the women wait in the kitchen, which is their separate physical and social space. At first, Minnie's "text"—the dirty towels, the mishandled stitching on her quilt, the act of violence of which she is suspected, and so on—is alien to them. That is, the dominant tradition that the women bring to Minnie's house, a tradition that they share with their husbands, forms a background of preunderstandings that does not help them reconstitute the self-understanding of this text. The men have called Minnie "mad," and the women at this point can articulate no other reading, even though they sense that more is at stake here for them.

Slowly the women start to put together an *explanation* of the strangeness in Minnie's text—the systematic psychological torture to which her husband subjected her, a torture that culminated in the strangulation of Minnie's double, her pet bird. The process of coming to this explanation forces them to transform their self-understandings (the texts of their own lives and indeed of the entire culture of the time). Minnie's text asks them disturbing questions, not just the other way around. They discover that Minnie's husband was not only "a cruel man" but also a typical one and that Minnie's responses differ only in degree, not in kind, from the ones they have had but have repressed. That their husbands share Minnie's husband's ideology is brought home to them when, every time the men pass the kitchen, they make a condescending remark about the triviality of women's occupations, considering the issue is murder. The women recognize that the values and textures of their own lives are neither read nor appreciated by their husbands and that the forces that drove Minnie mad operate around and within them as well. Their husbands' remarks help push the women toward an understanding of the distinctiveness of *their tradition*, a tradition that goes unread by the men and by the tradition that dominates their culture. The women do not just empathize with Minnie; they discover the narrow social space in which they have been forced to live and the anger

19

that they have been forced to ignore. The tradition through which they have lived, which has nourished them into the particular cultural shapes they now inhabit, suddenly appears as a crippling force as well.[24] Now Minnie's text speaks not only *to* them but *for* them: "It was as if something within her not herself had spoken, and it found in Mrs. Peters something she did not know as herself" (Glaspell, 272). When Mrs. Peters discovers the strangled bird, she understands it by recalling what a boy with a hatchet had done to her cat many years ago, and she gets back the feeling of that past moment. Mrs. Hale and Mrs. Peters arrive at their explanation not by detaching themselves from the situation, by striving to be "objective," but by engaging their personal feelings and the particularities of their individual lives. It is only by letting Minnie's text speak to them, by *applying* it to themselves and the present situation, that they can understand. Minnie's text forces them to see themselves and their husbands in a new way that requires a new language, a language that draws on the particular ways that the women have of understanding. Unlike Minnie, they are able to create a way of speaking that unites them and separates them from the men. They choose to hide the bird (conceal evidence) and betray their husbands. The circle in which they come to understand Minnie's dead bird—a circle, in which all three women stand together—is quite different from the circle they would have drawn around the dead bird at the beginning of the story. Interpretation is not just about what we do to texts but also about what texts do to us.

What Minnie's text asks cannot be answered within the tradition but only by a break with the tradition that defined the nature and importance of these activities. The holistic claim of Heidegger and Gadamer that there are no "radical" breaks in our beliefs, since such breaks would be unintelligible, does not account for the ethical/political and ontological force of the change. The critical awareness the women achieve of the meaning of canning, sewing, and the other activities of their lives is not the objectifying distance that Heidegger discusses in the example of the hammer that breaks. In directing their arguments at an objectivist, scientistic understanding of philosophy, Heidegger and Gadamer ignore the often crippling effects of linguistic practices. The women's relationship to Minnie's text is not a dialogical play but a violent, wrenching experience.[25] Closing the hermeneutical circle requires them to leave the tradition and betray their husbands. The dialogue between the women and their husbands thematizes the role of power outside and inside them. The women silently resist, reinterpreting their husbands' discourse internally. Mrs. Peters begins by almost quoting her husband to Mrs. Hale and by resisting the latter's sympathy for Minnie. By the end of the story, Mrs. Peters initiates the concealment of the bird. The fact that they hide the bird rather than confront their husbands shows how far their empowerment has to go. Moreover, the story's long exile from the canon repeats the way the tradition suppresses language and values.[26]

But if the story dramatizes some of the shortcomings of Gadamer's hermeneutics, it also dramatizes the need for a new one that works at smaller levels than the "tradition" so that islands of community and difference can be theorized. Moreover, a new hermeneutics needs to be open to more radical notions of critique and difference than the ones Gadamer puts forward. These revisions will bring with them new characterizations of the dialogue between texts and readers, characterizations that give a place to differences in traditions and in critical orientations. The value of hermeneutics for contemporary theory does not stand or fall on Gadamer's narrow characterization of dialogue and tradition. Gadamer directs his argument at a tradition of philosophy that deracinates the subject from language and history. No one seriously defends a theory of the deracinated subject today, but a new argument has taken its place. The question is no longer whether the subject is embedded or not but what the subject is embedded in and what theory (or theories) we should use to characterize this embeddedness. A story of oppression that emphasized only patriarchal power and the women's constructedness—for example, poststructuralism—would not account for the women's achievement or the conditions necessary for that achievement, such as an awareness of their own traditions. (Gadamer's understanding of language and tradition has been used by theorists of excluded traditions).[27] The task of contemporary hermeneutics is to bring together the idea of tradition as a nurturing resource with the antihermeneutic views that read our being in language as evidence of our subjection to the networks of power. Before examining the most widespread theories of subjection, those of the poststructuralists (chapter 3), we need to discuss two other important challenges to hermeneutics, the critical theory of Jürgen Habermas and the structuralist project.

2

Challenges to Hermeneutics

STRUCTURALISM AND PSYCHOANALYSIS

This chapter will look at challenges to the hermeneutical approach to interpretation from two types of explanation, structural and causal. The basis for structuralism comes from linguistics, and in the first part of the chapter, I discuss the structural linguistics of Ferdinand de Saussure and some of the ways literary theory uses his work. I then look at the hermeneutic philosophers who dialogue with structuralism: Paul Ricoeur, who appropriates it, and Mikhail Bakhtin, who attacks it. The productiveness of Bakhtin's approach is illustrated through a reading of Ralph Ellison's "Flying Home." In the second part of the chapter, I will examine, through the example of Jürgen Habermas, the ways that the causal explanations of post-Marxist social theory challenge hermeneutics. I begin with Habermas's use of psychoanalytic dialogue as a critique of Gadamer's hermeneutics and then offer a hermeneutic response to Habermas.

Structuralism

Like Gadamer, structuralism offers a critique of the phenomenological quest to find the origin of meaning in the subject. However, while Gadamer gives a new role for the subject as part of the tradition, structuralism abandons the subject and the act of interpretation as the focus of critical interest. Roland Barthes characterizes structuralism's new critical orientation as follows: "The critic is not responsible for reconstructing the work's message but only its system, just as the linguist is not responsible for deciphering the sentence's meaning but for establishing the formal structure that permits this meaning to be transmitted" (*Essais critique*, cited in Culler 1983, 79–80). Meaning is in language itself, not in the subject. Saussure asks of language a Kantian question— What makes speech possible?—and he seeks an answer not through the self-understanding of individual speakers but in a structural explanation that operates independently of the speaker's awareness: "The distinguishing characteristic of the sign—but the one that is least apparent at first sight—is that in some way it always eludes the individual or social will" (17).[1] Unlike Gadamer, structuralism puts explanation before understanding. That is, when structuralism looks at what makes understanding possible, it does not look at our being in the world; rather, it abstracts language from human embodiment and searches for the rules and laws that make linguistic utterances possible.

Saussure makes this break with an existential approach to language through his distinction between the system of language, called *la langue*, and the individual speech act, *la parole*. He is not interested in the infinite variations in speech, in the use of language by speakers and the worlds disclosed by their language; instead, he concerns himself with the systemic background, the principles and processes that make speech within a linguistic community possible. *La langue* is a coherent analyzable object, "a system of signs in which the only essential thing is the union of meanings and acoustic images (15). This system is a self-contained set of relational structures whose parts get their significance from the whole. It can be investigated if it is considered to be stable for a slice of time, if it is considered to be synchronic. This kind of study is "concerned with the logical and psychological relations that bind together terms and form a system in the collective mind of speakers" (99–100), and it must be distinguished from the historical study of linguistic change, or diachronic linguistics. Any change in one element of the synchronic system produces a change in the entire system.

The system is a set of conventions that link sounds or signifiers and concepts or signifieds. Signifiers and signifieds combine to form the basic unit of the system, the sign. There is no natural or inevitable link between the signifier and the signified. We use the signifier "table" to talk about a certain piece of furniture, but we could use another word if the community accepted it. (There are exceptions, such as onomatopeia.) In addition to being arbitrary, linguistic signs are also differential and relational. To explain these two characteristics, Saussure uses the example of colors. When we try to understand the concept of brown, we must compare it with the surrounding colors of red and green. There is no concept of brown that exists prior to its articulation in language. Thus the meaning of the linguistic sign comes not from its physical properties but from its place in the system: "Language is a system of interdependent terms in which the value of each term results solely from the simultaneous presence of the others" (114). Concepts or signifieds are hence neither essences nor nomenclature: "In all cases, then, we discover not ideas given in advance but values emanating from the system. When we say that these values correspond to concepts, it is understood that these concepts are purely differential, not positively defined by their content but negatively defined by their relations with other terms of the system. Their most precise characteristic is that they are what others are not" (117). The same is true of signifiers. The acoustic material gets its importance only from the presence of the surrounding sounds. The value of the *p* in "pit" is that it is unlike the *b* in "bit." There is a slot available in the system.

Translation illustrates these points well, for it shows how "impossible it is to fix even the value of the word signifying 'sun' without first considering its surroundings: in some languages it is not possible to say 'sit in the sun'" (116).

23

Saussure gives the example of the French "mouton" and the English "sheep." Because English uses "mutton" to talk about meat to be served and French does not, "mouton" and "sheep" have a different value even though they may have the same signification when a French speaker and an English speaker discuss farming. Jonathan Culler gives another example in his discussion of the translation of the English "river" into French (1986, 15). French does not have exactly the same concept but instead two concepts, "fleuve" and "riviére," which are differentiated on the basis of the direction of their flow (to the sea or not). The "surroundings," to recall Saussure's phrase, of the concept associated with "river" differentially articulate the concept on the basis of size—that is, compared to a stream—but not on the basis of direction. Saussure concludes that different languages are different systems that articulate the world differently. These Saussurean ideas have been developed in many directions. I will talk briefly about literature as a system, as narrative, and as intertextuality.

In "Literary Competence," Culler looks at the practice of literary criticism as *paroles*, for which a systemic explanation must be sought. Thus, after citing a passage of Harold Bloom's commentary on William Blake's "The Sunflower," Culler asks not whether Bloom's reading is good, correct, or productive but what assumptions about literature make this response possible. Culler grafts Noam Chomsky's notion of linguistic competence onto Saussure's notion of *langue* so that literary criticism becomes a peculiar way of speaking into which people are initiated. What Culler is after is not a new interpretation of Blake or a new theory of interpretation but an account of the institution of literature. The result will be a self-consciousness on the part of the reader about the way the discipline functions.

Structuralists also systematize the operations of narrative. One approach, developed by Gérard Genette and others, distinguishes between the *histoire*—or the content of the narrative—and the *récit*—the specific narrative text that manifests this content. Genette calls the *histoire* the "signified" (72) and the *récit* the "signifier." Genette deliberately conflates the *langue/parole* distinction with the signified/signifier distinction in order to talk about the different ways we can tell the same story and to compare the narrative technique of different texts. Although this approach has produced useful taxonomies of time, voice, and other qualities, there is a price for ignoring the world disclosed by the text. Saussure excludes reference and speakers from his system, but any narrative theory that works at the manifest level of the text must make a space for it since a text proposes a world.[2]

Another type of narrative analysis views the text as only a surface produced by a grammar, which, as Gerald Prince explains, "describes the rules and operations that allow one to process a particular representation as a narrative: if you process x as a narrative, it is because you make use of the following grammar or one that is formally equivalent to it" (80). Algirdas Greimas develops a semantics whose premise is that binary oppositions shape all thought, including narrative. His work seeks to draw out the fundamental oppositions of

texts and theorize the ways these oppositions combine to produce the narrative. Tzvetan Todorov sketches a narrative "syntax" of propositions and sequences, in which characters become nouns, their attributes become adjectives,
and their actions become verbs. He then works out the rules that determine
the formation of propositions and sequences. The antihermeneutic thrust of
these efforts is clear: a science of logical possibilities replaces the dialogue between text and reader. This kind of structuralist study is most successful with
schematic, formulaic bodies of texts—for example, fairy tales and *The
Decameron*—but is less satisfying when applied to complex, nuanced characters and plots, as Robert Scholes shows in his application of Todorov's method
to James Joyce's "Eveline."[3]

A third development of structuralism comes from the later work of Roland
Barthes, which represents a transition from structuralism to poststructuralism.
In *S/Z* he breaks Balzac's "Sarrasine" into short segments called "lexias." After
pulling out the codes that inform these lexias, he then shows how these codes
function. For example, a particular lexia could contribute to the enigma of the
narrative (hermeneutic code) and/or to the code of action (proairetic code)
that helps readers put discrete events into plot sequences. In examining the
codes that lie behind a given text, Barthes breaks down the idea that authorial
intention defines the identity of the text: "The text is not a line of words re-
leasing a single 'theological' meaning (the 'message' of an Author-God) but a
multidimensional space in which a variety of writings, none of them original,
blend and clash. The text is a tissue of quotations drawn from innumerable
centres of culture" (1989, 52–53). With the death of an author-based hermeneutics comes a new activity for the critic. The critic no longer seeks to "decipher" meaning but to "disentangle" textual threads: "In multiple writing, in
effect, everything is to be *disentangled*, but nothing *deciphered*, structure can be
followed, 'threaded' (as we say of a run in a stocking) in all its reprises, in all its
stages, but there is no end to it, no end to it, no bottom: the space of writing is
to be traversed, not pierced. . . . Thereby, literature (it would be better, from
now on, to say *writing*), by refusing to assign a 'secret,' an ultimate meaning, to
the text (and to the world as text), liberates an activity we may call anti-theo-
logical" (54). The text does not stop with the work or even body of works; it
extends to the reader as well: "The 'I' that approaches the text is itself already
a plurality of other texts, of codes which are infinite or, more precisely, lost
(whose origin is lost). . . . Subjectivity is generally imagined as a plenitude with
which I encumber the text, but in fact this faked plenitude is only the wake of
all the codes that constitute me, so that ultimately my subjectivity has the
generality of stereotypes" (1974, 10).

Barthes offers a view of existence as textuality here. His exploration of
intertextual relations is a long way from Saussure's notion of *la langue*. Barthes
reworks structuralism into a new view of language and subjectivity, into a
textuality of existence. The subject in the text is not the product of binary
oppositions but an implicate of institutions and codes. In the same way, the

reader is not the offstage scientific investigator (as in structuralism) but another text. Barthes's textuality abandons the subject and humanism as the point of departure. Language is not the instrument of the subject or the logical motor of a semiotics; it has a life of its own, a crucial point that poststructuralism will develop. Since Gadamer too thinks that language has it own life, the time has come for a quick Gadamerian response to structuralism.

First, Gadamer would insist on beginning with language in dialogue and history rather than accepting Saussure's methodological strictures. (Bakhtin will have much more to say on this point.) Second, Gadamer would agree with structuralism's critique of existing schools of interpretation—for example, New Criticism and Hirschian intentionalism. Third, he would point out that structural explanations depend first of all on our understandings of ourselves and our culture that are deeper than the explanatory vocabulary. The only reason that we even pick up Culler's book is that it speaks to our self-understandings, particularly our Enlightenment self-understandings as explainers. In the same way that Culler shows how subject (Bloom's commentary) and object (Blake's poem) are not set over against each other but mutually implicated, Gadamer would show that Culler's explanation of the institution is not detached from what it is critiquing. What structuralism seeks to unmask is the self-understanding of the institution of literary criticism so that a new self-understanding can replace it. We should not mistake the focus on critical explanation of culture, a focus that exposes the self-understandings of the time, with a claim to breaking with the hermeneutic circle. Only a positivistic claim that truth is independent of the culture that understands it—and structuralists certainly do not want to say this—would invalidate the hermeneutic circle. (I doubt that Culler and Barthes would deny much of this.)

Gadamer would agree with Barthes's project to decenter the subject and to bring language and being together. However, for Gadamer, unlike Barthes, the tradition is the focal point, not cultural codes. Moreover, Gadamer uses humanistic vocabulary of dialogue to talk about the text/reader relationship. For Barthes, "tradition" and "dialogue" make too many massive assumptions about textual dynamism that cover over the fascinating and multiple textual processes that continually remake us. Gadamer would insist on the historicity of our being that Barthes does not thematize. Thus Gadamer's decentering of the subject reads differently: "The focus of subjectivity is a distorting mirror. The self-awareness of the individual is only a flickering in the closed circuits of historical life. *That is why the prejudices of the individual, far more than his judgments, constitute the historical reality of his being*" (1994, 276–77, Gadamer's emphasis).

Ricoeur

Ricoeur negotiates the tension between hermeneutics and structuralism. In his works on metaphor (*The Rule of Metaphor*) and narrative (*Time and Narrative*), he strives to keep the competing claims of structuralism, with its search for rules and principles of combination, and hermeneutics, with its insistence on the priority of our language of existence, in a productive tension so that neither side can say it has the whole truth and thus make a totalizing claim. To structuralism, he makes the following reminder: "All objectifying knowledge about our position in society, in a social class, in a cultural tradition and in history is preceded by a relation of *belonging* upon which we can never entirely reflect. Before any critical distance, we belong to a history, to a class, to a nation, to a culture, to one or several traditions" (1981, 243). To the hermeneutical insistence on belonging, he brings the critical counterweight of distanciation, which, "Dialectically opposed to belonging, is the condition of the possibility of the critique of ideology, not outside or against hermeneutics, but within hermeneutics" (244).[4]

Although Ricoeur does not accept the Saussurean isolation of language from the world and history, he does not dismiss structuralism; instead he follows Emile Benveniste in supplementing the semiotic analysis of signs, the focus of Saussurean linguistics, with a semantic analysis of the sentence. Saussure theorizes the construction of language into sentences with the notions of the paradigmatic and syntagmatic dimensions. The paradigmatic is the axis of selection—that is, when we select a noun and verb from the vast possibilities of nouns and verbs available for the slots in the sentence "The player passed the ball," we could put a proper name in for "the player" or "threw" for "passed." The syntagmatic is the axis of combination. That is, this axis gives rules that govern the units that we can put together to make a sentence. We cannot say, "Player the," for the rules of syntax tell us where to put definite articles. Ricoeur says that Saussure's account "ignores entirely the properly logical difference between discourse and language, that is to say, the difference between the predicative relation in discourse and the opposition-relation between signs in the language system" (1977, 338). The structure of discourse is "not a structure in the analytic sense of structuralism—i.e., as a combinatory power based on the previous opposition of discrete units. Rather, it is a structure in the synthetic sense—i.e., intertwining and interplay of the functions of identification and predication in one and the same sentence" (1976, 11). By distinguishing the sentence from the sign, Ricoeur is able to bring in speakers, intentions, referents, and multifarious kinds of speech excluded by Saussure.

These features permit Ricoeur to reintroduce hermeneutics into his theory of language and to incorporate ideas from speech-act theory. He develops the distinction between a semiotics of the sign and semantics/pragmatics of the sentence in *The Rule of Metaphor,* where he shows how the history of metaphor from Aristotle to the date of the book's publication (1977) was dominated by a restricted understanding of metaphor as an issue of words as "deviant naming" (1983, 183). Ricoeur shows that we need to think of the production of sense in metaphor as a kind of predication, as an utterance. Moreover, by considering metaphor at the level of the sentence, we bring in metaphor's referential dimension, which structural analysis excludes.[5]

In *Time and Narrative*, Ricoeur places his work on narrative in the same frame he establishes for metaphor: "The epistemological problem for narrative or metaphor is to link the explanations of the semiotic and linguistic sciences with the pre-understanding that comes from an acquired familiarity with linguistic practice" (1984, I 12). "For a semiotic theory, the only operative concept is that of the literary text. Hermeneutics, however, is concerned with reconstructing the entire arc of operations by which practical experience provides itself with works, authors, and readers" (53). The center of Ricoeur's theory is his idea of triple mimesis, which is how he describes narrative in terms of the hermeneutic circle. Mimemis I is the precomprehension of the world of action that is necessary for the production or reception of narrative—for example, familiarity with such notions as "agent," "means," "goals," and the like. Here is where he is close to the grammar of narrative that structuralism investigates. Mimesis II is the "emplotment," the narrative text itself, which, Ricoeur emphasizes, is an act, not a thing. Mimesis III refers to the reception of the text where the world of the text and the world of the reader intersect. In sum, "we follow the destiny of a prefigured time to a refigured time by mediation of a configured time" (I 87).

Ricoeur sets up the importance of narrative by an analysis of the inevitable aporias that arise when the problem of time is discussed.[6] The basic aporia that is reworked by all major philosophers is between lived or phenomenological time and cosmological time. For example, Husserl, who tries to bracket objective or cosmological time in order to constitute time through consciousness, is forced to use language drawn from an already constituted objective time. Narrative time mediates between these two views of time: "Temporality cannot be spoken in the direct discourse of phenomenology but rather requires the mediation of the indirect discourse of narration" (Ricoeur 1988, III 242). This conclusion brings us back to the central hypothesis of the entire work: "Time becomes human time to the extent that it is articulated in a narrative; conversely, a narrative has significance to the extent that it portrays the characteristics of temporal experience" (1984, I 17). The aporias of narrative do not prevent them from disclosing a world and reconfiguring the world of the reader.

The narrative text provides a distinct mode of understanding since it gathers together or "emplots" episodic events with all their semantic heterogeneity and their temporal aporias into a story. Narrative thus articulates what would otherwise remain unutterable, for "there can be no thought about time without narrated time" (Ricoeur 1988, 241). Plot "is the intelligible unit that holds together circumstances, ends and means, initiatives and unwanted consequences. . . . From this intelligible character of the plot, it follows that the ability to follow a story constitutes a very sophisticated form of understanding" (1983, 178). Ricoeur does not assert that narrative produces a simple, stable closure, a "substantialist identity," but a narrative identity that permits other plots (1988, III, 248). His concern is not so much with the epistemological disputes between narrative historiographers (for example, Hayden White) and antinarrative ones. Instead, he wants to investigate what the activity of storytelling says about existence. His interest is in the ontological claim that the temporality of human action is the common ground between fiction and history (1984, 124). The commensurablity between these two is "assured by phenomenology, which [provides] a thematics common to both narrative modes" (1983, 180).[7]

Bakhtin

A more thoroughgoing hermeneutic critique of Saussure comes from Mikhail Bakhtin's dialogics. For Bakhtin, the irreducible unit of analysis is neither the sign nor the sentence but the utterance: "Speech can exist in reality only in the form of concrete utterances of individual speaking people, speech subjects" (1985, 75). The utterance is not the instantiation of a system of rules, as Saussure understands *parole*. Instead, the utterance requires an entirely different kind of critical vocabulary from the *langue/parole* opposition to characterize it.

The key to Bakhtin is his dialogical conception of language. Language is not about the construction of sentences but about dialoguing with others. Bakhtin uses the term "dialogue" in three senses that are sometimes confusing. The broadest claim is that dialogue is the nature of existence: "Life is by its very nature dialogical" (1984, 293). For Bakhtin, dialogue is a new conception of truth designed to replace the monologism that has dominated Western thought: "These basic [monologic] principles go far beyond the boundaries of artistic creativity alone; they are the principles behind the entire ideological culture of recent times" (80). But Bakhtin also speaks of dialogue in a more limited sense as an approach to the utterance. Last, he opposes dialogue and monologue. This last sense contradicts the first—how can there be monologic discourse if all language is dialogic? We can reconcile this apparent contradiction if we think of monologue as a theoretical and/or overtly ideological constraint—for example, linguistic hypotheses or authoritarian institutions, such as the church.[8]

A dialogic conception of language means that the structuralist speech models of Saussure and Roman Jakobson,[9] in which a message is encoded by a speaker and then decoded by a listener, miss fundamental aspects of language: "The word in living conversation is directly, blatantly, oriented toward a future answer-word: it provokes an answer, anticipates and structures itself in the answer's direction. Forming itself in an atmosphere of the already spoken, the word is at the same time determined by that which has not yet been said but which is needed and in fact anticipated by the answering word" (Bakhtin 1981, 280).[10] This means that language is charged and inflected with different values, with directions of meaning, and with genres of speech; language is not a system of differences articulated independently of subjects:

"Language is not a neutral medium that passes freely and easily into the private property of the speaker's intentions; it is populated—overpopulated—with the intentions of others" (294). When we speak, we are engaged with a variety of speakers of the past and present as well as with the speaker in front of us. Thus an utterance is shaped by what has already been said about a topic as well as by our immediate interlocutor: "No living word relates to its object in a singular way: between the word and its object, between the word and the speaking subject, there exists an elastic environment of other, alien words about the same object, the same theme" (276). Unlike Gadamer, whose dialogue emphasizes a common preunderstanding and an ultimate fusion of horizons, Bakhtin speaks of otherness as crucial to self-understanding, whether the dialogue is between speakers or between readers and texts: "A meaning only reveals its depth once it has encountered and come into contact with another, forming the meaning; they engage in a kind of dialogue, which surmounts the closedness and one-sidedness of these particular meanings, these cultures" (1986, 7). Bakhtin's discussion of the process of understanding uses Gadamerian language of question and answer, in which the speaker is neither imprisoned in his/her horizon nor capable of leaping into the other's horizon. The goal is not to find one's "home," as we saw in Gadamer (see chapter 1), but to discover a new relationship: "Without one's own questions one cannot creatively understand anything other or foreign. . . . Such a dialogic encounter of two cultures does not result in merging or mixing" (7).

The global concept that Bakhtin uses to talk about language is heteroglossia, and it produces a striking contrast to Saussure's *langue*: "At any given moment of its historical existence, language is heterglot from top to bottom: it represents the co-existence of socio-ideological contradictions between the present and past, between different socio-ideological groups in the present, between tendencies and schools, circles and so forth. . . . Each of these 'languages' of heteroglossia requires a methodology very different from the others; each is grounded in a completely different principle for marking differences and establishing units" (1981, 291). The structuralist idea of a holistic, interdependent system of a single language is replaced by multiple conglomeration of various sociolinguistic forces. Some of these forces push languages in new directions— what Bakhtin calls "centrifugal forces" (for example, innovations in literature or other institutions), while others, "centripetal forces" (such as the institutions of grammar, the church, and the courts), seek to maintain order.[11]

Bakhtin's heteroglossic critique of Saussure is markedly different from Ricoeur's supplementation of a pragmatic level of speech-acts to the semiotic level of *la langue*. This supplement grafts the phenomenological subject's intentionality onto the holistic systemic analysis rather than critiquing the holistic assumption itself. Ricoeur tries to keep dialogue and narrative in the problematic of phenomenology, in which the intentional act of the speaker is still the point of orientation.[12] Bakhtin rejects the system and the phenomenological subject as points of departure.

The heteroglossic understanding of language calls for a transformation of poetics, a field that has never come to terms with the novel: "The great poetics of the past—Aristotle, Horace, Boileau—are permeated with a deep sense of the wholeness of literature and the harmonious interaction of all genres within with this whole" (Bakhtin 1981, 5). Although Formalist and Structuralist poetics break with humanistic scholarship, their attempts to reduce literature to devices, functions, conventions, and binary oppositions overlook the dialogism at the heart of the novel just as previous poetics do.[13] For structuralists, the pendant of the deindividualized language system is the hyperindividualized concept of style, in which it is "understood in the spirit of Saussure: as an individualization of the general language" (1984, 264). For Bakhtin, only an entirely new conception of literary study, prosaics, is adequate to the dynamics of heteroglossia in the novel. Unlike poetics, prosaics opens the boundaries between the languages of life and the languages of art to make possible a critical hermeneutical consciousness that enlarges who we are: "What is realized in the novel is the process of coming to know one's own language as it is perceived in someone else's language, coming to know one's own conceptual horizon in someone else's conceptual horizon" (1981, 365).

However, the language of the novel is to be distinguished from everyday language, for the novel is concerned not with the transcription of ordinary speech but with the image of language behind the isolated utterances of daily life: "The image . . . reveals not only the reality of a given language but also, as it were, its potential, its ideal limits and its total meaning conceived as a whole, its truth together with its limitations" (Bakhtin 1981, 356). In order to do this, the novel requires at least two "linguistic consciousnesses to be present, one being represented and the other doing the representing, with each belonging to a different system of language" (359). The result is that the novel is a linguistic hybrid. A hybrid is not a mere mixing of different languages but is "stylized through and through, thoroughly premeditated, achieved, and distanced" (366). Hybridization is an "organized system for bringing different languages in contact with one another, a system having as its goal the illumination of one language by means of another, the carving out of a living image of another language" (361).

For Bakhtin, genres are not just rules and norms for the production of literary works but the cultural memory of ways of perceiving and representing the world, ways that inform literary and nonliterary utterances: "A genre lives in the present, always remembers its past, its beginning. Genre is a representative of creative memory in the process of literary development" (1984, 106). Thus the novel transforms the understanding of the world by making the present "the center of human orientation in time and in the world" (1981, 30). The past is not closed off and complete but open to continuous reinterpretation. In this view, "time and world lose completedness as a whole as well as in each of their parts" (3). We are in a "world where there is no first word (no ideal word), and the final word has not yet been spoken" (30). This is not a modernization,

31

for it gets to the pastness of the past by affirming its difference: "Reality as we have it in the novel is only one of many possible realities; it is not inevitable, not arbitrary, it bears within itself other possibilities" (37).[14] If reality were inevitable, it would be reducible to explanation, as Hegel and Marx claim. If it were completely random and arbitrary, it would escape all understanding. The relationship between past and present is mediated by genre: "Genres (of literature and speech) through the centuries of their life accumulate forms of seeing and interpreting particular aspects of the world" (1986, 5). Yet genres are not just about the relationship of past and present; considered synchronically, they are social shapes that articulate the character of a culture, that make possible some ways of being and foreclose others.

If Bakhtin introduces the speaking subject who is abstracted out of the structuralist system of language, he does not make the subject the point of departure. Instead, he begins with the heteroglot languages of the community from which the self emerges. He starts with the following premise: "For any individual consciousness living in it, language is not an abstract system of normative forms but rather a concrete heteroglot of conception of the world" (1981, 293). He explains this by beginning with a minimalist example of linguistic simplicity—"an illiterate peasant . . . naively immersed in an unmoving and for him unshakable everyday world" (295). Even this speaker "live[s] in several language systems" (295). He prays in one language, sings songs in another, speaks to his family in a third, and petitions the government in a fourth. When the speaker no longer takes these languages as scripted performances and begins to compare them, then a critical consciousness is born and the speaker faces "the necessity of actively choosing [his] orientation among" the various languages (296). That is, "consciousness must actively orient itself amidst heteroglossia" (295).

Such a view of language redefines the isolated subject of phenomenology in social space: "The word in language is half someone else's. It becomes 'one's own' only when the speaker populates it with his own intention, his own accent, when he appropriates the word, adapting it with his own accent, when he appropriates the word, adapting it to his own semantic expressive intention" (Bakhtin 1981, 293). The self is formed through the assimilation and reworking of one's discursive environment: "Our own discourse is gradually and slowly wrought out of the others' words that have been acknowledged and assimilated, and the boundaries between the two are at first scarcely perceptible" (345). Crucial to Bakhtin's idea of the self is the distinction between authoritative and innerly persuasive discourse. Authoritative discourse "demands that we acknowledge it, that we make it our own; it binds us, quite independent of any power it might have to persuade us internally; we encounter it with its authority already fused to it" (342). Authoritative discourse does not permit revision. It controls the subject from without. Innerly persuasive discourse develops through interaction with other voices, much like dialogue in the outside world, and it is always open, unfinalizable: "One's own discourse and one's own voice, although born of another or dynamically stimulated by another, will sooner or later begin to liberate themselves from the authority of the other's discourse" (348).

Bakhtin's views of language and the self require a new conception of authorship, which he finds in Dostoyevsky. The text is not the author's self-expression or monologic creation; instead, it is a polyphonic creation in which the author's voice or language does not control the heteroglossia. Characters are "not only objects of authorial discourse but also subjects of their own directly signifying discourse" (Bakhtin 1984, 7). The result is a "plurality of independent and unmerged voices and consciousnesses, a genuine polyphony" (6). The author does not disappear but rather places his/her language in dialogue with the languages of others and at the same time orchestrates the polyphony of the different voices.

Bakhtin's understanding of the subject in language makes him, like Gadamer, suspicious of structural explanation as well as the causal explanations of Freud and Marx. Bakhtin sees systemic accounts not just as abstractions that miss the character of speech; they also set themselves up as authoritative accounts that seek to demystify rather than dialogue with others. Whereas Gadamer sees only the forces of scientific rationalism in such explanations, Bakhtin sees the political forces of domination: "Forces that lie outside consciousness, externally (mechanically) defining it: from environment and violence to miracle, mystery, and authority. Consciousness under the influence of these forces loses its authentic freedom and personality is destroyed. There among these forces, must one also consign the unconscious (id)" (1986, 297). As Gary Saul Morson and Caryl Emerson say, "For Bakhtin, it appears political totalitarianism . . . and Freudianism were connected" (198). This connection between explanation and authority is a genuine concern, for theoretical monologism and political monologism work hand in hand in driving out the significance of the individual consciousness: "The monologic way of perceiving. . . . arises only where consciousness is placed out of existence" (Bakhtin 1984, 81). However, instead of thinking through the ways that the unconscious challenges and modifies his dialogism, Bakhtin tries to deny the importance of the idea of the unconscious: "The depths of consciousness are simultaneously its peaks. . . . Consciousness is much more terrifying than any unconscious complexes" (1986, 288).

Bakhtin's avoidance of the unconscious and of all external forces that construct the subject points to several shortcomings in his work. First, in arguing for the autonomy and liberty of the subject, he risks falling into a Kantian dualism in which the ethical subject is separated from the subject considered as part of the natural universe.[15] Explanation has no place in his work. Second, he has little to say about emotion, particularly pain, or embodiment in general. As Michael André Bernstein says, Bakhtin ignores "The immediate, intractable, and existence-embittering suffering" that inhabits the works that he studies (202).

Bakhtin's analysis of the Underground Man's spiraling speech "with a loop-hole" looks at dialogical relations only from the perspective of voice and never addresses the psychological wound that makes his speech part of a pattern of domination and submission. When Bakhtin says that Dostoyevsky's artistic form "liberates and de-reifies the human being" (1984, 63), he refers to the way Dostoyevsky refuses to shape monologically the voices of his characters; Bakhtin says nothing about the crippled beings in the texts. His linguistic idealism leaves him vulnerable to the same charge that Habermas makes against Gadamer, as we will see later in this chapter. Third, Bakhtin never recuperates the democratic political project to which he appeals—for example, the liberty and autonomy of the subject. He remains at the metaphilosophical level, in which he argues for dialogism against other theories of language. Thus he never inserts his theory of language into a historical argument in which the ethical and political heritage of the Enlightenment is criticized and recuperated. (Habermas's work is an example of this kind of work.) Instead, he tells a merely literary history about the triumph of the good of polyphony over the evil of monologism. When he defines critical linguistic consciousness in the well-known example of the peasant cited above, he detaches this person from the historical debates of his time so that critical consciousness per se is valorized rather than a specific kind of critical consciousness.[16]

In sum, we can say that Bakhtin's argument is, like Gadamer's, addressed to competing views of language—that is, his argument is metaphilosophical. He argues for a dialogical conception against other conceptions. He does not assess the linguistic reality that he discloses, except that he affirms diversity and dialogue and attacks monologism and authoritarianism. His values are thus tied to his claim to truth—language is dialogical and dialogue is good. The thinness of his normative claims has led some to accuse him, like Gadamer, of relativism since he does not tell us how to adjudicate among the multiple languages that inform our existence. It is better to say that Bakhtin is not worried about the issue of relativism and that he does not offer guidance on choosing one form of life over another except on the basis of liberty of dialogue. This is not a weakness but part of his critique of the debilitating effects of the narrow quest for truth. Giles Gunn articulates this Bakhtinian point as follows: "The aim of conversation is neither unanimity nor truth; its aim is rather the enlargement of consciousness through dialogic engagement with alterity" (145).[17] Bakhtin is at one with Gadamer on the linguistic constitution of the world as well as on the dialogic and historical character of language. But while Gadamer sees tradition as a unifying, authority-bearing, and nurturing force, Bakhtin sees language as an arena for conflicting and contradictory linguistic forces and voices. For Gadamer, "consciousness is more being than consciousness" (Gadamer 1977, 38).

We can see how productive Bakhtin's theory is when reading Ralph Ellison's short story "Flying Home." In this story, a black pilot named Todd is flying training missions in Alabama during World War II. He is not allowed to fly in combat because the army would then have to give him the recognition that its racist culture denies him. Nonetheless, Todd feels that his only hope for recognition or "for any real appreciation lay with his white officers" (152). Todd's inner speech tries to reconcile the irreconcilable, to cover over the contradiction in his attempt to show that he is good enough to be the white man's equal at the same time that he internalizes white standards and judgments in his internal and external speech. Indeed, we learn through Todd's recollection that his impulse to fly comes from a desire to fly over the conflicts produced by racism. He says of flying, "It's the only dignity I have" (151).

One day Todd crashes his plane, and he is met on the ground by Jefferson, a poor, elderly farmer. Todd is immediately ashamed because Jefferson is the kind of black man from whom he wants to dissociate himself: "Humiliation was when you could never simply be yourself, when you were always part of this old black ignorant man" (150). Jefferson "signifies" on Todd with an African American folk tale.[18] Jefferson claims to be telling an autobiographical incident about his own experience of flying in heaven, where we see the same kind of racism as on earth. The genre and language of Jefferson's story are quite different from the speech genres of white society; indeed, these tales are often designed to help their tellers and hearers cope with the language and power of the dominant culture. In this case, the story serves to unmask the internalization of the dominant discourse by an African American. Jefferson retells Todd's story in order to force the young pilot to see how he has let debilitating white judgments colonize his life. I say "forces" because Todd feels humiliated and angered by the tale but does not know what to say back. Jefferson's point is not simply to unmask Todd but to put him in touch with the resources of African American culture that he has lost. Jefferson does not "argue" with Todd on Todd's discursive terrain. Instead, he breaks with the genre in which Todd speaks. Jefferson goes after his entire self-understanding and urges him toward a new language for constituting himself and the world. The old man's story is one that Todd faintly remembers but cannot hear. Todd cannot help but "apply" the story as he understands it.

Ellison's story recounts the process of change within Todd after he hears the story. He passes out from the pain of his injury and has two sequences of recollection—one of his desire to fly and another of the force of racism that he has tried to deny. Ellison shifts to interior speech, in which the language of Todd's memories, with their emotional intensity, implicitly dialogues with the language in which he constitutes himself in the present. Jefferson serves as an analyst who fathers the boy by telling a story that coaxes him into the Freudian process of self-renewal, in which the repetition—his denial of the racism (flying)—is brought to the surface in a nurturing context so that Todd can return to the painful memory and work through it in a more efficacious way than he has done thus far. Jefferson's story does not tell Todd how to live his life; instead, it urges Todd toward a new language of self-constitution that only Todd can develop. Jefferson serves as an example for Todd of how African Americans can maintain their integrity in the face of oppression. Jefferson is treated with contempt by the whites, and he makes no idealistic protest, which would only get him beaten. However, he never lets white culture destroy the language through which he understands himself.

Bakhtin's dialogical hermeneutics helps lay out the linguistic dynamics of the story in a way that neither structuralism nor Gadamer's philosophy could ever do. At the same time, Ellison's story shows the limits of Bakhtinian analysis as well. Even though Bakhtin's dialogical theory is compatible with democratic values, the political dimension of Bakhtin's work is thin. He affirms the liberal values of tolerance, autonomy, and mutual recognition, but he does not go much farther. We will enrich the ethical/political context of hermeneutics by considering the arguments of Jürgen Habermas.

Habermas's Challenge to Hermeneutics: Rethinking Marxism and Psychoanalysis

Jürgen Habermas's work grows out of the Frankfurt School of Critical Theory, and he is committed to reworking the legacies of Marx, Freud, and Weber into a new understanding of democratic social theory. Unlike Gadamer, Habermas wants to redeem the Enlightenment's ethical/political dimensions— by rethinking the Enlightenment's epistemological project of grounding scientific reason, a project that modern philosophy has discredited.[19] By making this move, he rejects the wholesale critique of the Enlightenment made by his Frankfurt predecessors Horkheimer and Adorno in *The Dialectic of Enlightenment*.[20] He also rejects the move made by Richard Rorty and Chantal Mouffe in which the Enlightenment's democratic political project is separated from its epistemological project. Habermas wants to link democracy to an understanding of reason. Since the battle over the legacy of the Enlightenment is important not just for the Gadamer-Habermas debate but also for Habermas's arguments with poststructuralism, we need to give a brief sketch of the Enlightenment legacy as it reached Habermas.

The Enlightenment put its faith in reason to dispel illusions about science, ethics, and politics. The Enlightenment's ethical/political ideals—the dignity of the individual's reason, the right of the individual to develop a vision of the good, the ethical imperatives of equality and reciprocity—were important forces in cultural history, but there was an underside to this progress. First, the idea of scientific reason authorized an instrumental understanding of our relationship to nature. Capitalism became the means through which instrumental rationality invaded economic and social life. Kant's categorical imperative forbidding using people as means rather than ends was simply overwhelmed by an economic understanding of subjects as human capital. Non-Kantian ethical views, such as utilitarianism and social Darwinism, which authorized this understanding of society, often dominated public debate. In addition, Kantian ethics had internal problems of its own. First, it is a universal, formal, procedural ethics that is disconnected from daily ethical life. Second, it separates reason from desire so that morality is set against a selfish and tyrannizing human nature. As Freud points out, the categorical imperative is a perfect description of the superego, of the internalization of power.[21]

For the Frankfurt School, the Enlightenment vision of rational autonomy became a nightmarish social machine. As Horkheimer and Adorno put it, "Knowledge, which is power, knows no obstacles. . . . Technology is the essence of knowledge. . . . What men want to learn from nature is how to use it in order to dominate it and other men. That is its sole aim" (4). Habermas does not think this is the whole story. He wants to replace the Enlightenment's instrumental reason with a new conception of reason as communicative action. Unlike instrumental thinking that leads to social manipulation, communicative action, in his view, is "oriented toward understanding" (1979, 1). This communicative dimension of action is embedded in language itself; indeed, the fundamental mode of language is communicative, not strategic or instrumental. By rethinking reason in terms of intersubjectivity rather than subjectivity, Habermas tries to redeem the Enlightenment hope of linking democracy and critical reason.[22] It would overwhelm my exposition to lay out the rich and complex theories of language, history, society, and politics that Habermas elaborates to support his views. Instead, I will give a preliminary characterization of it here in the context of his argument with Gadamer and then a fuller account when I discuss his debate with the poststructuralists.

For our purposes in this chapter, the best way into Habermas's work is his rethinking of the opposition of explanation and understanding—that is, between the self-understanding of the agent and the observer's (theoretician's) explanation of the agent's self-understanding. This opposition, initiated by the Enlightenment, informs the work of Marx, Weber, and Freud as well as the entire sociological tradition.[23] Habermas follows the work of these thinkers in rejecting hermeneutic dialogue as the ultimate framework for understanding society and in insisting on an account of forces that do not lend themselves to the workings of language. To give some sense of how the problematic of explanation and understanding works, I will briefly describe Marx's account of these two stories and show how Habermas seeks to improve them.

In Marx's work, the opposition of explanation and understanding emerges in the difference between the story of capital, which transforms the relationships between human beings and their work (explanation), and the story of the experiences of the participants (understanding). Marx phrases the story of capital like this: "But capital has one single life impulse, the tendency to create value and surplus value, to make its constant fact, the means to production, absorb the greatest amount of surplus labor. . . . The capitalist then takes his stand on the law of the exchange of commodities. He, like all other buyers, seeks to get the greatest possible benefit out of the use value of his commodity" (cited in Benhabib 1986, 125). When the perspective shifts to the effects of this story on the working class, Marx adopts the voice of the worker:

Suddenly the voice of the laborer, which had been stifled in the storm and stress of the process of production, rises: The commodity that I have sold you differs from the crowd of other commodities, in that its use creates value, and a value greater than its own. This is why you bought it. . . . To you, therefore, belongs the use of my daily labor power. But by the means of the prices that you pay for it each day, I must be able to reproduce it daily, and to sell it again. . . . By an unlimited extension of the working day, you may in one day use up a quantity of labor power greater than I can restore in three. What you gain in labor I lose in substance. (Cited in Benhabib 1986, 125–26)

In Habermas's view, Marx never brings these two stories together but instead privileges explanation over understanding. The result is a reductive treatment of the subject in terms of class and work. The plurality of views held by different subjects becomes the monolithic idea of class consciousness. The subject's diverse modes of self-realization become simply work. Habermas replaces work with communicative action as the way to understand the realization of the individual and the community. This conception makes the multiple subject positions in any society available to theory. Moreover, the theory of communicative action does not begin with the isolated, individual consciousness, the Cartesian legacy that has crippled political and social theory; instead, Habermas draws on the philosophies of Ludwig Wittgenstein and John Searle to develop the idea of a common "life-world" in which subjects are embedded and which subtends their conversation.

Habermas does not abandon the third-person point of view of the theoretician, however; he splits the theoretical task into two parts. The first concerns the life-world, in which communicative action is the means in which daily life is reproduced. The second concerns those aspects of the modern world that are independent of the life-world, which Habermas calls the "system." By this latter term, he designates those modern institutions with a functional rationality that is independent of the intersubjective communication of individuals. The idea of system is Habermas's way of doing justice to Marx and Weber's analysis of the "iron cage" of capitalist instrumental reason that dominates so much of modern life.[24] We see this system in the bureaucracies of government and business, which direct society through the calculations of efficiency and output rather than through dialogue. I am not concerned with this dimension of Habermas's work but with the tension between explanation and understanding in his discussion of communicative action in the life-world.

Habermas also parts company with Marxism's wholesale critique of liberal democracy. Marx mounted a harsh attack on democratic ethical/political beliefs, and he did so in the name of his own ethical/political value of emancipation. Habermas also holds emancipation dear, but he does not think that a utopia on the other side of liberal democracy is the place to look for it. Marx thinks that *Recht* (roughly "liberalism") was an entire philosophy of human nature, society, and history. The three premises of *Recht* are: (1) scarcity is inevitable; (2) humans are egoistic; and (3) people have conflicting views of the good (Lukes, 29–35). Marx claimed that these ideas were not eternal truths about human nature—a belief that justified bourgeois ideology of property, rights, and the like—but the products of specific historical conditions that can be overcome in a future utopia. As Steven Lukes says,

> Marxism supposes that a transparent and unified society of abundance—a society in which the very distinctions between egoism and altruism, and between the public sphere of politics and the private sphere of civil society . . . have been overcome—is not merely capable of being brought about, but is on the historical agenda. . . . Thus, Marx scorns the "rights of man" as nothing but the rights of a member of civil society, i.e., the rights of egoistic man, of man separated from other men and from the community. By furnishing principles for the regulation of conflicting claims and interests, *Recht* serves to promote class compromise and delays the revolutionary change that will make possible a form of social life that no longer needs *Recht*. (35)[25]

Habermas believes that no such utopia is possible or desirable, that democratic politics can do better than the liberalism of the nineteenth and twentieth centuries, but that we cannot expect to bring about a unity of humanity and a dissolution of the political sphere.

Habermas brings these political concerns to the ontological conservatism of Gadamer's work. Gadamer is not directly concerned with politics, but his understanding of our cultural embedding disarms critique in a way that troubles Habermas. Habermas accepts much of Gadamer's hermeneutic critique of science and social science: "It makes good sense to conceive of language as a kind of metainstitution on which all social institutions are dependent; for social action is constituted only in ordinary language communication" (Habermas Review 1990, 239). Habermas thus rejects Marxism's positivistic science of society, in which the self-understandings of people are merely explained. However, Habermas thinks Gadamer abandons all critique by making the language of the present the untranscendable horizon. "Language is *also* a medium of domination and social power; it serves to legitimate relations of organized force" (239). If Marx makes the cultural superstructure a mere reflection of conditions of labor (base), then Gadamer opts for a linguistic idealism that evaporates all materials conditions. For Habermas, Gadamer gives "the ontological priority of tradition over all possible critique" (Habermas Claim, 266). Habermas cites Albrecht Wellmer to substantiate his point: "The Enlightenment knew what a philosophical hermeneutics forgets—that the 'dialogue' which we, according to Gadamer, 'are,' is also a context of domination and as such precisely no dialogue" (266).

In order to introduce explanation back into critical theory, Habermas distinguishes between self-reflection and rational reconstruction. In the former, the subject "becomes aware of unconscious presuppositions of completed acts. . . . Hermeneutic consciousness is thus the outcome of a process of self-reflection" (Habermas Claim, 249). Rational reconstruction, on the other hand, "is undertaken with the aim of explaining linguistic competence. It makes explicit those rules which a native speaker has an implicit command of " (249). However, the "speaker's subjectivity"—i.e., his/her self-reflection—remains excluded in principle" (249). Habermas seeks "a theory appropriate to the structure of natural languages on which methodological understanding of meaning can be based" (252). He thus wants something that Gadamer and Bakhtin think is both impossible and undesirable.

As an example of such an explanatory method, Habermas offers psycho-analysis.[26] Psychoanalysis presents itself as a possibility because it has to explain in order to understand utterances that are "systematically distorted" by forces that transcend the analysand's awareness. The analyst has techniques—free association, among others—as well as theories of development, what Habermas calls "general interpretations," to guide him/her. Psychoanalysis not only requires hermeneutical understanding "but also presupposes a theory of communicative competence . . . that covers the forms of intersubjectivity of language and the causes of its deformation" (Habermas Claim, 264). Psycho-analysis, like linguistic theory, requires "a systematic pre-understanding that extends into language in general, whereas hermeneutical understanding always proceeds from a pre-understanding that is shaped by tradition and which forms and changes itself within linguistic communication" (263).

Habermas is right in saying that we need metalanguages such as those of psychoanalytic theory so that we can capture the ways in which we are at the mercy of forces that transcend our awareness and powers of introspection. He is wrong insofar as he tries to universalize them and thus remove them from hermeneutic dialogue either with competing theories (reconstructive or otherwise) or first-order speech. As Mary Hesse says, "The difficulty with Habermas's description of reconstructive sciences is that it seems to presuppose that there is just one correct explication of linguistic competence, of logic, of human action, and even of theory of science and ethics" (cited in Benhabib 1986, 266).

Instead of reading Habermas's search for a prehermeneutic explanation as a failure to be dismissed, we can see it as a search for a critical explanation that can emancipate, as itself a particular hermeneutic tradition, a tradition that comes from the Enlightenment's use of scientific reason to demystify traditional religious and social beliefs and that stands next to the Romantic tradition in which Gadamer situates himself. Paul Ricoeur phrases this "reconciliation" of Gadamer and Habermas nicely: "Hermeneutics will say [to Habermas], from where do you speak when you appeal to *Selbstreflexion*, if it is not from the place that you yourself have denounced as a non-place. . . . It is indeed from the basis of tradition that you speak. This tradition is not perhaps the same as Gadamer's. It is perhaps that of the *Aufklarung*, whereas Gadamer's would be Romanticism . . . the tradition of emancipation rather than that of recollection. Critique is also a tradition" (1981, 99). Explanation is not opposed to hermeneutics; rather, it is a reading generated through the optic of an alternative tradition.[27]

This revision of the idea of explanation makes possible a reconciliation between Bakhtin and the need for explanatory critique. Certainly, Bakhtin would criticize Habermas's holistic assumption that there is a life-world that unites all speakers just as he would reject Gadamer's unconflicted characterization of tradition. Even though Habermas's view is not a Saussurean holism of *la langue* but a holism that includes speakers and different speech-acts, Habermas still factors out the diversity of languages that is at the heart of Bakhtin's view.[28] In Habermas's theory we can see Bakhtin's justifiable concern that the desire for monological explanation simplifies linguistic reality. At the same time, we need to recognize the need to explain utterances rather than just complicate their constitutions, as Bakhtin does. In the next section, I will consider how softening this tension between explanation and understanding lets cultural hermeneutics embrace the explanatory theories of psychoanalysis with the self-constitutions of individuals and cultures.

Explanation and Understanding Revisited: Bakhtin and Freud in Dialogue

The need to explain emerges in our everyday conversation. At times, we understand our interlocutor as an agent, and we seek to articulate the subject's intentions, the background assumptions, and the vocabularies used to constitute personal or communal identities. At other moments, however, we redescribe the subject's language or action in terms that do not respect the integrity of the subject's self-constitution. We do not leave our interlocutor's self-understanding as a truth that can never be paraphrased, nor do we simply dialogue with someone's conceptions in terms of our own self-understanding. We also employ explanations that work behind the backs of our interlocutors. Thus we come to understand that the habitual ways our friend talks about her mother, for example, point to wounds that control her speech in ways that she never thematizes. Sometimes we redescribe a person's virtuous or deprecating self-characterization in terms of a psychological mechanism—for example, guilt or masochism—or in terms of an economic/social system—for example, capitalism's ethic of consumption.

How should we think about the tension between of third-person accounts of explanation with first-and second-person accounts of agents? The advantage of such third-person accounts is that they can be used to cut across the various languages of self-understanding that individuals offer. Unlike Habermas in his attempt to reconstruct a general theory of linguistic competence that embraces and reduces self-interpretations, I would keep the tension in dialogue. Charles Taylor expresses this tension well: "One has to understand people's self-interpretations and their visions of the good if one is to explain how they arise; but the second task can't be collapsed into the first even as the first can't be elided in favor of the second" (1989, 203). Moreover, I would expand these third-person stories to include theories of psychological development, the histories of gender relations, the histories of ethics, the history of confessional practices (for example, Foucault's *History of Sexuality*). The tension between the two perspectives is ethical/political as well as theoretical. The function of third-person accounts is critique in the name of a better self-understanding.

These third-person accounts do not have to be fully developed, institutionalized theories that are studied in graduate school. In fact, everyone has such third-person assumptions embedded in his/her interpretations, and they are often quite fully articulated, as any episode of the television talk show *Oprah Winfrey* makes clear. These third-person theories can emerge implicitly from listening to another person's first-person story if this story makes one aware of agents operating behind his/her back. This is what happens to Mrs. Hale and Mrs. Peters in "A Jury of Her Peers" when they "hear" Minnie's story and become aware of an account about gender relations that transcends their situation but has not yet been told. In the same way in Ellison's "Flying Home," Todd becomes aware of a story about race after he listens to Jefferson's tale. The teller may also be the unconscious self, who comes out during the course of analysis. Indeed, the difference between the unconscious self and the outside teller always blurs. As we see in the cases of the women and Todd, there is a twisted unconscious story (or more than one story) of pain waiting to be made articulate by the stories that the characters are told.

However, what we have discussed thus far accounts only for the unmasking of the self-understanding of the old self and not the construction of a new one. The "hidden story" that the process of working through unfolds becomes available only through a utopian dimension involved in the projection of the new self. Making psychoanalysis simply a process of emancipation through understanding the repressed truth ignores the fact that understanding is always positioned within a linguistic and axiological space. Analyst and analysand work together to construct a new evaluative language of constitution so that the analysand not only accepts the unwelcome story of his/her unconscious self but discovers a self/language that constructs a meaningful existence. The analysand must not simply "understand" what the unconscious self is saying so that the split-off symbols can be reintegrated into the existing system. Rather, in Bakhtinian terms, the analysand, with the help of the analyst, must find a site within the complex languages and genres for authoring a new story that integrates the hidden story.[30]

In Glaspell's story, we see Mrs. Hale and Mrs. Peters grope toward a new language of self-interpretation. In a similar way in "Flying Home," we see how Todd starts to forge a new connection with Jefferson and his past. The idea of the language of constitution, a Bakhtinian point developed by Charles Taylor,[31] offers a new portrait of society as a collection of incommensurate and conflicting islands of linguistic difference in the same life-world. The need for explanation is not invalidated but complicated; this complexity comes not just from the diversity of what is to be explained but from the recognition that our explanations are not disinterested quests for truth but bound up with what we hope for.

Bakhtin's worry about the tyranny of explanatory monologism is certainly justified if we remain within Freud's own understanding of his work as a science that could be distinguished from ideology. (See his distinction between science and worldview in "The Question of a Weltanschauung" in *The New Introductory Lectures*.) The fact that Freud discussed almost every field in the social sciences and humanities does not mean that he retheorized these disciplines from within; rather, he challenged them from the outside. Ricoeur phrases this interdisciplinary dialogue well: "Freud grasps the whole of the phenomenon of culture—and even human reality—but he does so from a single point of view. We must therefore seek the limits of the principles of Freudian interpretation of culture in terms of the 'models'—topographic-economic and genetic—instead of in terms of the interpreted content" (1979, 323). For example, in "The Relation of the Poet to Daydreaming" Freud avoids the problem of creativity and "explores the limited problem of the relations between the pleasurable effect and the technique employed in producing the work of art" (Ricoeur 1970, 167).

Even Habermas's attempt to strip away Freud's positivism does not help us account for the dynamics of domination and achievement in Glaspell and Ellison in a way that would satisfy Bakhtin. If in "A Jury of Her Peers" we tried to reconstruct what the community believes linguistic competence to be—a competence that gives no place to gender or the incommensurability of different languages—the women's speech would not be intelligible. Habermas says, "The unity of knowledge and interest proves itself in a dialectic that takes the historical traces of repressed dialogue and reconstructs what has been suppressed" (1971, 315). Understanding Minnie's text does indeed require "explanation," but it is not an explanation made available by the dominant language. The power that Habermas seeks to analyze is in language itself in a way that reconstructive science cannot access. The women must draw on the resources of their own tradition, a tradition and genre that they did not hitherto understand as incommensurate with the one in which their husbands participate.

Moreover, Habermas's theory seeks to factor out only power; it does not assess achievement. A merely regressive story about causes does not address the recuperative aspect of Bakhtin's hermeneutic theory. He spells out this aspect of his hermeneutics in a comment on a study of Dostoyevksy that explains the novelist's works in terms of psychological and capitalist forces. Bakhtin points out that such explanations disregard Dostoyevsky's achievement and the hermeneutic language we use to articulate it: "The exceptionally acute contradictions of early Russian capitalism and the duality of Dostoevsky as a social personality, his personal inability to take a definite ideological stand, are if taken by themselves, something negative and historically transitory, but they proved to be the optimal conditions for creating the polyphonic novel . . . and this was without question a great step forward in the development of the Russian and European novel" (1984, 35). The tension between the third-person critical explanations that unmask a culture's self-interpretations and the need to reintegrate these critiques into new first- and second-person cultural ideals is at the heart of the controversy surrounding the poststructuralists, who are the subject of the next chapter.

3

The Poststructuralist Critiques of Interpretation

Poststructuralism develops from structuralism and turns against hermeneutics with an explicit vengeance. For poststructuralists, hermeneutics carries within it the humanist vision of "man," which has held the false promises of liberty and reason, promises that are screens for an oppressive culture. Structuralism's antihumanism called itself a new language of explanation, a new science; poststructuralism's antihumanism does not seek a new explanation but a critical unmasking of the coercive power of language and the discursive practices in the traditions of understanding and in the critical explanations of Marx and Freud. It is a political and revolutionary theory of freedom, or more specifically, negative freedom, as we will see later.

In philosophy, poststructuralists drew on the work of Heidegger. Approaching poststructuralism through Heidegger is much more difficult than going through structuralism, so I will limit myself to basic points about his connection to Derrida. Poststructuralists wanted to get beyond the humanist Marxism of Jean-Paul Sartre, the leading thinker of the previous generation. Even though Sartre was influenced by *Being and Time*, Heidegger's works develop in a totally different way from Sartre's.[1] Sartre's philosophy was "radical" only in a narrow political sense. Since poststructuralists sought a critique that cut right to the core of humanism, they turned to Heidegger. For Heidegger, what was wrong with the West was not just capitalism but an ontology of substance, a metaphysics of presence that continues from Plato's forms to modern philosophy. Heidegger's thought is so radical, the point of view from which he describes the present is so far away from received wisdom, that in his philosophy Marxism and capitalism, Nazism and democracy, all look pretty much the same.[2]

In the first part of the chapter, I will introduce the Heideggerian context of Derrida's work. I will devote the bulk of the section to a Sassurean approach to Derrida that compares deconstruction to Bakhtinian hermeneutics. I illustrate the strengths and weaknesses of Derrida's approach to reading by looking at writings by Barbara Johnson and Toni Morrison. In the second section of the chapter, I will examine a very different poststructuralist linguistic philosophy, the pragmatics of Jean François Lyotard. Lyotard's understanding of language is tied to his understanding of our postmodern condition and politics, and I introduce Lyotard by contrasting his position with Habermas's very different project of linking language and politics. The argument between these two is the best place to explore the competing claims of French poststructuralism and German Critical Theory. This argument will set up a discussion of Michel Foucault's antihermeneutic genealogies. I will conclude with a brief summary and assessment of poststructuralism that will set up the next two chapters.

Derrida and Heidegger

Derrida frequently writes about Heidegger,[3] and he openly acknowledges his influence: "What I have attempted would not have been possible without the opening of Heidegger's questions," and the question that is crucial is "what Heidegger calls the difference between Being and beings, the ontico-ontological difference such as, in a way, it remains unthought by philosophy" (Positions 1981, 9).[4] The ontic-ontological distinction is the critical lever that Heidegger uses to show how Western philosophy has covered over the problem of Being. Philosophy investigated the being of individual entities and then answered the question of Being by searching for what they all have in common. By neglecting Being, philosophy has left out the fundamental issue on which all understanding depends and has mistakenly thought of Being as presence contained in philosophical concepts.

In *Being and Time*, Heidegger gives a fundamental ontology that will provide a basis for ontic inquiries in the particular sciences. In his later work, he abandons the ahistorical anthropology of *Being and Time* for a deeper critique of Western ontology that links the objectification of Being into entities with the placement of "man" and his interests at the center of philosophy. In this view, we try to get clear and distinct ideas about the entities of the world so that we can control them for our use. This leads to a civilization based on the domination of nature and others. Heidegger calls this kind of thinking *Gestell*, which is objectifying, calculative thinking, in which language is an instrument of the subject. This kind of thinking is at the heart of humanism: "That period we call modern . . . is defined by the fact that man becomes the center and measure of all beings. Man is the *subjectum*, that which lies at the bottom of all beings, that is, in modern terms, at the bottom of all objectification and representation" (cited in Habermas 1987, 133).[5]

Heidegger tells a story in which the West has been massively off course, but he does not give us a clear program for changing this course. His alternative to calculative thinking is what he calls "poetic thinking," in which "man is not the lord of beings" but "the shepherd of Being" (1977, 221), who hearkens to the language through which Being speaks. Such thinking "surpasses all praxis" and "towers above action and production . . . through the humbleness of its inconsequential accomplishment" (239). Heidegger looks to poetry, not philosophy, for a new understanding of Being that will deliver us from the domain of *Gestell*.[6]

What interests Derrida is the radical deconstruction of philosophy that

Heidegger performs, not his poetic solution or his story of the West. Derrida does not think Heidegger was radical enough, for the latter remains attached to a quest for Being, to a nostalgia and hope produced by his own story of the decline of the West. Derrida looks at philosophy's failure to understand the ontic-ontological distinction as an opportunity for abandoning the quest for Being and delighting in the possibilities opened up therein. This perspective enables him to see Heidegger's false hope: "From the vantage of this laughter and this dance, from the affirmation foreign to all dualities, the other side of nostalgia, what I will call Heideggerian hope comes into question" (Margins 1982, 27).[7] Derrida's own point of view is not "inside" a story of how attunement to Being has been lost and must be found again; instead, his radical critique of philosophy's ontological underpinnings looks for renewal in language's disseminatory power and in the otherness that becomes available with the decentering of the logos governing Western philosophy.

Derrida and Hermeneutics

From a metatheoretical point of view, Derrida, Bakhtin and Gadamer share certain positions. For all three, the subject is embedded in historical and linguistic currents that mediate any interpretation of ourselves or texts. The scientific dream of stepping outside our historical situatedness is not only impossible but dangerously misguided. Derrida, like Bakhtin and Gadamer, rejects the structuralist model of communication in which the speaker formulates a private message and sends it to a receiver. Derrida characterizes this model as follows: "Communication presupposes subjects (whose identity and presences are constituted before the signifying operation) and objects (signified concepts, a thought meaning that the passage of communication will neither have to constitute, nor, by all rights, to transform). A communicates B to C. Through the sign the emitter communicates something to the receptor, etc." (Positions 1981, 23–24).

Derrida also shares with hermeneutics a critique of reference. His famous statement "There is nothing outside the text," which is often taken for a kind of textual solipsism that makes language merely self-referential, is really quite compatible with Gadamer's and Bakhtin's attacks on the naive notions of reference that place the physical world against language. Derrida's analysis urges "a revaluation of the relationship between the general text and what was believed to be, in the form of reality (history, politics, economics, sexuality, etc.) the simple referable exterior of language or writing" (91). Derrida reminds his critics that "to distance oneself thus from the habitual structure of reference, to challenge or complicate our common assumptions about it, does not amount to saying there is *nothing* beyond language" (1984, 24). Despite this agreement on our linguistic embedding, the way Derrida and the hermeneuts understand the relationship of language, subjectivity, and history is very different. Indeed, some of the "common assumptions" that Derrida wants to challenge are those of hermeneutics.

To make this challenge, Derrida draws on structuralism's vocabulary and antihumanistic thrust, but he does so in order to critique not just hermeneutics but structuralism itself. If structuralism decenters the subject through its theories of the signifying combinations that work behind the back of consciousness, it nonetheless sets itself up as a science that accurately describes the phenomena that consciousness-based problematics have misdescribed. In doing this, structuralism depends on the idea of a system with a center. This center, which serves the same ordering function as intention, holds the system in balance. The idea of *la langue* as a system depends on a center that is not itself part of the system, a center that permits signs to take on their identity in the field of signifiers and signifieds from which they emerge. As Derrida puts it, "Thus, it has always been thought that the center, which is by definition unique, constituted that very thing within a structure which while governing the structure, escapes structurality. This is why classical thought concerning structure could say that the center is, paradoxically, within the structure and outside it" (1978, 279). The idea of a center is not peculiar to structuralism; it has a legacy in Western philosophy. "Successively, and in a regulated fashion, the center receives different forms or names. The history of metaphysics is the history of these metaphors and metonymies. Its matrix . . . is the determination of Being as *presence* in all senses of this word. It could be shown that all the names related to fundamentals, to principles or to the centers have always designated an invariable presence—eidos, arche, telos, engergia, ousia (essence, existence, substance, subject), aletheia, transcendentality, consciousness, God, man and so forth" (279–80). Derrida treats these "centers" as rhetorical figures caught in a drama of signification, not as the ground for a system.

For Derrida, the center blocks out the dynamics of language and an alternative mode of interpretation: "The function of the center was not only to orient, balance, and organize the structure . . . but also to make sure that the organizing principle of the structure would limit what we might call the freeplay of the structure" (1978, 292). "Freeplay" designates a characteristic of language, which is more "primordial," to use Heideggerese, than the metaphysical dimension, and Derrida affirms a new mode of interpretation that is receptive to this characteristic of language.[8] "There are thus two interpretations of interpretation, of structure, of sign, of freeplay. The one seeks to decipher, dreams of deciphering, a truth or an origin which is free from freeplay and from the order of the sign, and lives like an exile the necessity of interpretation. The other, which is no longer turned toward the origin, affirms freeplay and tries to pass beyond man and humanism, the name man being the name of that being who, throughout the history of metaphysics or of ontotheology—in other words, through the history of his history—has dreamed of full presence, the reassuring foundation, the origin and end of the game" (294).

In his reading of Saussure, Derrida picks out the logocentric moment when the linguist moves from the play of difference to the sign as a positive term. Saussure says, "Although both the signifier and the signified are purely differential and negative when considered separately, their combination is a positive fact. . . . [Thus] when we compare signs—positive terms—with each other, we can no longer speak of difference. . . . Between them there is only *opposition*" (120–21). In other words, Saussure's assertion that language consists of "differences without positive terms" (120) holds only until the articulation process is complete; after that, we have positive terms. What lies behind the individuation of positive terms for Saussure is "the collective mind" (100).[9] Manfred Frank states the resulting problem for Saussure: if "the so-called collective consciousness of the participants in language is a result of articulation, it cannot appear at the same time as determining authority in the service of a system" (73).

Derrida's analysis draws on the critique of explanatory, third-person models of science that make no account of the interpreter, a critique that we saw in Heidegger and Gadamer. Heidegger's critique of scientific understanding is that it tries to avoid the hermeneutic circle by leaving out the interpreter's historical situatedness in particular practices so that claims to truth about the world could seem to transcend the practices that make these descriptions possible. But Derrida's stakes are different, for he wants to critique not just scientific understanding but all forms of closure or what he calls "logocentrism." For Derrida, concepts themselves have an oppressive desire for purity that seeks to drive out contamination from neighboring concepts. He tries to expose the way concepts seek to purge themselves of their "others." Thus he says that "to deconstruct a text is to disclose how it functions as desire, as a search for presence and fulfilment which is interminably deferred. One cannot read without opening oneself to the desire of language, to the search for that which remains absent and other than oneself" (1984, 126). For Derrida, the hermeneutics of Heidegger and Gadamer have their own form of closure since they bring interpretation back to our preunderstanding of the world.

In order for Derrida's critique to break with hermeneutics, he must create an alternative interpretive space, make a new transcendental argument about the nature of being in much the same way as Gadamer makes a transcendental argument about the conditions of the possibility of understanding. Unlike Gadamer, Derrida seeks a radical break with the vocabulary of the philosophical tradition. He says, "My central question is: from what site or non-site (non-lieu) can philosophy as such appear to itself as other than itself, so that it can interrogate and reflect upon itself in an original manner" (1984, 108). To do this, he introduces neologisms such as "différance" and iterability, which are the conditions of possibility of all being. These neologisms create a space for redescribing the world. He defines "différance" as follows: "*Différance* is . . . the production, if it can be put that way, of these differences of the diacriticity that the linguistics created by Saussure, and all the structural sciences modeled upon it, have recalled is the condition for any signification and any structure" (Positions 1981, 9). Derrida thus reworks Saussure's structuralism so that there is no totalizing closed system but a dynamic disseminating process at the heart of language itself:

The activity or productivity connoted by the *a* of *différance* refers to the generative movement in the play of differences. The latter are neither fallen from the sky nor inscribed once and for all in a closed system, a static structure that a synchronic and taxonomic operation could exhaust. . . . But it goes without saying that . . . the production of differences, *différance*, is not astructural: it produces systematic and regulated transformations which are able, at a certain point, to leave room for a structural science. The concept of *différance* even develops the most legitimate principle exigencies of "structuralism." (1978, 27–28)

If all of this sounds a little confusing, it is because Derrida is trying to give us a glimpse of a new understanding of Being that can be revealed only indirectly: "We can pronounce not a single deconstructive proposition which has not already had to slip into the form, the logic and the implicit postulation of precisely what it seeks to contest" (1978, 280–81). Thus he mounts a critique of the concept that necessarily manifests itself in his way of writing: "The notion of 'différance'. . . is a non-concept in that it cannot be defined by oppositional predicates; it is neither *this* nor *that*; but rather this *and* that (e.g., the act of differing and deferring) without being reducible to a dialectical logic either" (1984, 110).[10]

Derrida's "différance" has two background sources, Saussure and Heidegger. "Différance" breaks with Saussure's "difference," for it is not enclosed in any system, yet it permits Derrida to draw on the antihumanist structuralist vocabulary of signifiers and signifieds to talk about the production of meaning. "Différance" is also a new version of Heidegger's ontic-ontological difference, in which ontic labeling of beings confronts the ontological problem of Being. Derrida, however, is concerned not with creating a new philosophical anthropology, as Heidegger is in *Being and Time*, but with leaving behind all vestiges of humanism. Hence his definitions do not put a subject term, such as *Dasein*, in them, except as an effect: "Subjectivity—like objectivity—is an effect of *différance*" (Positions 1981, 28).

The best way to understand Derrida is to see how he reworks Saussure's idea of relational, differential identity of the sign within a system or economy, for the nature of identity of the sign—or the concept and its other—is Derrida's great theme: "Saussure powerfully contributed to turning against the metaphysical tradition the concept of the sign that he borrowed from it" (1981, 18). We can see this concern with identity and difference by various tactics. Derrida shows how what we took for unities are divided against themselves. Deconstructive analyses of the texts show how the central terms of a text suspend it between closure and openness, as we saw in Derrida's critique of Saussure's ideas of difference and system. In addition, he brings together unforeseen intertextual connections between entities so as to explode their boundaries or reverse accepted hierarchies—presence/absence, speech/writing, literal/metaphorical.[11] All these moves are concerned with the sign or the concept and its other. Derrida never lets identity close on itself, as Saussure does, but displaces it into a system of shifting relays.

For example, in "Signature Event Context," Derrida examines J. L. Austin's speech-act theory and explores the way Austin relegates certain kinds of discourse to a secondary status, such as fiction and citation. Derrida claims that these secondary features cannot be sequestered outside the core of the theory but infect the purity of the theoretical map itself. Thus "every sign . . . can be *cited*, put between quotation marks; thereby it can break with every given context, and engender infinitely new contexts in an absolutely nonsaturable fashion" (Margins 1982, 320). Derrida is not opposed to the systematizing operations of linguistics: "Formalisation is a fruitful, useful activity. . . . So the effort toward the formalisation of codes is indispensable" (1987, 252). His point is that such a project "cannot be completed" (252) because there is what might be called (from the logocentric point of view) a "logical virus" at the core of any such logocentric effort. (From Derrida's angle this "virus" is a disseminating energy.)

Derrida's project is to expose the hidden operations of these conceptual systems, not to correct them. He never comes up with an "improvement" in the characterization of speech-act theory or whatever he is investigating. He is like the explanatory theorists (for example, Marx and Freud) insofar as he is telling us what is going on behind our backs. Unlike the explanatory theorists, however, Derrida finds a truth that cannot be formulated as a theory about human nature or history. Instead, he makes available the contingent character of Being. However, in making this point he remains obsessed with the metaphilosophical argument against logocentrism's self-understanding rather than moving to what kinds of new first-order understandings might be better than the old ones.

The foregoing analysis sets up an opposition between Derrida's idea of language as signs and Bakhtin and Gadamer's view of language as dialogue. In the hermeneutic view, interpreter and text (or two speakers) achieve a fusion of their separate horizons by giving themselves over to the play of dialogue. Gadamer's understanding of our "embeddedness" in tradition employs a metaphor that evokes Derrida's suspicion: "We must remember that if we are *inside* metaphysics, we are not inside it as we might be inside a box or a milieu. . . . Our belonging to, and inherence in, the language of metaphysics is something that can only and adequately be thought about from another topos or space where our problematic rapport with the boundary of metaphysics can be seen in a more radical light" (1984, 111–12).

Derrida's critique is so profound that it has as its object the entire history of Western thought, including hermeneutics. It thus lumps together all previous philosophers, because from the Derridean perspective logocentrism makes Gadamer, Habermas, Bakhtin, and Marx bedfellows. Derrida rejects humanistic terms such as "dialogue," "understanding," "consciousness," and "tradition" because they occlude or cover over the dynamics of language that he wants to expose. Of course, Gadamer also rejects the way earlier philosophies including phenomenology made "understanding" a punctual, self-contained mental event; he wants to historicize and decenter this subject by placing it in the continuous process of reinterpretation known as "historically effective consciousness."

For Derrida, such a critique preserves too much of the old metaphysical structure that obscures the subtle and violent operations of language. The agent in his story is not the tradition or the subject but the logical drama of language: "A supplement is at the same time something you add as simply something more, another degree, *and* something which reveals a lack in the essence, in the integrity of an entity, so what I call the logic of the supplement is a principle of disorder at work in this very opposition. That's what I'm doing all the time, and it's not what *I* am doing, it is the principle of contamination or disorder which is at work everywhere" (1987, 259).[12] Derrida would make the same critique of Bakhtin's dialogic conception of language that he does of Austin's or Gadamer's, even though Bakhtin's conception is richer than either of theirs. Derrida's space of critique—the articulation of the identity of the concept and its other—is incommensurate with Bakhtin's. That is, Derrida works at the level of the sign, not the voice. Voice articulates difference with a vocabulary aimed at capturing the dynamics of dialogue and speech genres. The sign considers relationships among signifiers and signifieds that are shaped by the linguistic practices that underwrite dialogue. These relationships are logically prior to dialogue.

Whereas Gadamer writes against historical objectivists, Derrida sets deconstruction against all narrative understanding since it employs such unifying terms as "tradition" as the subjects of such narratives. Thus when an interviewer asks Derrida about deconstruction and modernity, he says that labeling inscribes the term "in a certain historical system of evolution or progress (a notion derived from Enlightenment rationalism) which tends to blind us to the fact that what confronts us today is also something ancient and hidden in history" (1984, 112). At the same time, he feels that we "must avoid the temptation of supposing that what occurs today somehow pre-existed in a latent form merely waiting to be unfolded or explicated. Such a view conceives of history as evolution and excludes the crucial notions of rupture and mutation in history" (113). Gadamer would agree with the rejection of the narrative of progress and the isolation of periods but would emphasize the development of a tradition through continuous reworkings rather than gaps and ruptures. Derrida's notion of "rupture" is not a historical concept but comes from his belief that identity is wrought by expulsion of and yet dependence on the other. He refuses to let the dissemination of meaning be contained within the teleology of narrative or englobing concepts such as the preunderstanding of an empirical or idealized speaker. But this then raises the question of whether Derrida denies that we understand each other at all.

When Derrida asks himself rhetorically in "Signature Event Context" whether there have been successful speech acts, he answers, "Perhaps. Here, we must first agree upon what the 'occurring' or the eventhood of the event consists in" (1982, 326). He then says, "I will not conclude from this that there is no relative specificity of the effects of consciousness, of the effects of speech. . . . It is simply that these effects do not exclude what is generally opposed to them term by term, but on the contrary presuppose it in dyssymmetrical fashion, as the general space of possibility" (327). "Relative specificity of the effects of consciousness" is Derrida's way of acknowledging that language does help us "get around in the world," that there are certain redundancies in our linguistic and nonlinguistic behavior. Derrida distinguishes these redundancies from transparent understanding of the meaning of speech and action. Saying that you can follow directions to the post office does not refute Derrida's claim about the dissemination of meaning. In "Limited Inc" (a response to a critique of "Signature Event Context" by John Searle), Derrida clarifies his distinction: "One of the things SEC is driving at is that the minimal making-sense of something (its conformity to the code, grammaticality, etc.) is incommensurate with the adequate understanding of intended meaning" (1977, 203). Derrida is trying to drive a critical space into the excessively grand hermeneutic notion of "understanding."[13] Thus we can say that Derrida does not ignore linguistic codes and textual intentions. He certainly does not urge that we interpret texts however we wish; rather, he looks at codes and intentions critically, and he is very quick to invoke these rules if he feels his own text has been misread, as he makes clear in his response to two of his critics: "The text of an appeal obeys certain rules; it has its grammar, its rhetoric, its pragmatics. . . . [A]s you did not take these rules into account, you quite simply *did not read* my text, in the most elementary and quasi-grammatical senses of what is called *reading*" (1986, 356, Derrida's emphasis).

The difference between deconstruction and hermeneutics can be clarified further by comparing the contrasting ways Derrida and Gadamer use the word "play" to talk about their approaches to reading. Both want to break away from the subject as operator on language and the world and to affirm alternative modes of being in the world, in which listening rather than speaking or dominating is brought to the fore. But for Gadamer, play is a new way of conceiving of the ontology of understanding, a way that replaces the epistemological view in which subject operates on an object through a method to arrive at a truth. We are played as much as we play, and this play takes the form of a dialogue. In Derrida, play is also ontological, but it does not emerge in dialogue but at the level of the sign itself. Play is logically prior to the subject and the tradition. With concepts such as "tradition" and "subject" the philosophical tradition tries to contain the play of language through the power of the concept. "Play" gets its being and its importance by escaping the logocentric understanding of language and shows a way of reading that is not associated with violent imposition of hierarchical relationships among signs. Even though Gadamer affirms the open-endedness of interpretation, he does not look with enough suspicion on the way power constitutes the articulation of meaning.

53

Like Foucault, as we will see (and unlike Gadamer), Derrida views the articulation of meaning as a question of power: "The repression at the origin of meaning is an irreducible violence" (1988, 150). The legibility of textual structures does not come from the norms available to the agents or the continuity of traditions, as hermeneutics would read them, but from "stratifications that are already differential and of very great stability with regard to the relations of forces and all the hierarchies they suppose and put into practice" (1988, 150). Like Foucault, Derrida does not think that power is in the control of a particular class or that there is a domain of reason or human nature that is repressed by power, as a Marxist philosophy of liberation does; rather, power is differentially articulated by signs: "There is never anything called power or force, but only differences of power and of force" (149).

Unlike Gadamer and Bakhtin, Derrida does not believe in the nourishing capacities of the tradition whether in Gadamerian unity or Bakhtinian multiplicity. In his view, the story of tradition is really about the multiple articulations of power that preclude recuperation and make "dialogue" a submission to the metaphysics of presence. Derrida's critique does not recuperate the values of these traditions but affirms only moments of rupture in previous texts. His emphasis on rupture and oppression seems to go beyond the exposure of the factitiousness of the status quo and point to revolutionary change. However, his stance makes any articulation of a new order simply another logocentric move. In addition, his philosophy provides no way of assessing the worth of competing logocentric systems, for it pushes texts to their moment of undecidability. This incapacity has provoked a good deal of critique. I will present this critique in two stages. First I will give a summary assessment of Derrida from a Bakhtinian perspective, and then I will clarify this critique by looking briefly at Barbara Johnson's *A World of Difference* and Toni Morrison's *Playing in the Dark* in which deconstructive reading strategies are brought ethical/political importance.

First, Derrida gives an account only of the *constructed* subject rather than the *constructing* subject. He tells us nothing about the very resources or the agency that enabled him to produce his own text. He never shows us how he closes the hermeneutic circle.[14] In other words, Derrida's theory offers us only a third-person vocabulary for the subject, a vocabulary that takes apart all of the subject's constitutive self-understandings (see chapter 2). Second, he offers an impoverished view of language as signs and systems, a view that overlooks the dynamics of dialogue, speech genres, and forms of life. Unlike the other in dialogue, Derrida's other is not at the level of the voice or the person, since this kind of grand assumption about the relationship of language and subjectivity blocks out his mode of critique. Derrida looks for otherness in the very process of linguistic articulation—for example, speech/writing, signifier/signified, woman/man—that works behind the backs of speakers.

This is indeed an important insight into the way power is articulated, an insight unavailable through competing views; however, Derrida's attention to difference is limited to the differences made available by his problematic of the sign, and he ignores (or deconstructs) differences articulated at other levels. It is important to remember that the discursive conflicts of a culture are not just about the hierarchical relationships of signs in systems—Derrida is still too wedded to Saussure—but about the different shapes provided by cultural institutions and traditions. "Différance" is thus a totalizing claim about language; that is, it takes other philosophical vocabularies such as "dialogue" and "understanding" as so seriously misguided that they cannot be recuperated. Derrida's linguistic philosophy becomes a kind of ontological terrorism that makes all other views of language incommensurate with his.

Third, Derrida's ethics and politics are limited to an ethics of difference and a politics of negative liberty—that is, freedom from oppressive structures rather than a positive freedom to become.[15] This ethical/political view follows from his assumption that power so corrupts cultural history that it totally defoliates the traditions of self-understandings. Derrida says that deconstruction is "a positive response to an alterity which necessarily calls, summons or motivates it" (1984, 118). "Deconstruction is not an enclosure in nothingness, but an openness toward the other" (124).

However, otherness as such does not discriminate among differences. The discourses of the Klan and the discourses of Chicanos are both "other" in American culture. Does this mean they both deserve the same attention? Furthermore, Derrida never articulates the ethical/political context of his work in which we could understand his work. He confesses that he has "never succeeded in directly relating deconstruction to existing political codes and programmes" (1984, 119). His refusal to recuperate any ethical/political tradition assures, as he says, that there is no "adequate political code to translate or incorporate the radical implications of deconstruction" (120). The force of his work is only purely critical, and the values that animate it are difference and negative freedom, two values that emerge from the traditions of liberal democracy and that Derrida is more interested in attacking than reworking. In fact, his problematic of the sign makes impossible a commitment to anything more than an ethics of difference and a politics of negative liberty. There can be no positive agenda.[16]

Barbara Johnson's deconstructive readings illustrate the strengths and weaknesses of this approach. In her essay "Thresholds of Difference: Structures of Address," on Zora Neale Hurston, she makes a fascinating analysis of the racial vocabulary in Hurston's text; however, her conclusion returns to the deconstructive truth of "undecidability": "If I initially approached Hurston out of a desire to re-referentialize difference, what Hurston gives me back seems to be difference as a suspension of reference" (Johnson 1986, 328). She hastens to add that race still matters despite its lack of reference: "Yet the terms 'black' and 'white,' 'inside' and 'outside' continue to matter. Hurston suspends the certainty of reference not by erasing these differences but by foregrounding the complex dynamism of their interaction" (328). Johnson never closes the hermeneutical circle with her own language of reference, which would simultaneously disclose the world and herself. Instead, she remains the deconstructor of textual decidability.

Limiting herself to the critique of decidability forces Johnson to leave out much of the context that makes her own reading possible, as her essay on feminist criticism makes clear. She says, "On the one hand, it would be impossible to deny that female experience has been undervalidated. On the other, the moment one assumes one knows what female experience is, one runs the risk of creating another reductive appropriation—an appropriation that consists in the reduction of experience as self-resistance. While deconstructive discourse may be in danger of over-valuing self-resistance, feminist discourse may be in danger of losing self-resistance" (Johnson 1987, 46). The key issues—how we know that female experience has been undervalued and what we will do about it—remain untheorized; yet such unannounced background knowledge clearly informs her reading. Deconstruction leaves unacknowledged all the preconditions of reading that interested Gadamer. Even worse, deconstruction seems to make a search for these preconditions a misguided logocentric project. But these preconditions are necessary if the changes made available by deconstructive critique are to be realized. Deconstruction deprives us of a sense of agency and of a historical understanding of resources that make this agency possible and meaningful.

Despite these weaknesses, deconstruction is an important avenue of critique, and a vivid example of its usefulness comes from someone who never calls herself a deconstuctor, Toni Morrison. She makes a case for a deconstructive mode of reading precisely because she is willing to place the results of a deconstructive reading in the service of a vision drawn from elsewhere. In *Playing in the Dark*, Morrison explores the way the self-understanding of white literary texts depends on unacknowledged black others, on the way that, in Derrida's words, "the rapport of self-identity is always a rapport of violence with the other" (1984, 117). She begins by talking about how she is situated in language in a way that does not make her the participant in a tradition but the site of discursive conflict: "The kind of work I have always wanted to do requires me to learn how to maneuver ways to free up the language from its sometimes sinister, frequently lazy, almost always predictable employment of racially informed and determined chains" (xi). Since texts and readers are woven in this fabric in ways that victimize them, there is no such thing as an "ideal reader" for a text, a reader who grasps its intentions. An appeal to such an ideal reader may ask the actual reader to stand up and be attacked by the same linguistic/textual structures from which he/she wishes to escape, and this is certainly the case for Morrison. Text and reader are positioned in many ways, and Morrison's particular concern is with racial positioning in language.

Morrison herself has wriggled free of these structures far enough to characterize them, and they form the "racial unconscious" of American literature. I say "unconscious" because they do not emerge in a thematized way in the text. Racial positioning is not a question posed by the self-understanding of canonical American literature, which holds that it "is free of, uninformed, and unshaped by the four-hundred-year-old presence of, first, Africans and then African-Americans in the United States. . . . Moreover, such knowledge assumes that the characteristics of our national literature emanate from a particular 'Americanness' that is separate from and unaccountable to this presence" (Morrison, 5). Moreover, this text of "Americanness" could not offer satisfying answers if Bakhtinian or Gadamerian questions were posed to it. "Americanness" is situated at such a deep level of the articulatory process that it cannot be brought to dialogue by existing subjects. Indeed, Morrison confesses that an earlier self held this view (15). Thus she needs to read against the grain of the text, a way of reading that she describes in Derridean terms: "Through significant and underscored omissions, startling contradictions, heavily and nuanced conflicts, through the way writers peopled their work with the signs and bodies of this presence—one can see that a real or fabricated Africanist presence was crucial to their sense of Americanness" (6).

Morrison gives a characterization of what deconstruction is when it speaks of a text/tradition being divided against itself. Thus she seeks to identify not only "those moments when American literature was complicit in racism" but also those in which "literature exploded and undermined it" (16). When she discusses Willa Cather's *Sapphira and the Slave Girl,* she probes the way plot and character contradict each other, the way "a breakdown in the logic and machinery of plot construction implies the powerful impact of race on narrative" (25). Clearly this is not a "dialogue" in any Gadamerian or Bakhtinian sense. Morrison does not situate herself "in" this American tradition; at the same time, she does not claim to be outside the discourses she is examining. Unlike Derrida, when she takes apart the self-understanding of others, she does not return to the grand Derridean truth about "différance" that makes all distinctions undecidable. Moreover, she brings her insights to a new understanding for herself and for others. That is, she cashes out the third-person insight into her first-person discourse rather than leaving all subjectivities as "effects" of discourse; she closes the hermeneutic circle. In this way, she implicitly makes a metatheoretical move in which she appropriates a third-person critique for a new, enriched self-understanding (first-and second-person).

Morrison's use of a critique of identity shows how the critique of identity at the level of the sign can be put to the service of change. The justifications for using the deconstructive approach have to come from the outside—that is, from the first-and second-person vocabularies that posit values, agents, and communities. They are not within deconstruction itself. That is, deconstruction itself provides no reason to choose racial oppression over a McDonald's ad as the object of criticism. This issue is the heart of the controversy surrounding another poststructuralist view of language, that of Jean-François Lyotard.

Lyotard Versus Habermas on the Politics of Language

The debate between Lyotard and Habermas over the nature of language goes back to their different readings of the Enlightenment. While Habermas wants to redeem Enlightenment reason and politics, Lyotard wants to move beyond them. I begin by developing Habermas's philosophy. While this was treated in the last chapter in the context of Habermas's debate with Gadamer, here I focus on the linguistic character of his project and contrast his understanding of language with Lyotard's and Derrida's.[17]

Habermas

The crux of Habermas's view of reason is that "the use of language with an orientation to reaching understanding is the *original mode* of language use, upon which indirect understanding, giving something to understand or letting something be understood, and the instrumental use of language in general, are parasitic" (Habermas 1983, I, 288). Giving priority to this communicative use of language enables Habermas to make a scientific claim that communicative discourse is fundamental and liberating. David Rasmussen articulates the stakes of Habermas's claim about language: "What may not be immediately apparent in Habermas's program . . . is that there is a certain kind of agenda that seems to be endorsed—i.e., egalitarian, universal rights, radical democracy . . . presented under the rubric of reconstructive science, the claims of which are read out of the philosophy of language" (3–4). Habermas wants to avoid normative and utopian claims; he does not say that we *should* use language communicatively or that we *will* do so in some future utopia but that we *do* use it that way. Moreover, he rejects pragmatism's context-dependent theories of meaning, such as Richard Rorty's, because he thinks that the Enlightenment political ideals need the backing of reason if they are to avoid being relativistic claims.

Habermas situates his account historically through many figures, but, for our purposes here, Kant and Hegel are the most important since these two philosophers play a major role in Lyotard's work. Habermas follows Kant in dividing the modern world into spheres of knowledge: "By the end of the eighteenth century, science, morality and art were even institutionally differentiated as realms of activity in which questions of truth, of justice, and of taste were autonomously elaborated, that is, each under its own specific aspect of validity" (1987, 19). However, Habermas also agrees with Hegel that "Kant does not perceive as diremptions the differentiations within reason, the formal divisions within culture, and in general the fissures among all those spheres" (19). That is, Hegel and Habermas read Kant's division of culture into separate spheres of rationality as a breakdown in the coherence of this culture's self-understanding. Kant's attempt to suture these splits together with an overarching Reason that marks out these domains and reconciles the morality and aesthetics of the time with the universal "is not powerful enough to regenerate the unifying power of religion in the medium of reason" (20). When Hegel restored this unity, he did so by historicizing the development of a self-conscious, universal subject.[18] In Habermas's view, Hegel thus continues the debilitating mistake of Western philosophy from Descartes to Heidegger that seeks to ground itself in the subject. Unlike Hegel, Habermas does not seek this unifying power in self-consciousness (20–44) but with the intersubjective idea of communicative reason.

Habermas presents his argument first in *The Theory of Communicative Action* and then in *The Philosophical Discourse of Modernity*, in which he develops his ideas while offering a critique of poststructuralism. The key unifying notions for his theory of language are the "life-world" (adapted from Husserl) and "background" (adapted from John Searle). Habermas does not begin with the isolated subject to ground his philosophy but with communicatively structured worlds that subjects inhabit: "Insofar as speakers and hearers straightforwardly achieve mutual understanding about something in the world, they move within the horizon of their common life-world; this remains in the background of the participants—as an intuitively known, unproblematic, and unanalyzable, holistic background" (1987, 298).[19] Unity is not in the subject but in the background, which can be studied by the reconstructive sciences so that "the pre-theoretical grasp of rules on the part of competently speaking, acting, and knowing subjects" can be made explicit (298). "Background" provides commensurability among different linguistic practices. This unity is the basis for a subject of competence as a defender of claims: "Rationality is understood to be a disposition of speaking and acting subjects that is expressed in modes of behavior for which there are good reasons or grounds" (1983, I, 22).

"Background" and "life-world" attempt to give a neutral, objective description of a holistic and homogeneous language, a language that Lyotard would describe as "naturally at peace with itself" (1983, 199–200). For Habermas, unlike Derrida and Lyotard, conflict emerges at the level of claims made by subjects, not in language itself. Linguistic practices permit us to make claims, but they do not become modes of being that shape what we are and exclude alternative shapes. He tries to block out the force and shape of practices by assuming that such conflicts take place only between but not within "forms of life."

The crux of Habermas's pragmatics, like that of John Searle's, is the double structure of the speech-act, in which the propositional content is distinguished from the illocutionary force. That is, the propositional content "Laura is running" may be part of an assertion ("I assert that Laura is running"), a question ("Are you [Laura] running?"), and so on. Habermas says that this double structure permits speakers to "combine the communication of content with communication about the role in which the communicated content is used" (1979, 42). The rules for illocutionary acts are constitutive of those acts, and the best-known are the performatives such as baptisms or marriage ceremonies, in which "saying is doing." Searle and Habermas use the double structure to make reference and content independent of the illocutionary act (Searle 1969, 123; Habermas 1979, 42).

Habermas adapts Searle's conception of this double structure to theorize the three major areas into which the life-world is divided: claims to truth (cognitive dimension), truthfulness (inner or expressive world), and normative rightness (the interactive dimensions of speech that establish legitimate interpersonal relations) (Habermas 1979, 68). Individual speech acts often engage all these claims simultaneously, but they usually thematize one. The divisions among sentence types are not incommensurable language games but differences among claims that are at the disposal of the competent subject (59). The entire problematic is built on the premise that communicative action—"action aimed at reaching an understanding" (1)—is the fundamental mode of action and is in fact "already embodied in the existing forms of interaction" (1982, 227). Communicative action is "the medium through which the life-world as a whole is reproduced" (1987, 299). Habermas assumes that these various "claims" can be discussed in a language of argument in which "content" moves easily among different sentences since all share the same "life-world."

For Habermas, the goals of emancipation and autonomy can be pursued through the notion of the ideal speech situation—that is, where there are no internal or external constraints on dialogue. This situation serves as a regulative ideal that can eliminate the inequalities of power and the linguistic differences that stand in the way of a rational consensus. Habermas's ideal speech situation "cannot judge the value of competing forms of life" (Habermas 1982, 227) because a common life-world is presupposed.

For poststructuralists such as Derrida and Lyotard, Habermas's problematic uses the notion of "successful communication" as a justification for bringing in an all-embracing idea of a shared system of practices that puts insidious forms of linguistic oppression and critical resistance to them out of play. Habermas fights off the linguistic claims of Heideggerians and poststructuralists by distinguishing between the problem-solving function of language, which is engaged with "the structural constraints and communicative functions of everyday life," and the "poetic world-disclosing functions of language" (1987, 204), whose role is simply to "enrich" the everyday world (207). Habermas claims that Derrida mistakenly privileges the world-disclosing function and thus ignores "the fact that everyday communicative practice makes learning processes possible (thanks to built-in idealizations) in relation to which the world-disclosive force of interpreting language has in turn to prove its worth" (205). Isolated from the "intramundance learning processes" (339) of everyday language, poetic language is given the facile role of enriching the "everyday world" through the mediation of literary criticism (207).

Habermas does not need the distinction between philosophy and literature that he argues for in order to offer a critique of Derrida. He uses the "everyday" as a metatype that provides a common core for all types. Habermas makes strong points against poststructuralism but to make them, he does not need the narrow, tendentious philosophy of language that he proposes but a Bakhtinian position on language. First, Habermas rightly claims that poststructuralists "can and want to give no account of their own position" (1987, 336). They never account for their own agency and thus participate in what he calls a "performative contradiction." He means by this that poststructuralists propose theories of the subject that treat it only as a dupe and hence do not account for the possibility of their own statements. Moreover, Habermas rightly claims that they implicitly appeal to democratic values but never tell us how these values emerge from the critique of the Enlightenment or what contexts they can be put into in the present or future. Against poststructuralist unmasking, Habermas makes the hermeneutic point that critique is understandable only if we "preserve at least one stand for [the] explanation of the corruption of *all* reasonable standards" (cited in Rorty 1991, 164).

Lyotard

The arguments at stake in Lyotard's *The Postmodern Condition* (1978) concern the Enlightenment tradition of Western philosophy from Kant through Hegel and Marx to Habermas. Lyotard reads the confrontation between the premodern world and the Enlightenment in terms of narrative. In the pre-Enlightenment world, societies' means of legitimating knowledge and politics was a religious or mythic narrative. During the Enlightenment, scientific reason changed this by setting itself up not as one more narrative but as a metanarrative of universal reason that transcended the particular stories of any individual culture. In Lyotard's view, this metatheoretical move was then repeated in different forms by Hegel, Marx, structuralism, and Habermas. This assumption is the cornerstone of Lyotard's definition of modernity: "I will use the term 'modern' to designate any science that legitimates itself with reference to a metadiscourse of this kind by making an explicit appeal to some grand narrative, such as the dialectics of the Spirit, the hermeneutics of meaning, the emancipation of the rational or working subject, or the creation of wealth" ("Interview," xxiii). By contrast, postmodernism displays "incredulity toward metanarratives" (1984b, xxiv). The postmodern does not seek to trump the patchwork of heterogeneous language games that make up society by setting up a tribunal of reason that unmasks and levels these different languages into a common discourse. On the contrary, the postmodern not only respects the incommensurabilities of these languages; it quests for the sublime, for the innovative that breaks with the current discursive map. This description of language forecloses the possibility of a unifying consensus. Indeed, to urge such a consensus, even theoretically, "does violence to the heterogeneity of language games" (Postmodern xxv). Lyotard gives a positive evaluation to this new paradigm of knowledge: "Postmodern knowledge is not simply a tool of the authorities; it refines our sensitivity to differences and reinforces our ability to tolerate the incommensurable. Its principle is not the expert's homology, but the inventor's paralogy" (xxv).

Lyotard's work is a critique of Habermas's argument for the unity of culture. In "Answering the Question: What Is Postmodernism?" Lyotard characterizes Habermas's project thus: "What Habermas requires from the arts and the experiences they provide is, in short, to bridge the gap between cognitive, ethical, and political discourse, thus opening the way to a unity of experience" (Postmodern, 72). Lyotard associates this project with Hegel and "the notion of a dialectically totalizing experience" (Question, 73). The cost of the totalizing schemes begun by Hegel and Marx and now revivified by Habermas is not error but terror: "We have paid a high enough price for the nostalgia of the whole and the one, for the reconciliation of the concept and the sensible, of the transparent and communicable experience. Under the general demand for slackening and for appeasement, we can hear the mutterings of the desire for a return of terror" (Postmodern, 81–82).

In Le Différend (1983), Lyotard develops the view of language announced in The Postmodern Condition and clarifies his rejection of the tradition of totalizers. He focuses on the delineation of various types of sentences and discourses so as to mark out the moves by which one type can silence or oppress the idiom of another. Lyotard wants to flush out the conflicts between sentences and reveal their "differends": "A différend takes place between two parties when the 'settlement' of the conflict that opposes them is made in the idiom of one while the injury from which the other suffers does not signify in that idiom" (23–24).[20] For example, before the capitalist tribunal, the worker is forced to use the "language of capital." He/she can complain in terms of wage earnings but cannot put into question the very category of wage earner (1987, 61). That is, the worker cannot complain about the identity assigned by the system of capitalism, only about inequities within the system.

Lyotard's study is divided into numbered paragraphs—like Wittgenstein's Philosophical Investigations—into which are inserted readings of various philosophers, such as Plato, Hegel, Lévinas, and especially Kant. These readings, which are done in terms of Lyotard's philosophy of the sentence, are not reconstructions of what these philosophers meant; rather, they are Lyotard's response to the questions these thinkers pose to him: "One writes because one hears a request [demande] and an order to answer it; I read Kant or Adorno or Aristotle not in order to detect the request they themselves tried to answer by writing but in order to hear what they are requesting from me while I write or so that I may write" ("Interview," 19). Lyotard shares with Gadamer and Derrida the emphasis on the appeal made by the text rather than the search for an authorial intention or self-assertion of the critic; however, Lyotard's view of language contrasts sharply with hermeneutic dialogics.

Lyotard distinguishes various incommensurable sentence types—cognitive, ethical, and aesthetic. He follows a Kantian scheme like Habermas but accentuates the differences, the incommensurabilities among the three areas. Un-like Habermas's model, in which the subject simply brings forward different claims, Lyotard's philosophy makes each sentence type a distinct universe with its own kind of subjectivity and reference. In Lyotard's view, unlike that of Habermas, the subject does not have a neutral propositional content that pro-vides the mediation necessary for him/her to move between sentences and gives agency to the subject. Lyotard puts the conflict within language itself, not be-tween competing claims by people who share a language: "The social bond is linguistic, but is not woven with a single thread. It is a fabric formed by the intersection of at least two (and in reality an indeterminate number) of lan-guage games, obeying different rules" (*Postmodern Condition*, 40). Individuals and institutions are assigned "agency" through discourse; they do not manipu-late language: "The conflict is not between humans or any other entities since they come about through sentences" (1983, 199–200). Lyotard does not rule out mediation of the types of sentences and genres he maps, but he wants to expose the cost of mediation by looking at mediation through Kantian rather than Hegelian eyes.

Lyotard's discussion of the politics of community will show how this works. "Community," he says, is a Kantian "Idea"—that is, a totality for which there is no ostensible referent or, in Kant's terms, there are no intuitions, as there are for concepts. The error of the Hegelian or the Habermasian is to take these statements about totalities—which are speculative, dialectical statements—for referential statements: "The speculative and dialectical sentence that em-ploys these Ideas "acts as if it referred to phenomena" (191). For Lyotard, there is no ethical community that can be formed from such an Idea (188). Plato and Marx make a parallel move when they violate the incommensurability between cognitive and ethical sentences, for they have "the conviction that there is a true being of society and that society will be just when it conforms to this true being. One can thus draw just prescriptions from true descriptions" (1979, 48). This argument leads Lyotard to the conclusion that "revolutionary politics rests on a transcendental illusion in the political domain; it confuses what is pre-sentable as an object for a cognitive sentence with what is presentable as an object for a speculative/and or ethical sentence" (1983, 233). Marxism con-fuses an ideal object, the proletariat, "with real working classes, the multiple referents of cognitive sentences" (248). The party masks this differend by mo-nopolizing the procedures that establish historical reality; however, "the re-pressed *différend* returns inside the works' movement" (248).

The Enlightenment itself produced one of the most notorious hidden *différends* in its confusion of the particular and the universal. Lyotard shows this through an analysis of the *Preamble to the Declaration of the Rights of Man and Citizen*. The text reads: "The representatives of the French people, orga-nized in National Assembly . . . have resolved to set forth in a solemn declara-tion the natural, inalienable, and sacred rights of man" (1983, 210). The authorization for this declaration goes beyond the French people to a metalanguage and a metanorm about "man" (210). Universal principles are thus attached to a particular nation. For the revolutionaries armed with universal principles, those who resist their uprooting of traditions are reactionaries. For those attached to traditions, these abstract principles are empty. The result is that "after 1789, international wars are also civil wars" because "one will not know if the law thus declared is French or human, if the war conducted in the name of rights is one of conquest or emancipation, if the violence carried out in the name of liberty is repressive or pedagogical (progressive)" (211–12).By exposing differends in what were taken for unproblematic statements, Lyotard challenges the communitarian assumption shared by Habermas and Gadamer in their notions of shared life-world and tradition. Lyotard dismisses Gadamer's hermeneutics with the cavalier comment that it "guarantees that there is a meaning to know and thus confers legitimacy on history" (*Postmodern Condition*, 35). As Gadamer says, "Is it not, in fact, the case that every misunderstanding presupposes a 'deep common accord'? . . . No assertion is possible that cannot be understood as an answer to a question, and assertions can only be understood in this way" (1977, 7, 11).

Like Derrida, Lyotard explodes the argument that uses a notion of shared assumptions (life-world, background) to put a common ground under our feet in a way that no difference can threaten. (Here Bakhtin can be included as well, since he never gives difference the same fracturing power as poststructuralists do. Bakhtin's idea of language as dialogue never looks at the predialogical constitution of subjects that interests poststructuralists.) The spatial metaphor of "common ground" that underwrites "sharing" collapses since heterogeneity emerges in unthematized ways within as well as between communities and their languages. Ontological differends emerge not simply between radically different cultures but in living rooms, where interlocutors can inhabit different argumentative spaces.[21] One of the most startling literary examples of how differends work appears in Henry James's *The Golden Bowl*, when Charlotte Stant visits her ex-lover, the Prince, on the eve of his marriage. In their conversation, a differend comes up in their ways of talking about what is happening in the present. She tries to get him to adopt her language of reference—at one point, she even says, "You don't refer . . . I refer" (James 1909, I, 109). But he is cautious and evasive because he senses what is at stake. When the prince finally consents to speak as she does—in fact, they repeat the same words (312)—they become lovers.

However, there are not just *sentences* in Lyotard's discursive universe but also *genres* of discourse that provide procedures for linking one sentence to another; hence genres resituate differends from the level of the sentence to the question of ends (Lyotard 1983, 52)—for example, narrative organizes various types of sentences into a temporal configuration. Genres of discourse do not overcome the heterogeneity of sentences that must be connected since there are no necessary links between any two sentences. At the same time, genres do not prevent linkage; rather, they expose the cost of mediation. Moving to the level of the sentence rather than the sign (word) does not present a sequence of static subject positions marked out by speech-act theory but provides a place for agency as linkage between sentences. "To link is necessary; how to link is contingent" (51, 200). For example, "The door is closed" can be followed by (1) "Yes, of course. What do you think doors are for?"; (2) "I know. They're trying to lock me up"; or (3) "Good, I want to talk to you" (123). The contingency of any sequence exposes the ideological leaps that connect sentences. Hence "Politics consists in the fact that language is not language but sentences" (200).

Lyotard opens a space for critique that shows the obfuscatory powers of narrative: "The multitude of types of sentences and genres of discourse find a way to . . . neutralize the differends in narratives" (1983, 228). The fact that narratives are inevitable ways of understanding does not mean that narrative is an irreducible point for thinking about cultural conflict. Narrativizing culture and identity resolves internal differends without thematizing them. (We will see this vividly in chapter 5 when we examine narratives of national identity.) Lyotard thus corrects a confusion created by *The Postmodern Condition* that the absence of metanarratives of legitimation collapsed a space for critique so that first-order "petits récits" were the irreducible category, the guarantor of heretogeneity against totalizing metanarratives.[22] Lyotard's idea of the differend creates a space of critique in three different areas: (1) between different types of sentences, (2) between different genres, and (3) between types and genres. Although these philosophical distinctions may seem far from literature, they can open up new paths to reading.

Henry James's *The Ambassadors* can be used to illustrate how differends occur among sentence types and narratives. In *The Ambassadors* the protagonist, Lambert Strether, is engaged with the conflicting claims of truth, beauty, and goodness, the same Kantian trio that we have seen in Habermas and Lyotard. As the reader will recall, Strether is sent from Woollett, Massachusetts, to Paris by his patron and fiancée, Mrs. Newsome, to bring her son back from the clutches of Parisian society and, in particular, Mme. de Vionnet. In Paris, Strether loses the cultural moorings that helped him to determine what truth, beauty, and goodness are and how they are supposed to go together. In order to discover the truth about Chad Newsome and his relationship with Mme. de Vionnet, he must give himself over to the Parisian practices of beauty. Strether recognizes that he must abandon "his odious suspicion of any form of beauty. . . . He periodically assured himself—for his reactions were sharp—that he shouldn't reach the truth of anything till he had at least got rid of that" (1964, 118). He slowly modifies the way he understands all three values, though in the process he falls in love with Mme. de Vionnet. In his reorientation, he locks himself into the aesthetic so that everything seems "beautiful," and he thus blinds himself to the sexual dimension of Chad's relationship with her, a dimension that is available to everyone but him. His ignorance (or denial) is the source of much knowledge, nonetheless. The dynamics of the novel turn on the ways that the three values conflict and yet are mutually informing.[23]

Lyotard's understanding of the ways that narratives cover over differends also works well with the text, for Strether is constantly striving to narrativize his life prospectively and retrospectively. However, there are always tensions in these stories, as we see in the very first sentence of the novel, where the story of the dutiful man of Woollett conflicts with the desire to break free: "Strether's first question, when he reached the hotel, was about his friend; yet on his learning that Waymarsh was apparently not to arrive till evening he was not wholly disconcerted" (1964, 17). In the closing scenes with Maria, Strether uses a narrative about his own "magnificence" to avoid the request that she is making of him to stay with her. This scene shows the ambiguity of narrative: we need narratives in order to understand ourselves, but narratives neutralize the conflicts between the competing parts of our selves and threaten to become prophecies in which we hide. Strether hides from Maria and himself with this narrative (340–45).[24]

However, if the sentence is the irreducible category, what is the site of critique where critical philosophy marks out pure sentence families and prescribes that we respect the integrity of each type? Does Lyotard talk about the context of his own project?[25] Most of his answers to these questions are couched in Kantian vocabulary. He finds in Kant's faculty of judgment a means of passage from among different language games: "Each of the genres of discourse is like an island; the faculty of judgment, at least in part, is like a ship-owner or an admiral who sends expeditions from one island to another, expeditions that are intended to present to one what they have found . . . in the other and that could serve for the first as an 'as if intuition' in order to validate it" (1983, 190). The "as if" neither accentuates nor obliterates the gap between sentences; rather, the phrase "takes the gap into consideration. . . . The 'as if' comes not from the transcendental imagination for the invention of the comparison but from the faculty of judgment for its regulation" (181). There is no totalization of faculties. Because analogies are part of a faculty (family of sentences), this faculty is always open, undetermined. The critic who adjudicates among these claims has no rule of judgment (Lyotard 1986, 11). Thus critical philosophy "does not come from a faculty but from a quasi-faculty or 'as if' faculty (the faculty of judgment, sentiment) in as much as its rule of determination of pertinent universes is indeterminate" (12). Lyotard insists that we not mistake his "passages" for "bridges." Such a reading would establish the unifying reason that Habermas seeks, a reason that undermines linguistic difference. Nonetheless, Lyotard cannot make these sentences so different as to be unintelligible to each other. There are no rules for crossing from one domain to another, but it is through these passages that "one sentence family finds in another the basis for presenting the case that would validate it in the form of the sign, the example, the symbol, the type, the monogram" (11).

Moreover, the notion of the "sea" in this metaphor is linkage, linkage that is at once necessary and contingent. The sea figures the space of indeterminate passage, not a community that embraces these various sentence families.[26]

Ultimately, however, Lyotard fails to lay out the stakes of his reading of Kant or his project. He fails to do the metaphilosophical work of showing the relevance of Kant's vocabulary in contemporary terms. For example, if cognitive and ethical judgments are considered to be cultural practices, is the distinction between them so clear-cut? Is there interaction between them? By merely maintaining that ethical and aesthetic judgments are indeterminate, he avoids addressing the question of what informs such judgments. Indeed, he never clarifies the problems of agency or the ethical/political agenda that motivates his critique.

Lyotard's view of agency remains incomplete. On the one hand, he appeals to the energy of the "request" and the "passage"; on the other hand, he gives an account only of the constructed subject, not the constructing one. For him, the subject is simply a discursive position: "Our 'intentions' are tensions to link a certain way that genres of discourse exercise on the senders, receivers, referents, and meanings. We think that we want to persuade, seduce, convince, ... but this is because a certain genre of discourse—dialectic, erotic, didactic— imposes itself on 'our' sentence and on 'us' its mode of linkage" (1983, 197). "Genres of discourse are strategies—that belong to no one" (198). Lyotard is so concerned about criticizing the humanist subject that he never gets to a point where he proposes an alternative. Thus in the beginning of Le Différend he makes one of his objectives an attack on a straw person: "to refute the reader's prejudice, reinforced by centuries of humanism and 'human sciences,' that there is 'man,' that there is language, and that man uses language for his ends" (11).

In the same way, Lyotard trades on the Kantian distinction between determinate and indeterminate judgments in order to insist that all judgments are indeterminate. He empties the subject by employing an almost Sartrean notion of nothingness to describe the ontological space between sentences. The "question 'how to link?' proceeds from the gap [néant] that 'separates' this sentence from the one that follows. There are différends because or just as there is Ereignis" (1983, 200). The recognition of this truth about the relationship among sentences is opposed to the mystifying powers of genres of discourse. That is, all links are "inauthentic" covering over of the nothingness, which is the true nature of being: "Genres of discourse are modes of forgetting the gap or the event; they fill the emptiness between sentences" (200). No matter what sentence appears in any text, all that we can say is that there is nothingness after it. As in Sartre's theory of radical choice where the "étre-pour-soi" contemplates the practices from which it is severed, Lyotard's metasubject of philosophical discourse has access to the ontological gap that opens a space for the ethical and for the disclosure of ideology.

This ontology is related to Lyotard's Lévinasian definition of the ethical sentence. The Other cannot be constituted as Other even though the self is tempted to do so. "The violence of the revelation [of otherness} is the expulsion of the self out of the instance of speaker." The universe of the ethical sentence presents "an I stripped of the illusion of being a speaker of sentences and gripped incomprehensibly by the instance of receiver" (1983, 164). This is a powerful and important formulation, but it also reduces the ethical to the unreadable request. In the gap between sentences, we find the call of the ethical, the truth of the ontological, and the disclosure of ideology; however, there is no acting subject to respond to these appeals. Lyotard shortcircuits any attempt to give content to this space. The disembodied philosophical subject of his text locks the empirical subject into an inflexible pragmatic position. He offers no account of changes in language games. How do linkages change over time? What is the relationship between discursive and prediscursive practices? The dynamic interchange of voices that we find in Bakhtinian dialogue is never discussed.

This brings us to the values that drive Lyotard's critique. *Le Différend* develops the proposal announced in the last line of *The Postmodern Condition*, which demands "a politics that would respect both the desire for justice and the desire for the unknown" (67). The quest for the unknown reappears in *Le Différend*: "Our destination . . . is to furnish a presentation for the unpresentable and thus, when Ideas are at issue, to exceed everything that can be presented" (238–39). He connects the quest to justice by showing how it contributes to the uncovering of silenced differends, the sentential means of oppression. Lyotard defends this kind of formulation by pointing to the homogenizing discourse of capitalism: "The only insurmountable obstacle that the hegemony of the economic genre encounters is the heterogeneity of regimes of sentences and of genres of discourse. . . . The obstacle does not depend on human will but the differend" (260). "The tribunal of capitalism makes the differends between regimes of sentences or genres of discourse insignificant" (255). Even if we leave aside this dubious characterization of capitalism, we could still ask why Lyotard remains within the horizon of the differend and sentences to talk about power.[27]

By calling up the specter of such a monolithic horror beyond recuperation, Lyotard justifies (but only implicitly) his refusal to characterize any positive ethical/political institution or way of life. The unpresentable, the beyond, is the counterpart of the differend, the suppressed, since they both are defined only negatively against existing discursive structures. He offers no discussion of how competing differends are to be adjudicated. Thus we find in his works statements such as "Politics cannot have for its stake the good but must have the least bad" (1983, 203). Is this a kind of liberalism, in which neutrality toward alternative views of the good is pursued? The "bad" is defined as the "interdiction of possible sentences at every moment" (204). These citations raise numerous questions about differends and value for which Lyotard has no satisfactory response. Are all differends equivalent? Does minimizing the bad mean simply reducing the number of differends? Lyotard, like Foucault and

Derrida, identifies the discursive and the oppressive. Politics and literature—which do not fit one of his generic categories—have as their stakes the discovery of their stakes: "When Cézanne takes his brush, the stakes of painting are questioned; when Schoenberg sits at the piano, the stakes of music; when Joyce grabs his pen, those of literature" (201). Art and politics are underdetermined discourses that bring together heterogeneous sentences and challenge the singular autonomy of the sentence types. The rules for these "quasi" genres do not preexist. The power of the text or the painting is not what it says or what it is but what it asks the receiver: "Painting will be good (will have achieved its end, will have approached it) if it demands the receiver to ask himself what it is" (201). Thus "the stakes of a certain literature, philosophy, and perhaps politics are to bear witness to differends by finding them idioms" (30). Lyotard's politics of the differend offers an avenue to discovering linguistic oppression but does little to link this critique to ethical and political practices. His critique is similar to Derrida's in that both are trying to show how unifying discourses misunderstand the nature of language; however, while Derrida makes his case in terms of the undoing of the concept, Lyotard makes his in terms of language games and pragmatics. Like Derrida, Lyotard accepts the ontology of power—that is, that the discursive is the oppressive—and they both share the ethic/political urge that accompanies this ontology—an ethics/politics of difference and negative freedom.

Even though these problems are serious, I do not think that they undermine Lyotard's project so much as limit its horizon. The analysis of differends can be an important critical moment in normative critical projects that offer democratic visions because it provides a means for locating discursive oppression: "In the differend, something cries out in respect to a name. Something demands to be put into phrases, and suffers from the wrong of this impossibility" (Lyotard 1987, 65). The philosophy of the sentence opens a new critical space not simply for articulating politics but for politicizing articulation.

Foucault

The work of Foucault, like that of Derrida and Lyotard, attacks Enlightenment premises about reason and humanism. However, Foucault is more concerned with the history of human practices than with the history of philosophy. He draws his inspiration from the work of Nietzsche, particularly the *Genealogy of Morals*. In an interview, Foucault says, "If I wanted to be pretentious, I would use the 'the genealogy of morals' as the general title of what I am doing" (cited in James Miller, 213–14). Although Foucault shares with Derrida an interest in unmasking the self-understandings of texts, Foucault does not focus on the rhetorical contradictions in the texts themselves, as does Derrida. Instead, he shows how texts are produced by social and/or discursive practices that are not thematized by the authors and their cultures: "I should like to know whether the subjects responsible for scientific discourse are not determined in their situation, their function, their perceptive capacity, and their practical possibilities by conditions that dominate and even overwhelm them" (1970).[28]

Foucault follows Nietzsche in exploding the self-understanding of the Enlightenment's rational, ethical subject. In *The Genealogy of Morals*, Nietzsche takes categories that moral theorists keep separate—body and soul, the physical and the spiritual—and ties them together into a story of self-deformation. Nietzsche claims that the internalized moral control of behavior can be brought about only through violence and threats. In Nietzsche's story, the spontaneous expression of instinct was blocked when humans formed societies, and this blockage made instincts turn inward: "All instincts that do not discharge themselves outwardly turn inward—this is what I call the internalization of man: thus it was that man first developed what was later called his 'soul'" (1956, 217).[29] For Nietzsche, this reversed instinct becomes hostility toward the self, which is the foundation of moral consciousness: "In its earliest phrase bad conscience is nothing other than the instinct of freedom forced to become latent, driven underground, and forced to vent its energy upon itself" (220).

While Nietzsche exposes the psychic price of morality, Foucault exposes the cost of the Enlightenment initiative to rationalize the life-world through the human sciences and their bureaucratic application. The Enlightenment heralds the autonomy and liberty of the individual, but at the same time, it releases insidious forms of control. Foucault's genealogy reads against the narrative of progress, in which the present looks complacently at a benighted past. As David Hoy says, "Genealogical histories are written to challenge others' histories of the same events written with the assumption of progress, precisely to disrupt this complacency about the present" (1991, 276–77; Foucault 1984, 91). Foucault unmasks the Enlightenment's false objectivity, its denial of the will to knowledge, which drives the inquiry itself (1984, 95–96). As he says, "The 'Enlightenment,' which discovered the liberties, also invented the disciplines" (1977, 222). These disciplines do not operate in the open as do the public, universal norms but in subtle, indirect ways. "In my book on the birth of the prison [*Discipline and Punish*], I tried to show precisely how the idea of a technology of individuals, a certain type of power, was exercised over individuals in order to tame them, shape them, and guide their conduct," as a kind of strict correlative to "the birth of a type of liberal regime" (cited in James Miller, 222).

To introduce his thesis, Foucault opens *Discipline and Punish* with a scene of violent execution and juxtaposes it to a scene of a man with prison timetables. He then reverses the reader's expectation by showing how the supposed less violent humanitarian prison system is in fact a deeper villain than its "barbarous" predecessor. The interest of the human sciences in documenting and categorizing all aspects of human behavior becomes a means of regulation, and this regulation is not imposed from without but internalized.[30] The most compelling metaphor for this internalization is the image of the panopticon. The administrators of prisons organized their populations so they could be seen but not see. In a "system of surveillance there is no need for arms, physical violence, material constraint. Just a gaze, a gaze which each individual under its weight will end by internalizing to the point that he is his own supervisor, each individual thus exercising this surveillance over, and against, himself" (Power/Knowledge, 155).

Unlike Marxists, Foucault does not see power as wielded by some over others. For him, power is constitutive of all social relations, relations that are not described in terms of self-understandings of individuals: "Power relations are both intentional and nonsubjective.... There is no power that is exercised without a series of aims and objectives. But this does not mean that it results from the choice or decision of an individual subject" (1978, 94–95). Intentionality is not situated in individual subjects but in institutional practices that are "deeper" than the self-reflection of the agents. The result is that the individual is neither the point of departure nor a necessary component of inquiry. The whole problematic of the "individual" is the product of a certain system: "The individual is not to be conceived as a sort of elementary nucleus, a primitive atom, a multiple and inert material on which power comes to fasten or against which it happens to strike, and in doing so subdues or crushes individuals. In fact, it is already one of the prime effects of power that certain bodies, certain gestures, certain discourses, certain desires, come to be defined and constituted as individuals" (1981, 98).

Moreover, Foucault does not discuss society in humanistic terms but through discursive categories that are not at the disposal of the agents in question. Indeed, these discursive categories produce the agents' consciousness and expose aspects of their beliefs that they never would suspect. This is a genealogical principle for Foucault: "Where the soul pretends unification or the self fabricates a coherent identity, the genealogist sets out to study the beginning—the numberless beginnings, whose faint traces and hints of color are readily seen by the historical eye" (1984, 81). The Cartesian tradition of the reflective, autonomous self that the Enlightenment continues covers over not just domination by the bourgeoisie but an autonomous and anonymous network of power. In Foucault's revision, the story of reason as the quest for truth becomes a tangled, contingent, and conflictual tale that has no singular beginning or ending and no evolutionary development: "It is not the activity of the subject of knowledge that produces a corpus of knowledge ... but power-knowledge, the processes and struggles that traverse it and of which it is made up, that determines the forms and possible domains of knowledge" (175). Moreover, Foucault's story traces the way power gets its teeth into us through our social practices and not just at the level of ideas and beliefs.

Foucault's decentering of the subject borrows from structuralism; but, unlike structuralism, Foucault is deeply interested in history. However, this interest is not the interest of typical historians who seek to narrate the historical development of a country or an idea. Foucault's critique of the traditional histories of value is made possible through two moves. First, he desubstantializes the identities of subjects and objects into a relational network. The second move is to take this Saussurean insight about the inseparability of individual identity from the system and transform it. Saussure's neutral system becomes a force that articulates—the will-to-power. The will-to-power is not a psychological principle but an ontological one that articulates the world: "To impose upon becoming the character of being, that is the supreme will power" (Nietzsche 1968, 179). The identity of signs is not just the differential product of an indifferent system whose signifiers and signifieds assemble around semiotic possibilities. The apparent "endurance" of things is a function of a given power structure (interpretation).

Contrary to Gadamer's view, history is not a tradition that evolves. Foucault does not see our heritage as "an acquisition, a possession that grows and solidifies; rather, it is an unstable assemblage of faults, fissures, and heterogeneous layers that threaten the fragile inheritor from within or from underneath" (1984, 82). Unlike Marx, the Frankfurt School, and Habermas, Foucault does not see power as simple repressive force from which the philosopher can liberate us. Power exercises control without a controller. Rather than being something that distorts who we really are, power, for Foucault, constitutes our being. Hence the relationship among texts or between readers and texts is not "the calm Platonic form of language and dialogue" but of a "violent, bloody, and lethal character" (57). The genealogical approach to the past exposes this violence that is masked by the agents' beliefs. As Foucault says in "Truth and Power," "the history which bears and determines us has the form of a war rather than that of a language: relations of power, not relations of meaning" (56).

A good way to understand the distinctiveness of Foucault's work is to compare his understanding of psychoanalysis with that of the Frankfurt School. When the Frankfurt School (Marcuse, Reich, Horkheimer, Adorno, and later Habermas) examined sexuality, they found the sources of repression in the family—that is, the family blocked the natural expression of sexuality. Freudian psychoanalysis seeks to uncover what is repressed by civilization and to bring it to consciousness, to replace the irrationality of the id with the rational consciousness of the ego. The Frankfurt School made alienation and neurosis the products of capitalism and our rationalizing society. (They thus broke with the Freudian assumption that such effects were just the inevitable consequences of civilizing our beastly instincts.) Therapy, in their view, was not local and private but global and revolutionary. Although Habermas abandons this revolutionary dimension, he still thinks that the philosopher and social scientist are capable of uncovering truths about us and straightening out ideologically distorted communication.

In volume 1 of the *History of Sexuality*, Foucault challenges the whole "repressive hypothesis" that informs not just psychoanalysis but all modern culture: "The question I would like to pose is not: why are we repressed? but rather: Why do we say, with so much passion and so much resentment against our most recent past, against our present, and against ourselves, that we are repressed?" (1978, 8–9). Foucault undermines this hypothesis, first, by historicizing the study of sexual practices so that recent interdictions imposed by Christianity and the needs of capitalism fold into earlier patterns of control. Second, he shows that the areas of sexuality that were morally problematic were not the areas forbidden. Third, he puts psychoanalysis in a history of practices of confession that goes back to the Greeks and is continued by Christianity. Psychoanalysis adds the Enlightenment twist of setting up the rational interest of the scientist against the moral about sexuality. (Pre-Enlightenment culture made no such division.) As Foucault says, "This need to take sex 'into account,' to pronounce a discourse on sex that would not derive from morality alone but from rationality as well, was sufficiently new that at first it wondered at itself and sought apologies for its own existence. How could a discourse based on reason speak of *that?*" (24).

For Foucault, psychoanalysis, the "talking cure," is just one more "incitement to discourse" (1978, 34), an incitement to "talk about sex" (24) that dates back to the eighteenth century. Discourse is not under the control of the subject but is part of the articulatory network of modern power. Hence our very desire to confess "is so deeply ingrained in us that we no longer perceive it as the effect of power that constrains us; on the contrary, it seems to us that truth, lodged in our most secret nature, 'demands' only to surface" (60). Thus Foucault turns around the question of repression. Instead of asking how our desires became alienated, he asks how practices to discover the truth about ourselves ever became part of the experience of sexuality. "The object in short is to define the discourse of knowledge-power-pleasure that sustains the discourse on human sexuality in our part of the world" (11).

Thus when Foucault writes the history of a topic—for example, morality or sexuality—he does not just look for what people have said about it; rather, he tries to account for how such a topic came about to begin with. He rejects the search for origins "because it is an attempt to capture the exact essence of things. . . , because this search assumes the existence of immobile forms that precede the external world of accident and succession" (1984, 78). In the same way, ends are also critiqued: "In placing present needs at the origin, the metaphysician would convince us of an obscure purpose that seeks its realization at the moment it arises" (83). Thinking in terms of origins obscures the dynamics of history. Concepts do not grow or develop over time; rather, history is a struggle for power not between individuals but between texts (86, 81). History is like a palimpsest in which one text seeks to supplant another: "If interpretation is the violent or surreptitious appropriation of a system of rules, which in itself has no essential meaning, in order to impose a direction, to bend it to a new will, to force participation, then the development of humanity is a series of interpretations" (86). Foucault's approach challenges the identity of an event— what Barthes in *S/Z* would call the proairetic code. He does not use the self-understandings of the past or present to code events: "An event . . . is not a

73

decision, a treaty, a reign, or a battle, but the reversal of a relationship of forces, the usurpation of power, the appropriation of a vocabulary turned against those who had once used it. . . . The forces operating in history are not controlled by destiny or regulative mechanisms but respond to haphazard conflicts" (88).

Foucault's critique of subjectivity and value raises important questions about the context from which he writes, about his own agency and the values that inform it. How did he slip out of the power/knowledge system in order to describe it? If all the values of the tradition are coopted, to what does he appeal? He avoids closing the hermeneutic circle by never letting us in on the position from which he writes. Moreover, his system of airtight oppression does not seem to leave any room for change. Nancy Fraser raises these issues pointedly: "Why is struggle preferable to submission? Why ought domination to be resisted? Only with the introduction of normative notions of some kind could Foucault begin to answer such questions . . . to tell us what is wrong with the modern power/knowledge regime and why we ought to oppose it" (1989, 29). Peter Dews, quite correctly, carries this critique to the entire poststructuralist assault on identity: "The rejection of any normative standpoint as complicit with the coercive imposition of identity, eventually leads to the malfunctioning and breakdown of the very concepts which were intended to expose the intrinsically coercive character of normativity. . . . In order to break this dialectic [of poststructuralist thought] the fundamental poststructuralist assumption that identity can never be anything other than the suppression of difference must be challenged" (169–70).[31] Foucault's response to such charges in a 1984 interview is worth quoting at length:

> R. Rorty points out that in these analyses [Forcault's earlier work] I do not appeal to any "we"—to any of those "we's" whose consensus, whose values, whose traditions constitute the framework for a thought and define the conditions in which it can be validated. But the problem is, precisely, to decide if it is actually suitable to place oneself within a "we" in order to assert the principles one recognizes and the values one accepts; or if it is not, rather, necessary to make the future formation of a "we" possible, by elaborating the question. Because it seems to me that the "we" must not be previous to the question; it can only be the result— and the temporary result—of the question as it is posed in the new terms in which one formulates it. (385)

Foucault's answer is that it is better not to close the hermeneutic circle because any closing will diminish the force of his critique by bringing it into the traditional web of discourse. He is thus placing his bets on a "total revolution,"[32] a revolution so profound that we cannot say anything about it. The value animating this hope is a freedom that can be conceived only negatively against the oppression of the present.

However, there was a change in Foucault's work after the publication of the first volume of the *History of Sexuality*. In an interview near the end of his life, he says, point-blank, "I changed my mind" (cited in McCarthy, 221, note 29). In his late work, Foucault talks about the self and its ethical constitution, what he calls a "ràpport à soi." I cannot follow this complex and ambiguous development, which has perplexed and fascinated many. Instead, I will focus on his renewed interest in Kant and the Enlightenment and use this interest as a way of cashing out his critique.

Foucault's interest in Kant began early, when he wrote a thesis on Kant's little-known *Anthropology*,[33] and Kant's transcendental method informs all of Foucault's work. Foucault revises this method so that instead of studying the logical and universal conditions necessary to make experience possible, as Kant did, one looks at the historical conditions necessary for various experiences to be possible. Unlike Habermas's reconstruction of the conditions necessary for speech, Foucault puts his reconstruction in the service of change, of freedom. We come to understand what brought us into being in order to break free of these constraints.[34] That is what Foucault means when, in an essay on Kant ("What Is Enlightenment?"), he speaks of "the critical ontology of ourselves" as being "an ethos, a philosophical life in which the critique of what we are is at one and the same time the historical analysis of the limits imposed on us and an experiment with the possibility of going beyond them" (1984, 50). Here Foucault recuperates the critical project of the Enlightenment and its hope of freedom. This freedom is not realized by trying to find the essence of humanity; "modern man" is the "man who tries to invent himself" (Foucault Reader, 42).

4

Feminist Theories

BEYOND CONSTRUCTIVISM AND ESSENTIALISM

This chapter focuses on the way feminist theories have established its own hermeneutic by challenging and reworking the theories we examined in the first half of the book. It does not survey feminist theories of recent years but rather examines those that pick up the thread of the argument developed thus far. I begin with an outline of three broad positions that inform various feminist theories: the liberal position, which argues for a difference of blind equality and a generalized subject of justice; the gynocentric position (which some call "essentialist"), which argues for the distinctiveness and value of women's practices and an embodied, situated subject; and the constructivist position, which sees gender distinctions as part of an oppressive linguistic/cultural system and problematizes all notions of agency by making them effects of an oppressive system. This rapid overview will set up the arguments of Iris Marion Young, Seyla Benhabib, bell hooks, Nancy Fraser, and Jessica Benjamin. Through the work of these thinkers, I develop a way of breaking down the bunkers among competing critical vocabularies that divide feminist theories so that women can talk about the nourishment of traditions, the forces of construction, and the claims of rights and justice. In the second half of the chapter, I describe how the problematic I develop can be used to read Marie Cardinal's *The Words to Say It*.

In her essay "Humanism, Gynocentrism, and Feminist Politics," Iris Marion Young provides a convenient articulation of long-standing debates within feminist theory. Humanist feminists, such as Simone de Beauvoir, argue for the equality of women and against the discriminatory practices of the past and present. De Beauvoir's standard for equality and the grounds for opposition come from the action and language of men. As Young says, "Humanist feminism defines women's oppression as the inhibition and distortion of women's human potential by a society that allows the self-development of men" (Feminist 1990, 231). De Beauvoir's *The Second Sex* shows how fruitful this approach can be, as she exposes the debased images and myths that men have created about women and the ways that the Western tradition has forced them to act as the passive, ornamental, and subordinate other to men. De Beauvoir argues that women ought to be thought of as free and equal agents, and her notions of "free" and "equal" come from the dominant male culture. The result is that women are separated from any gender-specific practices and that the existing value system is left in place.

Gynocentric feminism, on the other hand, sees, in Young's words, "women's oppression as the devaluation and expression of women's experience by a masculinist culture that exalts violence and individualism" (Feminist 1990, 231–32). Gynocentric feminism thus affirms women's practices against those of men. It does not ask for equality by male standards and access to a man's "world," as humanist feminists do. Rather, gynocentrism rejects these norms, which, in this view, have produced an exploitive, destructive, and egoistic world. Gynocentric feminists attack de Beauvoir for despising women's activities and accepting the patriarchy's view of what a human being is. As Young says, "Beauvoir's ontology reproduces the Western traditions oppression of nature and nurture, freedom and mere life, spirit and body" (235). Classic liberalism, prior to its most recent revisions,[1] accepts the male as the ideal; it leaves intact a conception of the subject as disembodied vessel of rationality. "Gynocentrism" is a loose category that includes a broad spectrum of thinkers from Carol Gilligan, who works on the distinctiveness of women's moral reasoning, to Luce Irigaray, who offers a feminist deconstruction of Lacanian psychology.

Gilligan's work contests the dominant model of development in moral psychology, which is proposed by Lawrence Kohlberg. Gilligan claims that girls in her research do not do as well as boys in Kohlberg's system because girls have a distinctive pattern of psychic individuation that involves self-articulation within relationships rather than through separation.[2] This psychological process produces a distinctive type of moral reasoning. While Kohlberg's highest stage of moral development is the dispassionate, detached, rule-governed subject of justice, girls tend to concern themselves with the maintenance and repair of relationships, a concern Gilligan calls an "ethics of care." Gilligan's claim is not just that Kohlberg's model is biased; she thinks rather that an ethics of care is an important complement to an ethics of justice.[3] Her work has been criticized by some feminists for its failure to account for racial difference and its glorification of traditional caregiving roles of women as well as other charges, and I will come back to them.[4]

The third major area of feminist theory is constructivism, which grows out of poststructuralism. Julia Kristeva, the French philosopher, linguist, psychoanalyst, and novelist, is a good representative of this view. Kristeva is self-conscious about her relationship to previous feminist theories, placing herself in a third generation of feminists, after the liberal humanists (exemplified by de Beauvoir) and the second generation gynocentrists such as Irigaray and Hélène Cixous (Kristeva 1986, 193–98). This third generation is suspicious of all languages of identity, collective or individual, and such feminists explore the discursive processes that construct gender identities behind the backs of subjects. In her early work, Kristeva adapts the poststructuralist psychoanalysis of Jacques Lacan to her understanding of language and subjectivity.[5] Lacan takes Saussure's concept of *la langue* and turns it into a linguistic nightmare: "Human beings are not masters of language. They have been flung into it, entangled in it, and are caught in its meshes. . . . We should wonder at the paradox. Man is not master in his own house here. There is something in which he integrates himself which largely reigns by its combinations" (Séminaire, 353). Lacan calls this linguistic mesh the symbolic order, which is associated with the law of the father. The child enters the symbolic order at the time of the Oedipal phase of development, when he/she is individuating. Prior to this, the child is in a pre-Oedipal stage that Lacan calls the Imaginary, a stage in which he/she is engaged in identificatory activity with the mother. The effect of the entry into the symbolic order is devastating. As Lacan says, "Woman is introduced into the symbolic pact of marriage as an object of exchange along basically androcentric and patriarchal lines. Thus, the woman is engaged in an order of exchange in which she is an object; indeed, this is what caused the fundamentally conflictual character of her position—I would say without exit. The symbolic order literally submerges and transcends her" (cited Leland, 123).

Even though she does not do away with Lacan's basic suppositions, Kristeva adds the semiotic to Lacan's symbolic. The semiotic is associated with the instinctual drives that operate most openly within the child before entry into the symbolic order, which shapes and represses these drives. The semiotic is not just connected to drives and to what Freud called the primary processes; it is also associated with the mother and her body (Grosz, 195). Both the symbolic and semiotic modes inform the subject's speech; however, poetry, for Kristeva, is more in touch with the semiotic than ordinary discourse: "One should begin by positing that there is within poetic language . . . a heterogeneousness to meaning and signification. This heterogeneousness, detected genetically in the echolalias of infants as rhythms and intonations anterior to the first phonemes, morphemes, lexemes, and sentences . . . operates through, despite, and in excess of [signification], producing in poetic language, 'musical' as well as nonsense effects that destroy not only accepted beliefs and significations but, in radical experiments, syntax itself, that guarantee of thetic consciousness" (1984, 133).

Our access to the semiotic is not direct but comes through the ruptures and overflows in the symbolic. Kristeva gives these ruptures in the symbolic a political charge, not just an aesthetic one: "The [avant-garde] text is a practice that can be compared to political revolution: the one brings about in the subject what the other brings about in society" (1984, 17). Through her readings, which are often devoted to male writers such as Joyce and Artaud, she connects the breakdowns in their signifying practices to socioeconomic crisis. Her proposal urges feminism to resist an identification with the father, in which women would hate themselves and their mothers, as well as an identification with the mother, in which case women would lose access to the symbolic order.[6]

What Kristeva's constructivist position enables us to do is to avoid the traps of humanist and gynocentric feminism, both of which remain hostage to existing gender categories. Humanists take existing patriarchal vocabularies as the standards for judging inequality, while gynocentrism takes women's practices as a source of critique. The constructivist steps outside this opposition and exposes the articulatory system of gender as a story of force. Constructivists, like Foucault, try to stand at right angles from the subject positions of culture so that accepted definitions of gender are problematized.

Despite these virtues, the constructivist position runs into difficulties of its own. First, it does not account for women's historical achievements. As Dorothy Leland says of Kristeva's theory: "The history of feminist interventions provides an empirical challenge to the view that we cannot transcend the identity options and laws definitive of the patriarchal Symbolic Order. The practice of consciousness raising provides just one example" (130). Second, the constructivist feminist, like Foucault, does not account for her own escape from the network she describes. Telling this story requires a break with the constructivist position, which talks only of the way language subjects us rather than how it enables us. Third, the constructivist does not recuperate the values to which she appeals. Kristeva's view of language leads to a wholesale critique of social norms rather than distinguishing between those that are emancipatory and those that are oppressive (Fraser 1992, 189). What goes with the one-sided critique of agency and norms is the failure to account for intersubjective relations to which the theorist's discourse appeals.

Feminist hermeneuts employ a metatheoretical reflection to assess and rework these conflicting claims. Feminist hermeneutics has two complementary but distinct metatheoretical aspects, which Seyla Benhabib articulates as follows: (1) the development of an "explanatory-diagnostic analysis of women's oppression across history, culture, and societies"; and (2) the articulation of "an anticipatory utopian critique of the norms and values of our current society and culture, such as to project new modes of togetherness, of creating to ourselves and to nature in the future" (1992, 152). These aspects are metatheoretical because they give the general shape that a theory must fit but do not specify which theory or theories must be filled into each aspect. These requirements are broad enough to include many different theoretical perspectives; however, they are also tight enough to break down the bunkers that divide current theories. The explanatory dimension can be broadened to include not just work in the social sciences but also poststructuralist accounts, since they too offer third-person insights. That is, they tell what is going on behind our backs. As Fraser says, we need a view of the subject "that integrates . . . poststructuralist emphasis on construction with . . . critical-theoretical stress on critique" (1991, 174).

This way of understanding the feminist project makes gender a relational identity, one that emerges from the historical context of signs and that will change in future contexts. Gendered vocabularies appear in the explanatory part of critique, and these vocabularies are those from which we want to escape. (This is the constructivist insight.) Gendered vocabularies also appear in the utopian dimension, and these are the vocabularies that we want to inhabit.

(This is the gynocentric insight.) Gender is, of course, only one thread of identity, and the way it figures in women's lives depends on a host of factors. What should concern us about any definition of "women" is not the metaphysical issue of "essentialism" but the ethics/politics of such an articulation in a given circumstance. Women need to be able to tell stories that depict their common suffering and their solidarity, and they also need to be able to tell stories that articulate the differences within and between themselves. These stories are partial and provisional constructs, not essences. As bell hooks says with regard to race, "There is a radical difference between a repudiation that there is a black 'essence' and recognition of the way black identity has been specifically constituted in the experience of exile and oppression" (29).

One of the most interesting places to test the two-pronged approach developed thus far is with the work of Judith Butler, which responds to the charge that poststructuralist feminists do not have a theory of agency. For her, "the critique of the subject is not a negation or repudiation of the subject, but, rather, a way of interrogating its construction as a pregiven or foundationalist premise" (1995, 42). Butler is suspicious of a vocabulary that merely "situates the self" because she fears that this formulation gives the self a kind of prediscursive unity or privilege outside the system of power: "the 'I' is not situated; the 'I,' this 'I,' is constituted by these positions" (42).[7] Butler's point is well taken insofar as one takes a vocabulary of the self in the way she describes. However, as we have seen, the notion of a linguistically embedded subject requires not simply a third-person vocabulary of its genealogical constitution but the dialogical vocabulary of its agency in, not outside, language. It is only the theorist's agency that makes possible a theory of constitution. When Butler moves from this constructivist formulation to agency, she tries to steer between the foundationalist idea that the subject is a ground and the constructivist notion that it is an effect: "The subject is neither a ground nor a product, but the permanent possibility of a certain resignifying process, one which gets detoured and stalled through other mechanisms of power, but which is power's own possibility of being reworked" (1995, 47).

The problem is that Butler does not characterize this possibility. As Nancy Fraser says, Butler assumes we have critical capacities but never says where they come from (1995, 66–67). Moreover, Butler does not give a shape to these acts of resignification since she eschews invoking any values or norms except negative liberty and difference, which, as we saw in the last chapter, give us nothing to work for except the undoing of systems. In brief, Butler tries to smudge the difference between the explanatory moment of critique in which the self-understanding of the agent is unmasked and the utopian moment in which agency is recuperated. Hence she loses the capacity to thematize the aspects of cultural history she wants to attack from those she wants to recover: "If performativity is construed as that power of discourse to produce effects through reiteration, how are we to understand the limits of such production, the constraints under which such production occurs?" (1993, 20). For Butler, the claim that there is no space of critique outside power means that all value terms are so complicitous with a kind of cultural mystification she wants to unmask that they must be avoided: "Power pervades the very conceptual apparatus that seeks to negotiate its terms, including the subject position of the critic" (1995, 39). But the presence of power in all ethical/political configurations does not mean that all ethical/political vocabularies are worthless.

The issue surrounding Butler's work—which problematics should be employed for understanding subjectivity and power?—informs the debates in different areas of feminist theory. The lesson from the above analysis is that feminist theory needs to keep the genealogical story of women's constitution in productive tension with the recuperative story of women's achievement. This is an important lesson for feminist historiography, which is also torn between the dilemma of constructivism and agency, as the argument between Joan Scott and Linda Gordon illustrates.[8] Our analysis enables us to say that the argument is not over the empirical question of whether this particular woman or group is best thought of as an agent or as a construct but on the transcendental issues with which the theorist must come to terms. She must make (or assume) an historical account of the possibility of her own agency in order to write a constructivist critique, and she must affirm (or assume) certain values in order for the critique to have any bite.

These transcendental guidelines can help us cut through the complex debate over the term "essentialism." For constructivists, such as Kristeva and Toril Moi, "to define 'woman' is necessarily to essentialize her" (Moi, cited in Fuss, 56), and such essentialism is an epistemological and political error. For liberal and gynocentric feminists, on the other hand, evaporating identity deprives women of the resources of solidarity they need to survive and thrive in a patriarchal world. The arguments between those who claim gender identity and those who read it as part of an oppressive order have produced a third view, "strategic essentialism," which tries to take something from each one. According to strategic essentialists, the constructivists win the epistemological battle over the relationship of language and identity: any definition is essentialism.[9] However, strategic essentialists think this position is politically vulnerable since groups need such definitions to survive.

The most extensive treatment of this debate is Diana Fuss's *Essentially Speaking,* in which there is a chapter on Irigaray. The charge often made against Irigaray is that her redescription and valorization of women's bodies turn "woman" into an essence. Here is a representative passage from Irigaray:

Woman's autoeroticism is very different from man's. In order to touch himself, man needs an instrument: his hand, a woman's body, language. . . . And this self-caressing requires at least a minimum of activity. As for woman, she touches herself in and of herself without any need for mediation, and before there is any way to distinguish activity from passivity. Woman 'touches herself' all the time, and moreover no one can forbid her to do so, for her genitals are formed of two lips in continuous contact. Thus, within herself, she is already two—but not divisible into one(s)—that caress each other. (cited in Fuss, 58)

Fuss defends Irigaray's "essentialism" by saying that "the point, for Irigaray, of defining women from an essentialist standpoint is not to imprison women within their bodies but to rescue them from enculturating definitions by men" (63). I wholeheartedly agree with this defense of the new self-understandings that Irigaray offers women but reject Fuss's shallow characterization of Irigaray's texts as "strategic essentialism" precisely because this label remains a hostage to the poststructuralist problematic that blocks out important vocabularies of agency, ethics, and politics by making the real truth about the subject what happens behind her back.

Such third-person vocabularies are useful, but women also need vocabularies that can articulate solidarities and conflicts, and they need ethical/political principles that inform these deliberations. The very word "difference" floats between two competing understandings—essentialist and constructivist. For Irigaray, "difference" is about the vocabulary of self-understanding, the valorized vocabulary that one wants to inhabit. For the constructivist, "difference" is a word that designates the unconscious of an oppressive system, what the system excludes once we see it through the eye of critique. The constructivist difference is not a voice or a person but a discursive feature such as the other of the concept. This capacity to work against humanistic categories is the strength of poststructuralism, but this strength in the explanatory aspect of hermeneutics becomes a weakness if it is not connected to a vocabulary that offers guidelines for change. The constructivist thesis makes any appeal to democratic traditions impossible, for these traditions are treated only critically. The constructivist tells us that we cannot or should not traffic in these vocabularies because we will be complicitous with a regime of power, but she provides no vocabulary for living now. Women can only say that they are oppressed; they cannot invoke their own traditions or existing political traditions to buttress their arguments. Such a problematic flattens the history of women's achievements into another chapter in the saga of logocentrism or the symbolic order.

Women have been constructed by the symbolic order, but they have also developed a critical consciousness, a power to rename that cannot and should not be trivialized by the constructivist unmasking of its essentialism or political naïveté. The changes in women's lives and texts over the years affirm the possibility of critically reworking the worlds into which we are born. bell hooks phrases this idea of positioned agency well: "Understanding marginality as position and place of resistance is crucial for oppressed, exploited, colonized people. If we only view the margin as a sign marking the despair, a deep nihilism penetrates in a destructive way the very ground of our being. . . . I am not trying to romantically re-inscribe the notion of that space of marginality where the oppressed live apart from the oppressors as 'pure.' I want to say that these margins have been both sites of repression and sites of resistance" (150–51).[10] Since constructivist accounts also do not tell the story of how they came to understand historical or present reality in this way—that is, they do not close the hermeneutic circle—they give no account of what previous self-understandings informed their own. The moments of history that are affirmed are only the moments of rupture with the system of power because there is no recuperation of the ethical/political vocabularies of previous epochs.

To get a handle on the roots of this confusion about gender, it helps to think back to the Saussurean notion of identity that informs poststructuralism. As we recall, Saussure asserts that all identities are relational notions defined through their differences with surrounding signs. For Derrida, the problem with Saussure comes when this third-person description of the linguistic system becomes speech and the signs become "positive terms." (See chapter 3.) This move marks the logocentric movement, which is where Derrida locates the oppressive misreading of the disseminatory character of Being. (Constructivist feminists often rename this idea "phallogocentrism.") Since we cannot avoid concepts, our task is, according to the ethics of deconstruction, to undo them as "we" use them, and this includes undoing the "I" that speaks. What this means is that the idea of relational identity can never be appropriated by the subject.[11] By never putting the subject of ethical/political deliberation who recognizes relational identity on the table, Derrida deprives identity of all the first-and second-person vocabularies that any politics needs. A critique of foundationalism—that is, the belief that philosophical reason can ground itself in the external world or in the subject—does not lead necessarily to the poststructuralist position. Fraser, hooks, Benhabib, and Benjamin join philosophers such as Gadamer, Charles Taylor, and Richard Rorty in separating out the critique of foundationalism and subjectivity from the dissolution of all first-and second-person vocabularies. Subjectivity does not collapse with the foundationalist enterprise; rather, it reemerges as an embedded, embodied subject that is composed of many threads, not just gender. Only the ontological terrorism of the constructivist position makes the employment of any concept an act of oppressive essentialism.

The importance of these first-and second-person vocabularies can be seen in Fuss's text, for they resurface without a theoretical place. Fuss is right when she says, "It is telling, I think, that constructionists are willing to displace 'identity,' 'self,' 'experience,' and virtually every other self-evident category *except* politics" (37). The problem is that a politics without any first- or second-person vocabularies, without any agents and norms, is impoverished and incoherent. For example, how do "we" know when and how to operate strategically and on what grounds? The political vocabulary we get is "displacing" or "disruptive": "When put into practice by the dispossessed themselves, essentialism can be powerfully displacing and disruptive" (32). Why is disruption per se good? Here we see how a total defoliation of all ethical/political traditions leads to an impoverished political/ethical and hermeneutical vocabulary. To what end is this displacement put? For whom and by whom? Without stories and theories about these issues, the entire debate is sterile. The underlying ethical/political appeal of stories of oppression and marginality is to some notion of justice and liberty; however, these values are not consciously accounted for—that is, if the story of construction unmasks all values, including liberty, then what sense does it make to say oppression is bad?[12]

It is difficult to conceive of freedom without some sort of agency, and we see the rhetoric of intentionality and agency creep back into Fuss's analysis when she addresses the question of when to use essentialism. In this passage, we find a subject who makes judgments about the motives of other subjects: "This, to me, signals an exciting way to rethink the problem of essentialism; it represents an approach which *evaluates the motivations behind the deployments of essentialism* rather than prematurely dismissing it as an unfathomable vestige of patriarchy (itself an essentialist category)" (32, my emphasis).

The dual need for third-person vocabularies and first-and second-person vocabularies that constitute and critique can be theoretically finessed by putting them into a complementary relationship. In this way, the relational identities of women do not rest on an essence but on the connections between the historical vocabularies in which we are embedded (the third-person voice) and the revisions we make in reworking them for ourselves (in the first-and second-person voices). Gendered vocabularies figure in stories of oppression, and these are uses from which we seek to escape. But gendered vocabularies also appear in stories of achievement that we tell in constructing our hopes. In other words, agency needs to be informed by the work of predecessors.

Our understanding is made possible by works such as Susan Glaspell's "A Jury of Her Peers," which chart the emergence of critical consciousness from a dominant discourse. The resources for women's agency come not only from their own practices but from the reinterpretation of canonical texts such as the Declaration of Independence.[13] There is a transcendental reason for this: our agency did not just drop from the sky; it is made possible by the struggles and practices of others. Yet there is also an ethical/political reason: we need the history of democratic struggle as a resource for understanding the present. The constructivist has to tell a story about the work that makes her own perspective possible, and this story will necessarily involve the recuperation (not the idealization) of women's efforts in the past.[14]

In *Justice and the Politics of Difference,* Young gives a good example of how a relational understanding of women's identity can function as critique. The easiest way to see how she works is to examine her discussion of the "ideal of impartiality" in liberal civic culture. She criticizes this ideal because it harbors all the presuppositions of dominant, male culture, leaving intact the cultural scripts that have had damaging effects on women and minorities. She calls for a new understanding of justice that is not difference-blind but self-conscious about difference. She characterizes difference as follows: "The alternative to an essentializing, stigmatizing meaning of difference as opposition is an understanding of difference as specificity, variation. In this logic . . . group differences should be conceived as relational rather than defined by substantive categories and attributes. A relational understanding of difference relativizes the previously universal position of privileged groups, which allows only the oppressed to be marked as different" (171).

What Young has done is let the first- and second-person vocabularies that inform the self-understanding of groups become part of the relational universe through which beings get identities. This provides an alternative to merely decrying identities as essentialist mystifications that cover over the "real truth" about identity that is revealed only through the vocabulary of the unspecified observer speaking from an unspecified site. Group identities are not totalized essences but a particular kind of story one tells about oneself in a given context. Moreover, difference does not mean that groups do not overlap in some respects. The group articulates itself "from a flowing process in which individuals identify themselves and others in terms of groups, and thus group identity itself flows and shifts with changes in social process" (172). Women have been stereotyped and devalued, and they do not simply want access to a world that is already scripted; they want to redefine the texts, "the symbolic order," in which we and our children will live. Moreover, Young's critique of liberalism's notion of justice is not a simple indictment of all previous notions of justice; instead, she further develops the concept of justice: "The achievement of formal equality does not eliminate social differences, and rhetorical commitment to the sameness of person makes it impossible even to name how those differences presently structure privilege and oppression" (164).

What follows from Young's understanding of justice and difference is a rethinking of questions of freedom and autonomy in ways that are neither liberal nor constructivist. Women need not only a theory that points out injustice and inequality, as liberals do, but a theory that empowers them, gives them access to a positive sense of freedom to shape their own lives and to challenge the so-called neutrality of existing norms. Autonomy is not just an assumption that goes automatically with being a subject in a democracy, for this leaves out the whole question of the kind of cultural nourishment that is necessary to become autonomous. Providing this nourishment is one of the tasks of education.

Autonomy needs to be rethought so that it means, in Fraser's words, "to be a member of a group or groups which achieved a degree of collective control over the means of interpretation and communication sufficient to enable one to participate on a par with members of other groups on moral and political deliberation" (1986, 428). Such a view does not deny the constructivist thesis that subjects are positioned by the oppressive histories and languages of race, gender, and class; instead, this view insists that this positioning be the place from which we negotiate our identities, take account of the resources that have made this oppression visible, and project new possibilities.

An important theoretical consequence of Young's, Fraser's, and Benhabib's theories is that feminists need to have access to the liberal democratic traditions of Western thought in ways that constructivist feminists working with the poststructuralist assumptions prevent. As we saw in chapter 3, poststructuralism criticized the liberal and Marxist understandings of these concepts. For poststructuralists, both of these theories overlook the deep constraints—whether through concepts (Derrida) or through disciplinary practices (Foucault)—that constitute their very definitions of liberty and autonomy. Poststructuralism appeals to a freedom from the discourses of power that make up the Western tradition. The poststructuralist affirmation of difference is part of its hope for a total revolution of our current society, not a positive assessment of the worth of groups or individuals.

Fraser, hooks, Young, and Benhabib, on the other hand, are committed to a reworking of democratic ideals, a critique and a recuperation, in which the past informs the projects of the future. For Benhabib, this involves going back to the Enlightenment, not merely to talk about its failures—for example, the disembodied self and the compromised public sphere—but to reconstruct its ideals: "The project of modernity can only be reformed from within the intellectual, moral and political resources made possible and available to us by the development of modernity on a global scale since the sixteenth century" (Benhabib 1992, 2). In *Situating the Self*, Benhabib phrases this project in hermeneutic vocabulary: "This book attempts a reconstruction of this [Enlightenment] legacy by addressing the following question: what is living and what is dead in universalist moral and political theories of the present, after the criticism in the hands of communitarians, feminists and post-modernists?" (2). In the same way, Fraser takes the early democratic concepts, such as the idea of the public sphere, and brings complex, nuanced questioning to them. She begins with the alternative of wholesale critique and recuperation: "Should we conclude that the very concept of the public sphere is a piece of bourgeois, masculinist ideology so thoroughly compromised that it can shed no genuinely critical light on the limits of actually existing democracy? Or should we conclude rather that the public sphere was a good idea that unfortunately was not realized in practice but retains some emancipatory force?" (Public Sphere, 117). Neither of these is satisfactory, for current research "neither undermines nor vindicates the concept of the public sphere simpliciter" (117).

Jessica Benjamin's *Bonds of Love: Psychoanalysis, Feminism, and the Problem of Domination* is a good work in which to examine the kind of feminist hermeneutics just described because she elaborates the movements of critical explanation and utopian revision more completely than do the other theorists discussed in this chapter. She "seeks to understand how domination is anchored in the hearts of the dominated" (Benjamin, 5). How is it that democracy's long-standing commitment to formal equality coexists with a cultural script that not only oppresses women but makes them complicitous with their oppression? She draws on Habermas and feminist psychoanalytic theory to understand domination through a problematic of intersubjectivity: "Domination and submission result from a breakdown of the necessary tension between self-assertion and mutual recognition that allows self and other to meet as sovereign equals" (12).

Benjamin is interested in reconstructing the concept of autonomy and in understanding where it went wrong and what we can do to improve it. While she credits Simone de Beauvoir with uncovering the bias in the cultural scripts of Western culture, Benjamin's stakes are much higher than demanding access to a liberal notion of autonomy; her critique shows that the very concept of autonomy is rooted in debilitating gender distinctions that cripple both men and women. As a warning to liberal feminists, such as Nina Baym,[15] Benjamin says that "the equation of masculinity with desire, femininity with the object of desire does reflect the existing situation; it is not simply a biased view" (90). She wants to go beyond the charge of bias to explain the root of bias. Benjamin also cautions gynocentric feminists that they need to critique the historical division of gender identities and not simply idealize women and their activities, since such an idealization ignores the ways that women have internalized their oppression. Benjamin thus joins constructivists in her radical critique of the fabrication of gender. However, she breaks with them in rejecting power as the whole story about culture and uses a problematic based on intersubjectivity to articulate a new conception of autonomy, a problematic that is developed in a line of Western philosophy from Hegel to Habermas.

When we look at theories of development—Freudian and others—we find that autonomy is understood as the slow separation of the child from an initial unity with the mother. Until the Oedipal phase, the child is considered to be an internal system of needs rather than a being who is formed through relationships with parents. Benjamin challenges this view by looking at the pre-Oedipal phase (a period she calls "rapprochement") in intersubjective terms that capture the child's complex need to have his/her identity recognized and defined during the process of individuation.

According to Freud and others, the process of individuation for a boy is achieved through an identification with the father, who represents independence and desire, and a rejection of the absorbing dependency on the mother. For the girl, individuation is problematic. Her desire for autonomy and agency also produces an identification with the father during rapprochement, but this identification conflicts with existing stories about what girls are supposed to be. The girl's pre-Oedipal identification with the father is driven out in the Oedipal phase, when she replaces identificatory love with object love: "When the girl realizes she cannot be the father, she wants to have him" (Benjamin, 110). This could lead her to marry the ideals she wants to achieve ("ideal love") or use "identification with her father to achieve liberation from a controlling and intrusive, although demeaned, mother" (96). In Freudian theory, such a paternal identification was a problem that had to be replaced by a "passive longing for the father—for his phallus, and his baby" (Benjamin, 115). The girl is also discouraged from placing herself in such stories by the behavior of her father, who tends to have an object love of his daughters, which denies them recognition, rather than the identificatory love he has with his sons.

What subtends these psychological dynamics is the cultural script that gives agency to men but not to women. The route to agency is based on avoiding engulfment by the mother, a being who has no clear wishes of her own apart from her care for others. "Separation-individuation thus becomes a gender issue, and recognition and independence are now organized within the frame of gender" (Benjamin, 104). This process damages the boy as well, for "recognition through identification is now substituted for the more conflictual need to be recognized directly by the primary parent on whom he feels dependent" (105). Autonomy is defined over against the relationship with the mother and indeed all others. The theory of autonomy carries domination within it. The way to overcome this is for each parent to integrate agency and care into him/herself rather than splitting along gender lines (114). This is not to say that Benjamin believes we can overcome gender oppression through shared parenting. She is aware of the objection frequently made to object-relations theory—that it ignores the effects of language and the unconscious. She does not, however, view language as an ironclad symbolic order.[16]

In Benjamin's view, the process of autonomy needs to be thought of in terms of the self-articulation through mutual recognition within relationships rather than as a separation from all relationships. The self does not have to be an isolated, needless fortress in order to have autonomy; rather, it needs the security and confidence to recognize the connections and conflicts between its identity and the identities of others: "The issue is not how we become free of the other, but how we actively engage and make ourselves known in relationship to the other" (18). Parents should not simply "mirror" their children, giving in to all their desires, until they can form a self and make a break. In order for children to have boundaries, they need to experience their parents and themselves as agents with their own needs and differences.

One of the sources for Benjamin's model is Hegel's discussion of mutual recognition. Hegel had theorized development in terms of intersubjectivity; but for him, the process of mutual recognition was doomed to failure. For Hegel, the self is assumed to want omnipotence, and others function only to confirm this sense. The paradox is that "to affirm itself it must acknowledge the other, and to acknowledge the other would be to deny the absoluteness of the self" (33). The result is domination: "When the conflict between dependence and independence becomes too intense, the psyche gives up the paradox in favor of opposition. Polarity, the conflict of opposites, replaces the balance within the self" (50). Trying to deny dependency leads to domination, for the boy denigrates the mother and his identificatory play with her. Instead of separating from the mother through mutual recognition, he is forced to give her up for fear of the father. Moreover, there is a tyrannical presupposition in Freud's and Hegel's conception of the self that makes our mutual dependence a menacing truth that the self tries to deny: "The hypothetical self presented by Hegel and Freud does not *want* to recognize the other, does not perceive him as a person like himself. He gives up omnipotence only when he has no other choice. His need for the other—in Freud physiological, in Hegel existential—seems to place him in the other's power, as if dependency were the equivalent of surrender" (53). Such a story of autonomy seeks to deny the relational character of the self and to make it a social atom.

Benjamin's discussion of the relational character of the self draws on the work of gynocentric feminists, such as Gilligan and Nancy Chodorow, who critique theories of development such as Freud's and Kohlberg's, in which the actual and ideal forms of the autonomous self are placed in opposition to human connection and human need. Autonomy becomes an isolated self-sufficiency that covers over personal and social needs. The ideal subject of democracy in liberal theory is the generalized self of justice, a self that is severed from its connections and that views others in the same way.[17] The result is an egoistic, competitive, and lonely individualism that feeds the processes of domination that democratic theories were supposed to overcome. The way in which Benjamin draws ethical/political conclusions from this view deserves a lengthy quotation:

> The moral subject can take the role of the other and can accept the principle of reciprocity in the abstract, but only by constituting a general point of view, not by taking the other's subjective point of view. . . . We may say that the reciprocity of rights is based on the most abstract common denominator—what makes a person like the other—and denies all that is "individual." This symmetry of rights presumes the competition of all against all. . . . Thus the individual is not "interested" in the other's needs, indeed, does not recognize them because they may oppose his own. Paradoxically, then, this abstraction from personal needs and the other's subjective viewpoint militates against the recognition of difference. Only the other (my complementary opposite) who does not have the same rights as I do, and against whom I do not compete, may claim respect for needs—in this category we find the helpless wife, the child, the deprived. Thus, the formal acceptance of differences opposes the intersubjective appreciation of it, which includes recognition of the particular, individual needs of the other. (Benjamin, 194–95)

Benjamin does not appropriate Gilligan's view without criticism, however, confessing that "there is an element of reversal in Gilligan's argument" and that her works contains "no explicit discussion of the historical "*constitution* of these gender differences . . . in light of woman's oppression'" (194).[18]

Benjamin's theory offers a comprehensive way of rethinking not just the question of women's domination but the whole question of subjectivity in a democracy. She exposes the complex process that damages men and women, and her theory can be used to critique the way our cultural narratives imprison men as well. Domination is not just a power wielded by men for their own benefit over women but a complex cultural system. She shows how feminist hermeneutics needs to go beyond pointing out bias and oppression to construct a theory of democratic subjectivity. She makes the metatheoretical moves necessary to draw on the resources of all three strands of feminist theory. She draws on liberalism's affirmation of equality, on gynocentrism's understanding of relational subjectivity, and on the constructivist practice of cutting beneath the existing understandings of subjectivity—liberal and gynocentric—to look at the forces that make them possible.

Marie Cardinal's *The Words to Say It* and some of the criticism that has been devoted to her work give concreteness to Benjamin's critical model. A look at this text moves us from the metatheoretical and theoretical levels to a first-order account of a particular woman's life. Cardinal's novel is the story of a woman's recovery from a severe neurosis during seven years of psychoanalytic treatment. The text works nicely with the critical model developed in this chapter because the damage done to the analysand is a result not only of the eccentricities of her life but of an ideology that cripples women. Her recovery is an ethical/political cure. The text moves between the voice of the narrating self—that is, the self that has recovered—and the fractured experiencing selves of the past. The character's healing results not in the dissolution of the old voices but with the emergence of a new voice that is strong enough to contain the old ones. As the narrator says early in *The Words to Say It*, "I am she. The mad one and I, we have begun a completely new life, full of expectations" (8–9).[19] The narrative moves forward in her analytic treatment and backward into the painful times of the past. The work of integration in the text is done by the analysand rather than the analyst, whose comments are infrequently reported. When they do appear, they serve to mark a powerful challenge to the self-understanding of the subject, a challenge that turns the analysand's pursuit of her past in a new direction. What counts in this text is not the third-person theoretical discourse but the analysand's efforts to escape from the debilitating narratives through which she understands her world and to invent new ones.[20]

At the beginning of the story, the unnamed heroine has uncontrollable menstrual bleeding, and her psychic life is dominated by a crushing anguish that she calls "The Thing": "How could I speak of the story that lived in me, 'the Thing,' that column of my being that was hermetically sealed and full of mobile blackness?" (1975, 10).[21] The Thing is the objectification of the many moments from her childhood that were too painful for her to process at the time, particularly her mother's confession that she did not want her daughter and had tried several times to abort the fetus. In Benjaminian terms, the narrator recovers a moment in which mutual recognition broke down, a moment in which she was so overpowered that she was forced to internalize the damage: "There on the street, in a few sentences, she put out my eyes, pierced my eardrums, scalped, cut off my hands, shattered my kneecaps, tortured my stomach, and mutilated my genitals. Today, I know that she was unaware of the harm she did me and I no longer hate her" (1983, 135).

The internalization of the narrator's rejection is so profound that it is somatized; she aborts herself through bleeding. Her first step in the cure is to confront her own attachment to her damage. In her very first session, she is prepared to speak of the blood, and the doctor says, "Speak about something else" (1983, 32). Her reaction reveals her investment in this narrative: "Never had I encountered such violence. Right in my face! My blood didn't interest him! If that was so, then everything is destroyed. . . . Apart from my blood there was only fear, nothing else, and I could no more speak of it than think about it" (32). By the time she gets home, she discovers that the bleeding has stopped. This kind of interpretive violence is crucial to her progress in analysis, for it involves a self-destruction in which the subject who comes to know is dislodged in the process of knowing in order to make a space for rebirth. For example, after deciphering the hallucination of an eye that had tormented her for years, she expects to be rejuvenated but instead finds a devastating loss: "Now it seemed to me that by putting out the eye at the end of the tube I had aborted myself. That eye was not only my mother's eye, and the eye of god, and of society, it was my own eye as well" (1983, 164–65).

The narrator's recovery depends on her understanding of the ideological encoding of these personal events. She goes beyond a mere remembrance of the events that took place between her and her mother to an understanding of the ideological oppression that informed her mother's life, the ideology that constructed her mother and their relationship: "I figured that the religion of my mother got all the blame; that is not the only thing in the way of her responding to these men to whom she was surely attracted. She was afraid of something else" (1983, 259). This "something else" turns out to be a fear of men's power, and this fear unites the analysand with her mother and all women: "This fear which paralyzed me, my mother and women in black, was not fear of the phallus, the *membrumvirile* (the penis), it was fear of male power" (268). Her resolution of this problem of power comes to her in the form of a dream: "Another nightmare came to my rescue" (265). In her dream, she and her husband grab a snake by the mouth and rip it in half. Her conclusion is that "to divide this power was sufficient to displace the fear. I was certain that that was the significance of my dream" (1983, 268). This completes her reconciliation with her husband and her family.[22]

The recovery gives her power to retell her life not just in analysis but in novels: "It was in the nature of a miracle out of fairy tale, magic. My life was completely transformed. Not only had I discovered a way to express myself, but on my own I had found a road which took me away from my family and my background, allowing me to build my own universe" (1983, 230). Writing is related to her positive transference onto the analyst and then her husband, who falls in love with the new woman he discovers in her manuscript.[23] Cardinal does contrast the experience of writing to the experience of analysis: "I was not in the yoke of truth, as in analysis. I was conscious of being more free than I had ever been" (1983, 215).

As does Benjamin, the novel weaves together strains of constructivist, gynocentric, and liberal forms of critique. Cardinal's narrator speaks the language of the constructivist when she speaks of her linguistic embeddedness before her recovery: "That is what writing was for me: to put correctly into words in accordance with the strict rules of grammar references and information that had been given to me. In this area, improvement consisted in expanding vocabulary in so far as it was possible, and learning Grevisse almost by heart. . . . Writing seemed to be an act of which I was unworthy" (1983, 215–16). However, she does not view this embeddedness monolithically as a Kristevean symbolic order: "Words could be inoffensive vehicles. . . . Words could be vibrating particles, constantly animating existence. . . . Words could be wounds or the scars from old wounds. . . . Words could also be giants . . . thanks to which one can get across the rapids. . . . Words could become monsters, finally, the SS of the unconscious, driving back the thought of the living into the prisons of oblivion" (240).

But this multiplicity does not lead her to deny the force of gender in language: "All words have two meanings, two sexes, depending on whether they are used by a man or a woman" (1977, 88). The force of the patriarchy does not so damage women as to vitiate all their practices, as the strict constructivist maintains. Instead, there is a space for a gynocentric affirmation of some of women's activities that are currently devalued (1983, 262–3) and for a revalorization of the body now that a patriarchal understanding has been cast off: "Now I had discovered my vagina, and I knew that henceforth, as with my anus, we were going to live together, in the same way as I lived with the hair on my head, the toes on my feet. . . . I lived with my own violence, deceit, sensuality, authority, capriciousness, courage, and high spirits. Harmoniously, without shame, distance and discrimination" (261).

The text of Cardinal's novel also adopts the liberal rhetoric of equality and the self to discuss gender relations: "Thirty-seven years of accepting the inequality and injustice, without flinching, without even being aware of it" (1983, 264). Autonomy is not conceptualized as an effect (as in constructivism) or simply a patriarchal ideal (as in gynocentrism); rather, it is a project that helps her to reconnect with rejected parts of herself, to define her own porous boundaries, and reconnect with others.

The importance of the critical model developed in this chapter can be seen by comparing it to a reading of Cardinal that dramatizes incoherent approaches to feminist hermeneutics. My example is Carolyn Durham's *The Contexture of Feminism*. Her chapter on *The Words to Say It* sets up an opposition between patriarchal practices (for example, "'classical' Freudian analysis," 211), which are oppressive, and women's practices, which are liberatory. This critical model sets up an opposition of bad/good and male/female that locks feminist criticism into gender point scoring that blocks the cultural reconstruction needed to rethink democratic culture.[24] By offering a blanket valorization of women's practices, Durham's gynocentrism denies the internalization of oppression as well as the often conflictual differences within women's practices. As Benjamin points out, radical politics takes a wrong turn when it tries "to idealize the oppressed, as if their politics and culture were untouched by the system of domination, as if people did not participate in their own submission" (9).

Hence Durham has no way of discussing the difference between the self at the beginning of Cardinal's novel and the self at the end. The self of the past needs to be liberated from her own inner monologue. Without a place for internalized oppression, Durham is forced to read the passage of the doctor's telling the analysand not to speak of blood any more as an example of his ignoring women's topics: "His [the analyst's] expression of personal (i.e., male) indifference immediately imposes silence on female reality" (228). She contrasts the analyst's request with Cardinal's conversation with Annie Leclerc in which Leclerc asks her to speak of some more of the blood: "In direct contrast, the reaction of Annie Leclerc demonstrates that the female analyst/reader fully understands the primacy of this story of women that the male would relegate to an insignificant digression" (Durham, 228; Cardinal 1977, 26). Durham ignores the difference between the damaged and healed selves in the text (and in Cardinal's life) as well as the difference between a conversation with a friend and the analytic relationship. The story of blood was imprisoning the self who goes in for treatment. The fact that this is a "female" topic is crucial, but this does not mean that it is in the interest of the analysand to let her repeat a story that reinforces her imprisonment. If, years before, the anguished and bleeding Cardinal had come to Leclerc, Leclerc may have asked her to change the subject.

Women's themes are not good in and of themselves, as any reader of Phyllis Schlafly knows. We have seen earlier, in the stories by Glaspell and Ellison, how the road to empowerment can mean the loss of a damaged self. The damaged selves of Mrs. Peters and Todd in these stories are silenced by their interlocutors (Minnie and Jefferson) so that new selves can emerge. By isolating and totalizing the female versus the male, Durham not only blurs the diversity of women's positions but also blocks out the positive resources of the democratic tradition. A critique of Freudian analysis becomes a straw man—who thinks that doctrinaire Freudianism is right?—that drives the exposition into an all too simple reading along gender lines. Durham falls into the trap that Nancy Fraser points out: "Either we limn the structural constraints of gender so well that we deny women any agency or we portray women's agency so glowingly that the power of subordination evaporates" (Introduction 1992, 17).

Cardinal's narrative also raises issues that emerge any time we move from a theory and the virtues it affirms to the life of a particular woman. One of the important dialogues in contemporary feminist theories concerns the way mainstream theories have ignored and suppressed differences among women. Women of color, lesbians, and working-class women have pointed out how feminist theories have reflected the interests of white middle-class feminists. There has been an unthematized complicity between feminist theories and the narratives of particular women. Does this mean that every group of women requires a different theory peculiar to its narratives? It depends. The answer is yes insofar as the issue of race, for example, needs a kind of theoretical attention that a theory addressing only the abstract issue of gender will not bring out. The answer is no insofar as we can construct the metatheoretical issues and values of the democratic subject, which is what this chapter has attempted to do. The work of metatheory is tied to the common issues that all democratic subjects share—for example, an interest in being recognized and in recognizing others, in having one's stories heard in the public sphere. In this way metatheory is openly linked to an ethical/political gesture that seeks to enrich the threads of the hermeneutic circle that lets people speak to each other in an ethical/political community.

In such a community, the articulation of difference does not lead immediately to invidious comparison or a nonnegotiable nationalism. One of the unfortunate effects of the poststructuralist/essentialism nexus is that it turns differences into a bunker. The oppressed protect themselves with new self-understandings against the dominant culture. The poststructuralist, suspicious of all languages of constitution and justification, intervenes strategically and without principles or waits for the birth of a radically new culture. Moreover, without a space for a democratic understanding of difference, the particular positions and choices of a women are taken to mean that all other possibilities are demeaned. Cardinal's novel, for instance, is concerned with heterocentric and middle-class issues. Does this mean that it is homophobic and insensitive to class differences? Not necessarily. We cannot say this simply because her life is particular. The closing of the hermeneutic circle means moving from metatheoretical model to first-order narrative, from the contemplation of one's situated agency to the actual choices. The subject is certainly multiple, but it cannot be everything. Every difference at the level of first-order narrative does not have to be a difference of principle. Differences become barriers when the culture provides no nourishment for public dialogue, when the public sphere becomes a platform for the demonization of other democratic subjects. Cardinal's heterocentrism is not something to be deplored unless it characterizes alternative relationships embodying mutual recognition in a deleterious way. First-order narratives participate in oppression when they are collectively canonized to exclude alternatives, such as lesbian narratives, as we see, for example, in the reception of Audre Lorde.[25] The threads of a particular subject can be connected to threads of another subject, as Cardinal herself works to retell the story her mother tells her about the connection between the colonizing French and the people of Algeria.[26] These threads can be composed of various things, from sexual preference to class, race, and occupation. What ought to guide theory and practice are democratic values of mutual recognition, attention to others, autonomy, freedom, equality, and care, values that the public sphere needs to support. In this way, a feminist democratic project reemerges from the constructivist and gynocentric critiques.

5

Exile or Rootedness

THE POLITICS OF DIFFERENCE IN EDWARD SAID AND CORNEL WEST

This chapter examines the new concern with global politics in recent theory. The issue is not just how Western culture has oppressed those inside its system, but how Western culture has colonized other cultures. Indeed, the most thorough critiques of Western culture that we have examined, such as Marxism and poststructuralism, are often criticized for being part of the imperialist tradition rather than a critique of it. Edward Said and Cornel West work through the limits of both Marxism and poststructuralism in their analysis of the dynamics of power and resistance. Their work appeals to the democratic values of liberty, justice, and self-determination and is thus a continuation of the issues about the subject of democracy that were discussed in the last chapter. West and Said must grapple with the ambiguous legacy of liberalism and the political significance of cultural difference. However, they take different stands on the relationship of the critic to the cultures in question. Is a democratic politics of difference best served by an exile position, in which the theorist pulls away from the particular traditions in which he/she is ideologically located, as Said does? Or does the critic assume a more satisfying intellectual and political position when he/she situates himself/herself in traditions that are inflected by democratic norms?

Edward Said

Edward Said's *Culture and Imperialism* (1993) is the realization of a critical project he began with *Orientalism* (1978). My approach in this chapter will be not to survey Said's work but to draw on his previous research in order to clarify the present. For Said, literary criticism and theory should have a worldly vocation, not float in a solipsistic universe. As he says in *The World, the Text, and the Critic* (1983), "The realities of power and authority—as well as the resistances offered by men, women, and social movements to institutions, authorities, and orthodoxies—are the realities that make texts possible, that deliver them to their readers, that solicit the attention of critics. I propose that these realities are what should be taken account of by criticism and the critical consciousness" (5). Said adds the adjective "secular" to this formulation to counter any privileged sense of identity deriving from religious or national narratives: "Men and women produce their own history, and therefore it must be possible to interpret that history in secular terms, under which religions are seen, you say as a token of submerged feelings of identity, of tribal solidarity. . . . But religion has its limits in the secular. Possibilities are extremely curtailed by the presence of other communities" (1992, 232).

Said's critical project is a metahermeneutical one that draws on a number of sources. He accepts the Gadamerian premise concerning the embeddedness of the interpreter in a particular cultural position: "There is no vantage outside the actuality of relationships among cultures. . . . We are, so to speak, of the connections, not outside and beyond them" (1993, 55). However, Said directs this claim about positionality against the very theorists of positionality, for he points out how the stories narrated by hermeneutics, Marxism, and poststructuralism are Eurocentric.[1] Said's sense of positioning is not just spatial but also temporal, like Gadamer's. Said reminds us that "we should keep before us the prerogative of the present as signposts and paradigms for the study of the past" (61). Reciprocally, "how we formulate or represent the past shapes our understanding and views of the present" (4).

Unlike poststructuralists, Said connects his hermeneutics to the Marxist project of ideology critique and utopian projection. First, he wants to expose the ideologies of Western imperialism and of those cultures that fought against it. These ideologies have prevented us from seeing how power and cultural identity work together to carve up the world into competing islands. Second, he hopes to reconnect these islands by retelling their stories in a way that recognizes both Western culture and the marginalized cultures of the Third World. Said wants to forge a new cultural dialogue made possible by his unmasking operations.[2]

In articulating the dynamics of imperialism, Said draws on the genealogical method of Foucault to expose workings of a particular discursive network. In *Orientalism* he studies the way the concept and discipline of the Orient function. As Said says of his approach, "The phenomenon of Orientalism as I study it here deals principally, not with the correspondence between Orientalism and Orient, but with the internal consistency of Orientalism and its ideas about the Orient (the East as a career) despite or beyond any correspondence, or lack thereof, with a 'real' Orient" (5). In examining the "constitution of a new geographical entity called the Orient" (222), Said makes a Foucaultian exposure of what he called in *Culture and Imperialism* "the dependence of what appeared to be detached and apolitical cultural disciplines upon a quite sordid history of imperialist ideology and colonialist practice" (1993, 41). Foucaultian genealogy lends itself to this project because there is a "parallel between Foucault's carceral system and Orientalism . . . for as a discourse Orientalism, like all discourse, is 'composed of signs; but what they [discourses] do is more than use these signs to designate things. It is this 'more' that renders them irreducible to the language and to speech. It is this 'more' that we must reveal and describe" (1983, 222–23). What Said likes in Foucault is the idea that "we can best understand language by making discourse visible not as a historical task but as a political one" (219).[3]

However, Said departs from Foucault's analysis of power and resistance in terms of discourse rather than agents because discourse analysis leaves out too much of the story that he wants to tell: "Yet despite the extraordinary worldliness of this work, Foucault takes a curiously passive and sterile view not so much of the uses of power, but of how and why power is gained, used and held onto" (1983, 221). Said believes we still need to think in terms of "who holds power and who dominates whom" (221). Foucault "underestimates such motive forces in history as project, ambition, ideas, the sheer love of power." Moreover, "he seems unaware of the extent to which the ideas of discourse and discipline are assertively European and how . . . discipline was used also to administer, study, and reconstruct—and then subsequently to occupy, rule and exploit—almost the whole of the non-European world" (222).

In *Culture and Imperialism*, Said moves beyond the exposure of imperialism to the contrapuntal strategy of juxtaposing stories of imperialism (chapter 2) with stories of "resistance and opposition" (chapter 3). He develops his alternative to the antihumanist ontologies of Foucault and Derrida that have been influential in the postcolonial work of Gayatri Spivak and Homi Bhabha. Said rejects Spivak's hypothesis that imperial discourse does not just oppress but completely coopts the native subject into complicity with his/her own oppression.[4] National resistance, in Spivak's view, provides evidence of how thoroughly the hegemonic discourse has been internalized: "No perspective critical of imperialism can turn the Other into a self, because the project of imperialism has always already historically refracted what might have been the absolutely Other into a domesticated Other that consolidates the imperial self" (Spivak cited in Parry, 36). Said rejects poststructuralist ontologies of power that rewrite agents as movements of signification. He refuses to deny agency to resistance movements just as he insists on addressing the motives of imperialists. As Benita Parry says, "In Said's account, signs of the counter-hegemonic opposition are located not within the interstices of the dominant discourses or the ruptures of the imperialist representation [that is, the way poststructuralist theory locates opposition] but in acts and articulations of native defiance" (36).

Said's commitment to a critical ontology that does not dissolve agency into signs is reflected in his understanding of the critic's position, which he discusses with the Marxist humanist idea of "critical consciousness": "Critical consciousness stands between the temptations represented by two formidable and related powers engaging critical attention. One is the culture to which critics are bound filiatively (by birth, nationality, profession); the other is a method or system acquired affiliatively (by social and political conviction, economic and historical circumstances, voluntary effort and willed deliberation)" (1983, 26). The problem here is that Said views this positioning only negatively, only from the point of view of a hermeneutics of suspicion. He is so afraid of being coopted, of reducing this complexity of the past and the possibilities of the future by using gross categories of self-understanding such as national or theoretical allegiance, that he gives no positive vocabulary to describe his theoretical location. The specter of the Gadamerian maxim that "consciousness is more Being than consciousness" pushes him into an unmappable exile.

To talk about critique, Said develops a spatial metaphor that includes both distance (the Foucaultian dimension) and closeness: "To stand between culture and system is therefore to stand close to—closeness itself having a particular value for me—a concrete reality about which political, moral, and social judgments have to be made" (1983, 26). One can only get close to reality, however, when one is an exile, when one pursues a nomadic form of thought. "On the one hand, the individual mind registers and is very much aware of the collective whole, context, or situation in which it finds itself. On the other hand, precisely because of this awareness . . . the individual consciousness is not naturally and easily a mere child of the culture, but a historical and social actor in it. And because of that perspective, which introduces circumstance and distinction where there had only been conformity and belonging, there is distance, or what we might also call criticism" (15). What is interesting is that Said uses "closeness" instead of "rootedness" as the opposite of distance and exile. What the use of "closeness" permits him to do is affirm engagement but never specify the traditions that inform this engagement so that "distance" per se is valorized. At the beginning of *Culture and Imperialism*, he affirms, "This book is an exile's book" (1993, xxvi). Said's critics have called him on the meaning of "exile" in his work. As Catherine Gallagher says, "He notes that knowledge is always bounded by place but insists that there is an epistemologically privileged locus of displacement called exile" (cited in McGowan, 170).

In *The World, the Text, and the Critic* Said's model is Erich Auerbach, while in *Culture and Imperialism* his models are Frantz Fanon and C. L. R. James, critics who thematize their heteroglot and contrapuntal critical languages.[5] It is over the question of rootedness and nationality that he criticizes Raymond Williams precisely because of Williams's Englishness, his sense of home: "The power of Williams's work is intrinsically at one with its rootedness and even its insularity, qualities that stimulate in the variously unhoused and rootless energies of people like myself—by origin un-English, un-European, un-Western— a combination of admiring regard and puzzled envy" (cited in Parry, 21).

Although Said insists on rootlessness, the values to which he appeals are those of humanism and democracy. In *The World, the Text, and the Critic* he says, "For in the main—and I shall be explicit—criticism must think of itself as life-enhancing and constitutively opposed to every form of tyranny, domination, and abuse; its social goals are noncoercive knowledge produced in the interests of human freedom" (29). Said recognizes that these values put him at odds with Foucault and in line with the cultural criticism of Noam Chomsky. In an interview Said says, "I've always felt that one in fact could incorporate both of them [Foucault and Chomsky]. In the end, I think Chomsky's is the more honorable and admirable position. . . . Orientalism is theoretically in-consistent, and I designed it that way: I didn't want Foucault's method . . . or anybody's method, to override what I was trying to put forward. The notion of a kind of non-coercive knowledge, which I come to at the end of the book, was deliberately anti-Foucault" (Salusinsky, 134, 137).[6] The problem is that Said tells no story about these values and how he understands them. He refuses to locate himself in ethical/political traditions. The result is that his political philosophy has no bite. As John McGowan says, "What's odd here is the insis-tence on a dichotomy between the 'oppositional' critic and the oppressors, as if to take a stand for life enhancement and human freedom is controversial. Ev-eryone claims to be working for such goals. At issue is how to activate these rather vague norms in specific circumstance so that they can serve to limit actual tyrannies" (176).

Said does counterbalance his insistence on exile with a call to adopt a holistic perspective on the cultures of the world, and the word he uses for this holism is "community." He builds his idea of community on empirical and uto-pian claims. The empirical claim concerns the interconnectedness of the world's experiences: "To ignore or otherwise discount the overlapping experience of Westerners and Orientals, the interdependence of the cultural terrains in which colonizer and colonized co-existed and battled each other through projections as well as rival geographies, narratives, and histories, is to miss what is essential about the world in the past century" (1993, xx). At the utopian level, Said wants to bring about noncoercive dialogue among heteroglot beings with po-rous boundaries. He wants "to bind the European as well as the native together in a new non-adversarial community of awareness and antiimperialism" (274). Said tries to get us away from the actual self-understandings and narratives that have crippled world dialogue to a space where a new understanding of culture can be opened. Here we recognize the familiar hermeneutic pattern of critique and utopia: "I want first to consider the actualities of the intellectual terrains both common and discrepant in post-imperial public discourse, espe-cially, on what in this discourse gives rise to and encourages the rhetoric and politics of blame. Then, using the perspectives and methods of what might be called a comparative literature of imperialism, I shall consider the ways in which a reconsidered or revised notion of how a post-imperial intellectual attitude might expand the overlapping community between metropolitan and former colonized societies" (18).

Said's new stories require that he break with the homogenizing premise that usually goes with holism, as we saw with Habermas. Said's utopian dimen-sion has space for conflicting and incommensurate stories and ontologies. Un-like Habermas, Said does not try to straighten out "distorted communication" with a utopia of communicative transparence. Moreover, Said's critique resists any dialectical conclusion, for he is suspicious of narrative itself: "Stories are at the heart of what explorers and novels say about the strange regions of the world; they also become the method colonized people use to assert their own identity and the existence of their own history" (1993, xii). Said squeezes critique and utopia together by what he calls a "contrapuntal" strategy that brings together stories that imperialist and nationalist narratives have isolated: "We must be able to think through and interpret together experiences that are discrepant, each with its particular agenda and pace of development, its own internal formations, its internal coherence and system of external relationships" (32). Said offers no help on how to "think through" or orchestrate these different stories, only the hope that juxtaposing incommensurate stories will produce political change: "My interpretative political aim (in the broadest sense) [is] to make concurrent those views and experiences that are ideologically and culturally closed to each other and that attempt to distance and suppress other views and experiences" (33). Contrapuntalism establishes a synchronic unity between incommensurate stories.

Said shows how such a contrapuntal reading might look when he analyzes Jane Austen's *Mansfield Park*. He begins by situating his own reading: "Interpreting Jane Austen depends on who does the interpreting, when it is done, and no less important, from where it is done" (1993, 93). If feminists and Marxists have brought out issues of gender and class, they have neglected "the geographical division of the world" (93). In his reading of *Mansfield Park,* Said focuses on the connection between the Bertram family's life in England and the estate in Antigua from which the family draws its income. "Austen sees what Fanny [the protagonist] does as a domestic or small-scale movement in space that corresponds to the larger, more openly colonial movements of Sir Thomas, her mentor, the man whose estate she inherits" (89). Since we never hear Sir Thomas comment on Antigua, Said goes to John Stuart Mill to give us a feel for Austen's use of Antigua: "These [outlying possessions of ours] are hardly to be looked upon as countries . . . but more properly as outlying agricultural or manufacturing estates belonging to a larger community" (cited in Said 1993, 90).

Said then isolates a moment of silence in the novel when Sir Thomas is asked about the slave trade: "In order more accurately to read works like *Mansfield Park*, we have to see them in the main as resisting or avoiding that other setting, which their formal inclusiveness, historical honesty, and prophetic suggestiveness cannot completely hide. In time there would no longer be a dead silence when slavery was spoken of " (1993, 96). Said juxtaposes in contrapuntal fashion this silence about Sir Thomas's activities in the colony to the textual richness of his appearances in Mansfield Park: "From our later perspective we can interpret Sir Thomas's power to come and go in Antigua as stemming from the muted national experience of individual identity, behavior, and 'ordination,' enacted with such irony and taste at Mansfield Park. The task is to lose neither a true historical sense of the first, nor a full enjoyment or appreciation of the second, all the while seeing both together" (97).

As important as Said's disclosure of the imperial story is, his reading also begs questions. What does "full enjoyment or appreciation" mean here? It seems to be a kind of aesthetic sense that is opposed to the knowledge claim made by the historical story. He rejects any simpleminded dismissal of Austen's work: "Yes, Austen belonged to a slave-owning society, but do we therefore jettison her novels as so many trivial exercises in aesthetic frumpery? Not at all, I would argue" (1993, 96). But what values from Austen's work can be recuperated for Said's project? We never find out. Said's contrapuntalism has no recuperative dimension.

The failure to recuperate any traditions deprives the nonadversarial community of concreteness and Said's critical ideals of any argumentative location in contemporary debates. Said is, of course, eloquent on his empirical positionality—that is, his upbringing in Palestine, Egypt, and America—but he says little about how he situates his thought in any traditions. Community is a regulative ideal that is not connected to any ethical/political traditions, and I use this Kantian term to emphasize how Said's "community" is deracinated from history and traditions. Its deracination is facilitated by the location of his critique at the metaphilosophical level. His vocabulary remains at the metatheoretical level. "Imperialism," "resistance," and "contrapuntalism" are terms that factor out all aspects of culture except identity and difference: "Culture" is one of the determinants of the subject that "critical consciousness" needs to watch, but it is defined only negatively as entrapment.[7]

Said confesses that he is deeply suspicious of the concept: "As for me, though perhaps I am putting it too strongly, culture has been used as essentially not a cooperative and communal term but rather as a term of exclusion" (cited in Parry, 21). In *Culture and Imperialism* he says, "Culture is a concept that includes a refining and elevating element, each society's reservoir of the best that has been known and thought, as Matthew Arnold put it" (xiii). For Said, this concept of culture "is a source of identity, and a rather combative one at that," a conception that leads culture to separate itself from "the everyday world" (xiii). His discussion of the concept of tradition is similar, for he considers it only as an ideological fabrication designed to produce a national or ethnic purity, not as a source of rationality as Gadamer, Alasdair MacIntyre, and Cornel West would see them (xii–xiii, 4–5, 15–16, 32–33).[8] Said is so concerned that any ethical/political shape, whether at the individual or the community level, will become a reified enclave that he gives no theoretical or narrative space to the positive construction of identity, including the identity of his ideal community. But some notion of identity is inescapable. As Charles Taylor says, "To know who you are is to be oriented in moral space, a space in which questions arise about what is good or bad, what is worth doing and what not, what has meaning and importance for you and what is trivial and secondary" (1989, 28).

Said's readings of Fanon and C. L. R. James do not clarify this picture very much. He valorizes these thinkers because they take a contrapuntal view of "history that sees Western and non-Western experiences as belonging together because they are connected by imperialism" and because they employ "nomadic, migratory, and anti-narrative energy" (1993, 279). Yet his discussion of

James does not do the metatheoretical analysis of the different strains in James's thought; instead, Said praises him only for his ability to juxtapose discrepant experiences, and this praise is all too thin.[9] The value of contrapuntalism has to be connected to first-order values and stories that guide the political interpretation of culture.

Ultimately, the value of Said's project comes from his unmasking of the imperialism and not from his ethical/political position or his theory. His stories challenge the self-understanding of Western democracies and of those cultures that fought off Western hegemony. Perhaps it is asking too much of him to provide the ethical/political and cultural resources for thinking through the dilemmas he has posed, for this would require a very different kind of book from the ones he has written.[10]

Cornel West

West's work is existentially and philosophically rooted in a way that Said's criticism of exile is not. West's approach is a polyglot hermeneutics developed from pragmatism, Marxism, African American culture, and Christianity. From our perspective, what is crucial about his work is the way he helps us think about the politics of difference, perhaps the most vexing issue facing theory today.

Marxism plays an important role in West's theory because it gives him an explanatory power that he finds in neither humanism nor poststructuralism. In his essay "On Georg Lukacs" in *Keeping Faith* (1993), West outlines a three-pronged defense of the dialectical tradition against humanism and poststructuralism. First, Marxist critique cuts through the surface dialogue of humanist criticism to reveal underlying social processes rather than simply deconstructing the truth-producing apparatus of all thought in the manner of Derrida and Foucault. Second, Marxism's effort to think the totality society—what West calls its "synechdocal" mode of thought, as opposed to humanism's metaphoric mode and deconstruction's metonymic mode—is an important critical moment, even if it is not the only one. Moreover, Marxist thought is always focused on the transformation of the structures of social and political domination, not on the individual will (humanism) or "the philosophical antinomies of humanist thought" (144).

West is sensitive to the poststructuralist critique of Marxism's reductive emphasis on class, its simplified understanding of history, and its totalizing theory. In fact, West's thought recuperates Foucault's genealogical critique for his own project. Foucault "delves into the specificity of the political, economic and cultural matrices within which regimes of truth are produced, distributed, circulated and consumed. No longer should intellectuals deceive themselves by believing—as do humanist and Marxist intellectuals—that they are struggling 'on behalf' of the truth; rather, the problem is the struggle over the very status of truth and the vast institutional mechanisms which account for this status"

(1993, 81). Yet he rejects Foucault's ironic skepticism and detachment from politics. Foucault's critique is debilitating, he believes, insofar as it rejects "any form of utopianism and any positing of a telos" (84).[11] West affirms the possibility of agency and change, and the direction of social change is "unashamedly guided by moral ideals of creative democracy and individuality" (1989, 226).

But how does West square these ideals with Marxism, which is notoriously hostile to liberal democracy?[12] The Marxist thinker who helps West with this transition is Antonio Gramsci, a figure who is important for Said as well. In Said's reading, Gramsci is a precursor of Foucault who tells us about the complexities of authority in modern states: "Well before Foucault, Gramsci had grasped the idea that culture serves authority, and ultimately the national State, not because it represses and coerces but because it is affirmative, positive, and persuasive. Culture is productive, Gramsci says, and this—much more than the monopoly of coercion held by the State—is what makes a national Western society strong, difficult for the revolutionary to conquer" (Said 1983, 171).

West's reading of Gramsci, by contrast, emphasizes how culture can offer ethical/political resources that resist domination: "In Gramsci's view, culture is both tradition and current practices. Tradition is understood, not as the mere remnants of the past or the lingering inert elements in the present, but rather as active formative and transformative modalities of a society. Current practices are viewed as actualizations of particular modalities, creating new habits, sensibilities, and world views against the pressures and limits of dominant ones" (West 1982, 119). Said affirms resistance, of course, but it is resistance per se rather than an examination of the shapes of these traditions and their democratic potential. West is concerned with our cultural nourishment in the present, and he finds this nourishment in various places from the blues to John Dewey.

For West, any thinker who neglects the ethical/political needs of the present is not politically responsible. And while he never says anything about the absence of recuperation in Said, West does not hesitate to criticize the important contemporary Marxist thinker Fredric Jameson precisely because Jameson never connects his critique of the forces that dominate our world to the political agents capable of changing it: "Jameson's basis for a positive hermeneutic is utopian in a bad sense; for this is a utopianism that rests either on no specifiable historical forces potentially capable of actualizing it or on the notion that every conceivable historical force embodies it" (1993, 188). By making no recuperative gestures, Jameson places all his bets on a massive revolution that takes nothing from our present political institutions (189).

Moreover, West's reading of Gramsci helps him drop Marxism's wholesale critique of liberal democracy: "To 'trash' liberalism as a political ideology in the modern world is to overlook its revolutionary beginnings and oppositional potential. . . . To ignore the ambitious legacy of liberalism and thereby downplay its grand achievements is to be not only historically forgetful but also politically naive" (1993, 201). West's interest in liberal democracy is not just about setting the record straight; for him, it serves as a point of departure for thinking through our own political future. Here West joins other political theorists, such as Chantal Mouffe,[13] who urge the Left to give up the idea of a revolution that would annihilate liberal democracy: "There simply is no intellectually accept-able, morally preferable and practically realizable Left social vision and pro-gram that does not take liberalism as a starting point in order to rethink, revise and reform it in a creative manner" (223). West does not ignore the failures of liberalism, particularly its insensitivity to "capitalist practices" that undermine democracy (223) and to the racism and sexism of our cultural institutions. Yet despite liberalism's complicity with oppression, West insists that it is not "the possession of white, male elites in high places, but rather a dynamic and mal-leable tradition, the best of which has been made vital and potent by struggling victims of class exploitation, racist subjugation and patriarchal subordination" (223).

West's most sustained defense of the liberal democratic tradition comes in *The American Evasion of Philosophy: A Genealogy of Pragmatism*, which is "the best America has to offer itself and the world" (8). He begins his story with Emerson, Peirce, William James, and John Dewey before tracing their legacy in the work of W. E. B. Du Bois, Sidney Hook, Reinhold Niebuhr, W. V. Quine, and Richard Rorty. West's reading of this tradition emphasizes the way Ameri-can thought steers clear of philosophy's obsession with epistemological ques-tions that are deracinated from social and political practices. American pragmatism's "common denominator consists of a future-oriented instrumen-talism that tries to deploy thought as a weapon to enable more effective ac-tion" (5). His treatment of Emerson is typical of the way West tries to revise our understandings of these thinkers to give them a greater social/political weight. West rejects the standard reading of Emerson as a figure of the Ameri-can Renaissance (11) and puts him in a different intellectual trajectory by associating him with Marx: "Similar to Marx, Emerson focuses on the pressing concerns unleashed by the American, French, and industrial revolution: the scope of human powers and the contingency of human societies. . . . What separates Marx and Emerson from most of their contemporaries is their stress on the dynamic character of selves and structures, the malleability of tradition and the transformative potential in human history" (10). The last figure in the genealogy of pragmatism is West himself with his philosophy of "prophetic pragmatism": "Prophetic pragmatism makes this political motivation and po-litical substance of American evasion of philosophy explicit. Like Dewey, it understands pragmatism as a political form of cultural criticism and locates politics in the everyday experiences of ordinary people" (213).[14]

Yet West's attempts to draw together such diverse figures has drawn criti-cism. I will focus on the way he conflates competing problematics for the inter-pretation of culture, particularly the tradition-based problematic and the genealogical problematic. This conflict is raised nicely by Robert Gooding-Williams, who says that West's organic conception of the pragmatist tradition "contradicts the conception of genealogy he advocates" (519). He discusses the development of pragmatism through the organic metaphors of growth, and yet he calls his writing a genealogy. This conception, as we recall from the discussion of Nietzsche and Foucault in chapter 3, is designed to critique such organic conceptions of history.[15]

This theoretical conflation is connected to West's avoidance of pragmatism's failure to address feminist, black, or international concerns. Only Du Bois, by West's own admission, gives pragmatism what it sorely lacks—that is, "an international perspective . . . that highlights the plight of the wretched of the earth, namely, the majority of humanity who own no property or wealth, participate in no democratic arrangements, and whose individualities are crushed by hard labor and harsh living conditions" (1989, 147–48). Gooding-Williams puts his finger on the problem when he says that "the figure of Du Bois bears the full weight of West's effort to link progressive feminist, racial and third world preoccupations of prophetic pragmatism to what otherwise appears to be the received history of the pragmatist tradition" (530). Gooding-Williams goes on to show how Du Bois is better read as part of another tradition altogether, one that works through Hegel and Marx.[16]

This critique points to the need for a kind of metacritical thinking that we did in chapter 4, in which the potential of competing theoretical problematics is placed on the table. West does not make much of the theoretical leap necessary to make Foucault work with a tradition-based problematic, and self-consciousness about this leap would complicate the story of pragmatism in productive ways. Making such a leap would require that the genealogist thematize his/her position so that the narrative position of the genealogist and the narrative position of the apologist for the tradition dialogue with each other. This dialogue is possible because there is a shadow narrator in the genealogical perspective who can be flushed out. As Alasdair MacIntyre says, "Behind the genealogical narrative there is always a shadow self-congratulatory narrative" (209). Bringing out this self and its concepts, which can provide the bridge between tradition and genealogy, requires that we expose "the extent to which the genealogical stance is dependent for its concepts and its modes of arguments, for its theses and its style, upon a set of contrasts between it and that which it aspires to overcome" (215).

What contributes to West's evasiveness on metatheoretical issues is the instrumental understanding of language and culture that is at the heart of pragmatism. Although I cannot develop here a critique of pragmatism, the key issue is that pragmatism tries to dissolve philosophical controversies so that the ideas are simply tools that we can use or discard according to the purposes at hand. Thus West and his fellow pragmatist Richard Rorty move easily among competing and incommensurate philosophies without attending to their differences. Pragmatism's understanding of language is a very different from Gadamer's, and yet West considers it insignificant. However, since my goal in this book is to foreground the metatheoretical moves necessary to overcome the bunkers of contemporary theory rather than to develop my own theory, I will not pursue the issue further.[17]

These shortcomings do not diminish West's contribution to contemporary theory—his defense of the importance of a tradition-based problematic of culture for radical politics: "Following the pioneering work of Hans-Georg Gadamer and Edward Shils, prophetic pragmatism acknowledges the inescapable and inexpungible character of tradition, the burden and buoyancy of that which is transmitted from the past to the present" (West 1989, 228). Tradition is an important way of conceiving of cultural memory because the past becomes a resource of narratives: "To keep alive a sense of alternative ways of life and of struggle requires memory of those who prefigured such life and struggle in the past. In this sense, tradition is to be associated not solely with ignorance and intolerance, prejudice and parochialism. . . . Rather, tradition is also to be identified with insight and intelligence, rationality and resistance, critique and contestation" (230). West recognizes that the concept of tradition is usually defended by cultural conservatives, not critics with his leftist political agenda. However, he locates the reactionary politics with particular traditions, not with the theoretical problematic: "Tradition per se is never a problem, but rather those traditions that have been and are hegemonic over other traditions" (230). The metaquestion that enables one to assess the value of these traditions for us today is whether they are "enhancing individuality and expanding democracy" (230). West's sensitivity to tradition helps him to develop a hermeneutics of recuperation as he ranges across popular culture, political theory, literary theory, sociology, legal studies, and theology, looking at ways theorists in these disciplines enrich our self-understandings of democracy.

West's use of a tradition-based problematic for culture is important for two reasons. First, it enables him to recuperate the achievements of marginalized culture. Liberalism, Marxism, and poststructuralism are theoretical vocabularies that have often served the interests of the marginalized, but they have not often been the vocabularies that inform the life-worlds of the marginalized. This is not just because these theoretical vocabularies are developed inside academies but because these three theoretical schools are hostile to the vocabularies of traditions. Liberalism views traditions as proposing dogmatic, narrow understandings of public life that ignore pluralism and fairness. Marxism views traditions as mystifications of the true needs of the people. Poststructuralism ignores marginal traditions altogether, focusing all its energies on exposing the exclusions and incoherences in the dominant theoretical languages.

Another advantage of the tradition-based problematic is that it treats pragmatism (liberalism) and Marxism as traditions rather than antitraditions. This advantage enables West to tell developmental stories about the dynamic interaction among the different strains of thought that are important to him rather than viewing them as mutually exclusive. Some of the most important of these stories are the ones that West tells about the development of the African American traditions through Christianity, Marxism, and liberalism. In *Prophesy Deliverance!* (1982) he maps African American thought as a distinctive yet heteroglot tradition. At the outset West places his own telling inside this tradition and defines its function: "The major function of Afro-American critical thought is to reshape the contours of Afro-American history and provide a new self-understanding of the Afro-American experience which suggests guidelines for action in the present" (22). This is a very Gadamerian formulation of critical thought, for it speaks of dialogue between past and present, in which the past is reconfigured (critique) and new possibilities are opened for a specific interpretive community. Like Said, West wants to do the work of critique, of genealogical investigation, as we see in his analysis of racism in chapter 2 of *Prophesy Deliverance!*; however, West does not view culture and tradition only as traps and limits, as we saw in Said. He wants to offer new languages of self-constitution to the African American community rather than merely dissolve all identities into genealogies.

The key figure in this discussion is West's intellectual and political model, Martin Luther King, whose social movement, in West's view, "represents the best of what the political dimension of prophetic pragmatism is all about" (1989, 234). King, too, is a dialectical hermeneut, as the following quotation illustrates: "I read Marx as I read all of the influential historical thinkers—from a dialectical point of view, combining a partial yes and a partial no. In so far as Marx posited a metaphysical materialism, an ethical relativism, and a strangulating totalitarianism, I responded with an unambiguous 'no'; but in so far as he pointed to weaknesses of traditional capitalism, contributed to the growth of a definite self-consciousness in the masses, and challenged the social conscience of the Christian churches, I responded with a definite 'yes'" (cited in West 1982, 93). Like King's, West's attitude toward Marxism is dialectical, for West wants to retrieve Marx's "stress on structural constraints, class formations and racial democratic values" while rejecting his "privileging of the industrial working class and the metaphysical posting of a relatively harmonious socialist society" (1993, 83).

The common ground for Christianity and Marxism, and indeed for all of West's recuperative moves, is democracy. Democratic norms enable us to decide what is worth keeping and what should be rejected in either of these traditions: "Regardless of the basic differences and subtle disagreements between the Christian viewpoint and the Marxist viewpoint, their prophetic and progressive wings share one fundamental similarity: commitment to the negation of what is and the transformation of prevailing realities in the light of the norms of individuality and democracy" (West 1982, 101).

What attracts West in prophetic Christianity is its affirmation of hope and the language of constitution it offers to him and many other African Americans. "Unlike Gramsci," he writes, "I am religious not simply for political aims but also by personal commitment. To put it crudely, I find existential sustenance in many of the narratives in the biblical scriptures" (1989, 232–233). Yet West's commitment is not about his private needs but about the progressive tradition of the black church, whose legacy of public political achievement is crucial. It is impossible to overlook the "contribution black churches have made toward the survival, dignity, and self-worth of black people" (1982, 116), regardless of one's religious beliefs. Yet West's is no simple affirmation of the self-understanding of the black church. His recuperation of this tradition is always informed by democratic norms. Hence, when he claims the Christian epic "remains a rich source of existential empowerment and political engagement," he adds that it must be "stripped of static dogmas and decrepit doctrines" (1989, 233). Moreover, he finds Christianity's narratives of struggle noble because they "elevate the notion of struggle—personal and collective struggle regulated by the norms of individuality and democracy—to the highest priority" (1982, 19).

West's hermeneutics clarifies not only the relationship between religion and democracy but also the relationship between race and democracy. Racial politics has been deadlocked by the essentialism/constructivism opposition that informs critical discussions of race just as it informs the analysis of gender, as we saw in chapter 4. The best starting point for tracing West's thinking is "Black Leadership and the Pitfalls of Racial Reasoning," in which he chastises the black community for its appeal to an amorphous and politically dangerous notion of racial authenticity during the Clarence Thomas hearings. This appeal kept Thomas's judicial record and important ethical issues off the table. In order to rework the relationship of ethics/politics to race, West gives a three-part definition of "blackness" that comports well with the discussion of the subject of democracy we examined in chapter 4, for it includes accounts of our construction and our agency. In the first part, he articulates the oppressive dimension of racial vocabularies: "Blackness means being minimally subject to white supremacist abuse" (393). The second part gives a place to the positive racial vocabularies generated by the oppressed, vocabularies that establish community, for "blackness" also means "being part of a rich culture and community that has struggled against such abuse" (393). The third part of the definition moves from a communitarian identity to the democratic agents who animate this identity: "All black Americans have some interest in resisting racism. . . . Yet how this 'interest' is defined and how individuals and communities are understood vary. So any claim to black authenticity—beyond black struggle— is contingent on one's political definition of black interest and one's ethical understanding of how this interest relates to individuals and communities in and outside black America" (394).

It is clear how West's hermeneutics illuminates racial politics in his readings of Malcolm X and Henry Louis Gates, Jr. In "Malcolm X and Black Rage," West appropriates Malcolm X's desire to transform black self-understanding, to produce "psychic conversion," so that African Americans would "affirm themselves as human beings, no longer viewing their bodies, minds, and souls through white lenses, but believing themselves capable of taking control of their own destinies" (Malcolm 1992, 49). Malcolm is making a critique of Du Bois's well-known idea of "double consciousness": "The Negro is a sort of seventh son, born with a veil and gifted with second-sight in this America—a world which yields him no true self-consciousness, but only lets him see himself through the revelation of the other world. It is a peculiar sensation, this double-consciousness, this sense of always looking at one's self through the eyes of others, of measuring one's soul by the tape of the world that looks on in amused contempt and pity. One ever feels his twoness,—an American, a Negro" (Du Bois, 45). For Malcolm X, this definition was disempowering because it left black subjectivity vacillating between the demands of two communities, one of which had a degrading power. Malcolm criticized integrationists for ignoring the damage being done to African Americans by the dominant culture.

While West recuperates this moment in Malcolm X's work, he also criticizes the black leader's nationalism and essentialism as parasitic on white racism: "This preoccupation with white supremacy still allowed white people to be the principal point of reference" (Malcolm 1992, 52).[18] Moreover, this nationalism ignored the cultural hybridity of black (and white) culture. "The Black church and Black music . . . [are a] complex mixture of African, European, and Amerindian elements," which "are constitutive of something new and Black in the modern world" (54). The mixture of cultures is not just an empirical fact but an ideal for West. Yet for West, unlike Said, this hybridity does not mean that all identities are suspect. West recuperates Malcolm X's recognition of the need for black identity: "Malcolm's notion of psychic conversion can be understood and used such that it does not necessarily entail Black supremacy" (53). Nationalism is not an illusion to be dismissed but a need that demands to be recognized in vocabularies of black pride that neither essentialize nor demonize. West explains his nationalism as a means of addressing the "existential dimension of black rage" (53) in a way that other forms of black culture, such as religion and music, were not doing. "If we are to build on the best of Malcolm X, we must preserve and expand his notion of psychic conversion (best seen in the works of bell hooks) that cements networks and groups in which Black community, humanity, love, care, and concern can take root and grow" (56–57).

West's sensitivity to the dangers of identity politics leads him to criticize the work of Gates, who calls for distinctive African American "vernacular criticism" and for a distinctive African American canon. For West, such a move "is but a shift from Euro-American elitist formalism to African American populist formalism, and it continues to resist viewing political conflict and cultural contestation within the forms themselves" (1993, 42). West insists on the hybrid character of African American culture; hence, to treat someone such as Ralph Ellison merely as representative of "a post-Wright school of black writing" misses his "sources in African American music, folklore, Western literary humanism, and American pluralist ideology" (41). Moreover, West resists any exclusive concern with literature for the wider focus of a cultural critique that addresses the "larger institutional and structural battles occurring in and across societies, culture and economies" (43).

Thus the great merit of West's democratic hermeneutics is that it shows us how to affirm our differences without resorting to relativism or ethnic bunkers. This requires that we give space to the work of critique, in which the discourses of oppression are unmasked and the marginalized are given a voice. The work of critique draws on Marxism and poststructuralism to expose what the humanist liberal tradition has glossed over and driven out. Yet with this work of critique goes the labor of recuperation. This recuperation opens up the particularities of our different backgrounds at the same time that it retrieves the democratic political culture that underwrites and nourishes such a community. As West says of his prophetic pragmatism, "It is possible to be a prophetic pragmatist and belong to different political movements, e.g., feminist, Chicano, black, socialist, left-liberal ones. It is also possible to subscribe to prophetical pragmatism and belong to different religious and/or secular traditions. This is so because a prophetic pragmatist commitment to individuality and democracy, historical consciousness and systemic social analyses, and tragic action in an evil ridden world can take place in . . . a variety of traditions" (1989, 232).

In discussing the ways in which West's work handles certain theoretical issues more successfully than does Said's, I do not mean to say that West's work as a critic is better than Said's. West is more a philosopher than a literary critic, while Said is more of a critic. The value of a critic's readings does not rest entirely on his/her theoretical coherence. The scope and complexity of the criticism in *Culture and Imperialism* transcends its theoretical problems. My point has been to place their work in the metatheoretical ideas developed over the preceding chapters.

Whereas Said resists all forms of cultural location as undermining his democratic norms, West offers a different reading of democracy and particularity. In West's philosophy, we need the particulars of our traditions to understand ourselves in the private and public spheres. Our traditions enable us to make claims in the public sphere, for without them we are faceless atoms controlled by the dominant discourses. Unlike Richard Rorty and the liberal tradition, West does not think that our views of the good life need to be private affairs.[19] However, what makes our public dialogue a democratic conversation and not a cacophony of incommensurate voices is that the claims of our traditions are inflected by democratic norms. The virtues of our different traditions are not driven out of the public sphere, nor should they simply be tolerated; rather, they must be challenged and defended in the rhetoric of democracy.[20]

Conclusion

The conflicts in contemporary critical theory are not just internal disputes about the correct model of interpretation but intensely political discussions that have consequences for the teaching of the humanities and the public understanding of the links between culture and democracy. The analysis in the preceding chapters is a metatheoretical story that seeks to cut through the contradictions in the theoretical tangles of contemporary debates. While my analysis is not neutral, it also does not seek to vindicate a particular theory or to articulate my own. Instead, I have attempted to present and assess the claims of the major paradigms. I have been guided by two theoretical assumptions. First, any theory must leave a space for the recuperation of democratic ethical/political values since these values are the horizon of appeal for all theories. This is not to say that there is consensus about the interpretation of these values; but what this does mean is that any theory that makes such an appeal must show how these values emerge from their troubled histories. The second theoretical goal is to bring to light an understanding of the subject that permits us to discuss the way language *both* cripples *and* enables us. The first three chapters show how these two assumptions can break down theoretical bunkers and broaden the interpretive space of theory so that we can examine the conflicts and the complementarities in the major paradigms.

I began with hermeneutics because it offers an indispensable insight that has been lost in recent discussions. Heidegger and Gadamer argue for an understanding of ourselves as linguistic and historical beings who are embedded in traditions. All too often when we hear about the famous "linguistic turn" in theory we think only of poststructuralism. If someone wants to talk about the subject as agent, it is assumed that this person will have to go "outside" language, back to some benighted paradigm of the subject, to find such a view. Gadamerian hermeneutics shows that this is not the case.

However, Gadamer's insights cannot simply stand unmodified, for critical social theories challenge this hermeneutic perspective by making the hermeneut examine the way that psychological and historical forces contort dialogue. Explanatory models, such as psychoanalysis and Marxism, can access the contortions of our personal and collective histories in ways not possible in Gadamerian dialogue. Gadamer's philosophy of interpretation is more about what an ideal interpretive dialogue ought to be than it is an account of the processes of cultural history. This unacknowledged utopian dimension also informs his idea of tradition, which avoids the role of power and diversity in the articulation of historical understanding.

Hermeneutics responds to these challenges by acknowledging the contributions of the social sciences but at the same time maintaining that these explanatory insights are derivative of the first-order languages through which we live and talk, the very languages that are the object of explanation. Social theory can uncover important features of these languages, and the discoveries it facilitates can lead to changes in the way we talk; however, the hermeneutic circle begins with the first-order languages and closes with these first-order languages, even if these languages are transformed in the process. We saw just such a transformation of the languages of understanding in the women of Glaspell's "A Jury of Her Peers" and in Ellison's "Flying Home." Both of these stories demonstrate how power and linguistic difference are best understood within an expanded hermeneutic space rather than an antihermeneutic one.

Chapter 3 raises the stakes of the antihermeneutic challenge. What poststructuralism shares with the hermeneutics we explored in chapter 2 is that neither stays within the model of the isolated subject on one side and the models of explanation on the other. Like hermeneutics, poststructuralism shows how the explainer who holds himself/herself outside of the sociohistorical process under consideration is part of this social text. However, poststructuralism does not read this social text as a dialogical hermeneutics any more than it does as data for explanation. Instead, the explainer's language is read as part of a palimpsest of power in which the web of interconnections breaks down the existing divisions between the language of the interpreter and the object of interpretation. Thus Foucault shows how "repression" is not an atemporal truth about human nature but part of a system of interlocking and unthematized presuppositions that came into existence at a particular time. Derrida shows how philosophy's treatment of primary and secondary elements such as presence and absence, nature and culture, fiction and nonfiction is part of a system of assumptions about the nature of being, not just a localized claim about one particular sphere.

The antihermeneutical ontologies of poststructuralism thematize the presuppositions of literature, philosophy, and social science in ways that demand the attention of any democratic hermeneutics. Yet the problems disclosed by Foucault and Derrida do not admit of solution through revisions because the problems are too deep. For Foucault, the system of power and knowledge in the modern world cuts so far into the construction of our identities that we cannot imagine an alternative to the present. Our imaginations are coopted. For Derrida, the logocentrism that tyrannizes the articulation of the world through concepts is inevitable. The best we can do is to hold on to the idea that the truth of language is dissemination, not closure, so that we can attend to the ways closure shapes the world with violence. We cannot transcend logocentrism, only work to subvert it. Such a conception breaks with the democratic hermeneutics, for poststructuralism does not leave a space for recuperation in the interpreter's present or in the past. Thus poststructuralism does not account for its own critical capacities or for the democratic values—for example, liberty and justice—to which it implicitly appeals. These failures provide a wedge that breaks down the poststructuralists' claim that their work is opposed to the hermeneutic project. Democratic hermeneutics does not reject poststructuralism but instead considers the challenge offered by stories of power to the facile recuperation of democratic traditions. Democratic hermeneutics gets points of contact with poststructuralism by filling the blanks in their texts—that is, by telling the stories that have enabled us to make available this critical perspective. The opposition between hermeneutics and poststructuralism becomes a creative tension.

Chapters 4 and 5 five looked at the ways that poststructuralism informs feminist and postcolonial theories. Here our concern with the ethical and political dimensions of poststructuralism comes to the fore, and it is in these chapters that the exposition moves from a critical presentation to negotiation. Feminist theories look for ways to talk about women's exclusion, domination, and achievement, and to do this, these theories cannot simply adopt a poststructuralist or hermeneutic theory. We saw the problems that result from a poststructuralist story, which depicts women only as constructed, or from a gynocentric or essentialist one, which sees them as creating a special space of value. The solution I proposed was to recast the "essentialism/constructivism debate" by replacing "essentialism" with dialogism. Such a move sees the new vocabularies that women use to talk about their lives not as an essence but as a hermeneutical reworking of the existing vocabularies so that women are enabled, not crippled. The constructivist looks at historical traditions only from the outside and exposing the twisted shapes of gender in them. Such an exposure is crucial, but it does not account for how the theorist escaped what she is describing, what positive antecedents made this critique possible. Moreover, the constructivist exposure leaves women without vocabularies for living in the present. The solution is a democratic hermeneutics that makes these enabling historical antecedents available and closes the hermeneutic circle by showing how the interpreter lives through these reworked vocabularies in the present. The discussion of Marie Cardinal's text showed how feminist theory can bring together liberal, gynocentric, and poststructuralist analyses.

Edward Said's work illustrates how postcolonial theory is haunted by the poststructuralist legacy, for Said never recuperates the value to which he appeals. His brilliant analysis of how imperialism infects all aspects of culture in Western and third-world countries leaves out the story of achievement that makes his analysis possible. Cornel West's hermeneutic pragmatism seeks to weave together poststructuralist and Marxist theories of domination with a hermeneutic concept of tradition. My agreement with West is a metatheoretical agreement; that is, he brings to the foreground the necessity of thinking about domination and achievement together. However, I have theoretical problems with West's pragmatic solution—his view of language and his understanding of the role of philosophy. Since these disagreements are about theory rather than metatheory, I have excluded them from discussion in this book. An exposition of my own theory would have taken us down a different path filled with dense arguments, which I have made elsewhere.[1]

My hope for this book is that the reader has emerged with an understanding of the competing claims of contemporary theory and a way of thinking about these claims. The anchor of my story has been my focus on the conditions of democratic interpretation. These conditions require us to recognize the differences and the atrocities of the past along with the resources that make this recognition possible and desirable. For without an account of the resources of democratic interpretation, we cannot give a satisfying justification of the study of the humanities. Is there anything more urgent at a time when the standards for American history are read as a balance sheet of good and bad characteristics and when "democratic interpretation" means handing the humanities over to the forces of the market?[2]

Notes

Introduction

1. See Sedgwick's *The Epistemology of the Closet*, 48–52. Elaine Showalter's *A Literature of Their Own: British Women Novelists from Brontë to Lessing* is one of the first examples, while Joanne Braxton's *Black Women Writing Autobiography: A Tradition Within a Tradition* is a recent one. Nancy Hartsock expresses frustration at poststructuralist theories that deny agency: "Why is it, exactly at the moment when so many of us who have been silenced begin to demand the right to name ourselves, to act as subjects rather than objects of history, that just then the concept of subjecthood becomes 'problematic'?" (26).

2. This opposition is often called the constructivism/essentialism debate, and it cuts across the discussion of gender and race. See Diana Fuss's *Essentially Speaking* for a recent examination of these issues. Her study illustrates perfectly the blockage in contemporary theory. In her case, the blockage results from her unthematized commitment to poststructuralism. I discuss Fuss's work in chapter 4.

3. In "Language and African American Culture: The Need for Meta-Philosophical Reflection," I discuss how Henry Louis Gates, Jr., attempts unsuccessfully to marry poststructuralism with a tradition-based problematic.

4. Theorists who defend traditions have been the object of critique for many years because their views have supported a racist and sexist canon, and these critiques have certainly been justified. However, what they do is conflate a critique of a particular tradition with a critique of tradition as a theoretical problematic. Cornel West is one of the few prominent theorists to make this crucial distinction. "Tradition," he writes, "is to be associated not solely with ignorance and intolerance, prejudice and parochialism, dogmatism and docility. Rather, tradition is to be identified with insight and intelligence, rationality and resistance, critique and contestation. Tradition per se is never a problem, but rather traditions that have been and are hegemonic over other traditions" (1989, 230).

5. See Selden's *A Reader's Guide to Contemporary Theory* and his *Practicing Theory and Reading Literature* as well as Eagleton's *Literary Theory*.

6. See Jonathan Culler's 1984 review of Eagleton's *Literary Theory*.

7. Eagleton's critique of Gadamer's view of tradition is typical: "History for Gadamer is not a place of struggle, discontinuity and exclusion but a continuing chain, an ever-flowing river, almost, one might say, a club of the like-minded" (72–73). Selden omits him entirely. Donald G. Marshall's *Contemporary Critical Theory: A Selective Bibliography* shows how Gadamer is reduced to a figure of only historical interest, despite the author's opinion, which I share, that Gadamer is "arguably the most important philosopher of the humanities in this century" (82).

Chapter 1:
The Background to Contemporary Interpretation

1. There have been many discussions of Hirsch and the New Critics over the years that treat their positions in much more detail than I will give here. See, for example, David Hoy's analysis in *The Critical Circle*.

2. Kant's three critiques are *The Critique of Pure Reason*, in which his concern is science; *The Critique of Practical Reason*, in which his concern his morality; and *The Critique of Judgment*, in which his concern is aesthetics. Kant is a key figure in the book since he plays such an important role in the work of all the theorists I will discuss. In this chapter, I will keep most of the references in the notes.

3. Kant's role in the argument over modernity in contemporary theory is crucial. In *The Order of Things*, Foucault points out the aporias in Kant's efforts to account for an empirical and transcendental subject. Hubert Dreyfus and Paul Rabinow phrase Foucault's critique nicely: "Modernity begins with the incredible and ultimately workable idea of a being who is sovereign precisely by virtue of being enslaved, a being whose very finitude allows him to take the place of God" (30). Habermas, on the other hand, tries to redeem the project of modernity by shifting the ground from the subject to intersubjectivity.

4. Kant's view of ethics was not, of course, the only Enlightenment view. Benjamin Franklin's utilitarianism is another notable ethical theory that emerged during this period.

5. For a discussion of the opposition between the human and natural sciences, see Richard Rorty's *Philosophy and the Mirror of Nature* and Paul Ricoeur's *Hermeneutics and the Human Sciences*. For a hermeneutic critique of reductive behaviorism in the human sciences, see Charles Taylor's "Interpretation and the Sciences of Man" and "Neutrality in Political Science" in *Philosophy and the Human Sciences*. In this chapter, my reading of the Enlightenment will focus on epistemological issues; this reading is primarily critical. In the subsequent chapters, I will look at the ethical and political aspects of the Enlightenment's democratic project, and my interest will be recuperative as well as critical.

6. Kant investigates the universal subjective conditions that inform aesthetic judgments. Kant wants disinterestedness in the reader, which will keep the

faculties at play rather than engaging them. He bases his claim about the universality of the aesthetic judgment on the common mental faculties shared by all humans.Gadamer attacks what he calls Kant's "radical subjectivization" of aesthetics: "In discrediting any kind of theoretical knowledge apart from that of natural science, it compelled the human sciences to rely on the methodology of the natural sciences in conceptualizing themselves. But it made this reliance easier by offering as a subsidiary contribution 'artistic element,' 'feeling,' and 'empathy,' as subsidiary elements" (1994, 41). Later in the same work Gadamer asks, "Is there no knowledge in art? Does not the experience of art contain a claim to truth which is certainly different from that of science, but just as certainly is not inferior to it?" (97).

7. See Brooks, "The Heresy of Paraphrase," *The Well-Wrought Urn*.

8. There is a direct parallel here to Kant's idea that "beauty is an object of purposiveness insofar as it is perceived in the object without the presentation of a purpose" (1987, 84).

9. Unlike the New Critics' view, Wellek and Warren's understanding of the work of art is informed by Roman Ingarden's phenomenology. Nonetheless, the internal/external distinction parallels the assumptions of New Criticism. See Graff's discussion of this distinction in *Professing Literature*, 183–95.

10. An excellent way to see the assumptions of New Criticism is to juxtapose Robert Heilman's "Hawthorne's 'The Birthmark': Science as Religion" with Judith Fetterley's reading of the same story in *The Resisting Reader*. (Both essays are conveniently collected in Shirley Staton's *Literary Theories in Praxis*.) Heilman's essay exemplifies the traits of New Criticism very well. He says that the story presents great, universal themes—e.g., the Faustian and the nature of pride—and that it does this through its imagery, technique, and symbols. He never thematizes his own position as a reader. Is he reconstructing Hawthorne's intention? Is he endorsing these themes or describing? The work is assumed to be part of the museum of Western culture. Fetterley's essay brings out the sexism of these themes in a way that problematizes the values of the text and forces out the position of the reader.

11. Hirsch calls "explanation" "interpretation" (1967, 209–210). For further discussion of the three dimensions of hermeneutics prior to Gadamer, see Richard Palmer's *Hermeneutics*, chapter 2. See Hirsch's recent concessions to Gadamer in "Meaning and Significance Reinterpreted."

12. Heidegger says, "'Understanding' in the sense of one possible kind of cognizing among others (as distinguished, for instance, from 'explaining') must, like explaining, be interpreted as an existential derivative of that primary understanding which is one of the constituents of the Being of the 'there' in general" (1962, 182).

13. See Kaelin's *Heidegger's Being and Time* for a discussion of these ideas.

14. Hoy sums up what I mean about Kant's emptying of the subject. He urges us to "read Kant not as a precursor of the phenomenological emergence of consciousness, but as the beginning of the disappearance of consciousness"

(1991, 264). Kant seeks to expose Descartes's "I think, therefore, I am" by showing that there is an invalid inference "from the existence of consciousness to the existence of the thing that is conscious" (Hoy 1991, 264). For Kant, the unifying "I think" that must accompany all experience is a logical condition (the transcendental unity of apperception), but this logically necessary "I think" is not the *I* that is experienced.

Heidegger's understanding of existence is where existentialism gets its name, even though Heidegger himself repudiated this label. See Jean-Paul Sartre's *Existentialism Is a Humanism* and Heidegger's response in the "Letter on Humanism."

15. For examples of theorists who think that Heidegger and poststructuralists are not arguing at all, see Richard Rorty's essay "Is Derrida a Transcendental Philosopher?" (1971) and Jürgen Habermas's *The Philosophical Discourse of Modernity*. Rorty thinks the failure to conform to the existence of argument makes these writers interesting, while Habermas deplores it. I will discuss Heidegger's late work and his connection to poststructuralism in chapter 3.

16. See Victor Farias, *Heidegger and Nazism*; Richard Wolin, *The Politics of Being: The Political Thought of Martin Heidegger*; Hans Sluga; and Heidegger's *Crisis*.

17. See Joel Weinsheimer's *Philosophical Hermeneutics and Literary Theory*, in which he develops the difference between Gadamer's work and theory: "In principle, hermeneutic theory offers legitimate methods, which interpreters ought to and can apply in order to avoid errors" (29). He thinks that the "animus against interpretation has coincided with the rise of theory" (29). However, the major opponent of hermeneutics, poststructuralism, would not call itself a theory in Weinsheimer's sense. In my reading, poststructuralism pursues the "ontological turn" that Heidegger initiated and Gadamer followed, in which arguments about method are replaced by a new kind of discussion. In this discussion, a new vocabulary that is incommensurate with existing vocabularies is introduced and then used to redescribe the subject, the language, and the world. See chapter 3.

18. Gadamer distinguishes his idea of play from Kant's in *The Critique of Judgment* and Schiller's in *Letters on the Aesthetic Education of Man*: "I wish to free this concept from the subjective meaning which it has in Kant and Schiller and which dominates the whole of modern aesthetics and philosophy of man" (1994, 101). For Gadamer, play "means neither the orientation nor even the state of mind of the creator or of those enjoying the work of art, nor the freedom of a subjectivity expressed in play, but the mode of being of the work of art itself" (107).

19. An example of this is Barbara Smith's *Contingencies of Value*. See my review of Smith in *Comparative Literature*.

20. See Rorty, *Philosophy and the Mirror of Nature*.

21. Heidegger says that "assertion cannot disown its ontological origins from an interpretation which understands" (1962, 201).

22. See Charles Taylor's "Self-Interpreting Animals" in *Human Agency and Language*. I will return to Taylor's work later and the question of explanation and understanding. Gadamer's characterization unnecessarily exaggerates the differences between human and natural science. See Richard Bernstein's *Beyond Objectivism and Relativism* for a discussion.

23. See Donald Davidson's "On the Very Idea of a Conceptual Scheme" in *Inquiries into Truth and Interpretation*, where he explodes the notion that people can have radically different schemes of the world and still be intelligible to each other.

24. In "Two Moral Orientations" in *In a Different Voice*, Carol Gilligan discusses Glaspell's story in the context of her theory of care, which she develops in this work. Gilligan claims that the women dramatize the ethic of care, while the men dramatize the ethic of justice. What this leaves out is the question of power and the revolutionary change that the women undergo while they are at Minnie's house.

25. Gadamer's ontology has norms embedded in it. Thus play is not an optional or possible interpretive event but what the interpretive event is. People who do not give themselves up to "play" are inauthentic. In "Whose Home Is It Anyway? A Feminist Response to Gadamer's Hermeneutics," Robin Schott offers a critique of the masculine metaphors that inform Gadamer's work. In addition to her discussion of play, she points out that Gadamer's preferred metaphor "for understanding our fundamental relation to language" is "being at home" (205). Gadamer says, "Is not language always the language of the homeland, the process of becoming at home in the world?" (1977, 238–39). In *Critical Theory*, Thomas McCarthy argues against Gadamer's "fallacy of treating ontological conditions as normative principles" (41) from a Habermasian perspective.

26. For perceptive discussions of Glaspell's story, see Annette Kolodny's "A Map of Misreading: Gender and the Interpretation of Literary Texts" and Judith Fetterley's "Reading about Reading: 'A Jury of Her Peers,' 'The Murders in the Rue Morgue,' and 'The Yellow Wallpaper.'"

27. See Mae Gwendolyn Henderson, "Speaking in Tongues: Dialogics, Dialects and the Black Woman Writer's Tradition"; and Alice Templeton, "The Dream and the Dialogue: Rich's Feminist Poetics and Gadamer's Hermeneutics."

Chapter 2:
Challenges to Hermeneutics

1. Paul Ricoeur calls structuralism "Kantianism without a transcendental subject" (1974, 52). That is, "linguistic laws designate an unconscious level . . . a categorical, combinative unconscious" (33). Claude Levi-Strauss gives this structuralist notion its antihumanist edge: "Language, an unreflecting totalization, is human reason which has its reasons and of which man knows nothing" (cited in Ricoeur, 52).

2. See Emile Benveniste's discussion of the limits of Saussure's semiotics in *Problémes de linguistique générale*. For a critique of Genette's narrative theory, see my essay "The Limits of Structuralist Narratology: Genette's Misinterpretation of Proust."

3. See Robert Scholes, "Semiotic Approaches to a Fictional Text: Joyce's 'Eveline'" in *Semiotics and Interpretation*.

4. Ricoeur's comment is an attempt to negotiate Gadamer's hermeneutics and Habermas's critical theory, rather than structuralism, but the argument for the priority of understanding over explanation is the same.

5. Saussure clearly distinguishes the signified from the referent, but critics run these together. Structuralist narratology's conflation of signified and referent is partially responsible.

6. Ricoeur is making an implicit reply to Derrida, who leaves aporias where they are. Unfortunately, Ricoeur never addresses deconstruction directly, aside from some brief comments in *The Rule of Metaphor*. J. Hillis Miller, in his review of *Time and Narrative*, offers a deconstructive attack on Ricoeur: "All Ricoeur's presuppositions are mistaken. There is no such thing as an 'experience of being in the world and in time' prior to language. All our 'experience' is permeated through and through by language. The aporias of temporality are a displaced name for a linguistic predicament that exists as much in narrative as in any other mode of language" (1105). Ricoeur would not, of course, deny that experience is "permeated through and through by language," but he would differ about what language is. For Miller, we cannot close the hermeneutic circle and speak of an "I" or a "we" because of language's "heterogeneity," which is "the interference of rhetoric (in the sense of figurative language) in the functioning of grammar and logic" (1105). I will examine this standoff between hermeneutics and deconstruction in the next chapter.

7. In considering historical and fictional narratives, Ricoeur neither separates nor collapses the two but instead interweaves them. Traces of the past are not direct references; rather, these traces "take the place of" or "stand for" the past, so that history depends on imaginative schematization in its configuration of the past and in its reinscription of lived time on cosmic time through the use of the calendar.

8. Morson and Emerson make a helpful distinction among three ways that Bakhtin discusses dialogue: (1) "as a view of truth and the world" (131); (2) as an approach to the utterance; and (3) as opposed to monologic utterances (Morson and Emerson, 130–33).

9. See Roman Jakobson's well-known essay "Concluding Statement: Linguistics and Poetics."

10. Bakhtin says, "Linguistics and philosophy of language acknowledge only a passive understanding of discourse and moreover this takes place by and large on the level of common language, that is, it is understanding of an utterance's *neutral signification* and not its actual meaning" (1981, 281).

11. In "Linguistic Utopias," Mary Louise Pratt challenges the holistic idealism of Sassurean linguistics and speech-act theory, since both assume a homogeneous

language, unmarked by differences in class, gender, race, or local speech community.

12. Ricoeur is ontologically conservative. He is against "plurality of centers" (cited in Clark, 157). As Giles Gunn says, "Ricoeur sounds as if he wants to absorb alterity" (142). Moreover, Ricoeur's idea of narrative identity is often linked with a theological search for the "recovery of a founding symbolism" (Ricoeur 1988, 247–49).

13. See, for example, Victor Shlovsky's "Art as Device." For a survey of Russian Formalism, see Peter Steiner's *Russian Formalism: A Metapoetics*.

14. The novel is also about the discovery of the future that began in the Renaissance: "In that era, the present [that is, a reality that was contemporaneous] for the first time began to sense itself not only as an incomplete continuation of the past but as something like a new and heroic beginning" (Bakhtin 1981, 40).

15. Kant makes the distinction between these "two standpoints" in the *Groundwork of the Metaphysic of Morals* and *Critique of Practical Reason*.

16. I develop this critique of Bakhtin at greater length in "Ontologie linguistique et dialogue politique chez Bakhtine."

17. The following passage clarifies this notion of Bakhtinian "enlargement": "Languages of heteroglossia, like mirrors that face each other, each reflecting in its own way a piece, a tiny corner of the world, force us to guess at and grasp for a world behind their mutually reflecting aspects that is broader, more multileveled, containing more and varied horizons than would be available to a single language or single mirror" (Bakhtin 1981, 414–15). At the metalevel only diversity, per se, can appear as value. Gunn says, "The goal of human experience is not to name, explain, or verify the existence of the sacred or singularly other but to have a relationship with it" (145).

18. See Henry Louis Gates, Jr., *The Signifying Monkey*, for the role of signifying in African American literature. I will return to Gates's work in chapter 5.

19. We have already seen this critique of the Enlightenment in the work of Heidegger and Gadamer. For an account of how this change takes place in the Anglo-American tradition of philosophy, see Richard Rorty's *Philosophy and the Mirror of Nature*.

20. Horkheimer and Adorno articulate their position as follows: "For the Enlightenment, whatever does conform to the rule of computation and utility is suspect. So long as it can develop undisturbed by any outward repression, there is no holding it. In the process, it treats its own ideas of human rights exactly as it does older universals. . . . Enlightenment is totalitarian" (6).

21. In "The Economic Problem of Masochism," Freud says that Kant's categorical imperative is "a direct inheritance from the Oedipus complex" (XIX, 169). Herbert Marcuse's *Eros and Civilization: A Philosophical Inquiry into Freud* is the most influential of the Frankfurt School's readings of Freud.

22. I discuss Habermas's views of language and modernity further in the next chapter, where I contrast them with Lyotard's.

23. Clauss Offe says, "All social systems reproduce themselves through the normatively regulated and meaningful action of their members on the one hand,

and the effectiveness of objective functional contexts on the other. This differentiation between 'social integration' and 'system integration,' between rules and rule-like regularities that assert themselves beyond subjects, is the basis for the entire sociological tradition" (cited in Benhabib 1986, 127).

24. See Albrecht Wellmer's "Reason, Utopia, and the *Dialectic of Enlightenment*" for a good account of this.

25. The work of the contemporary Marxist theorists continues this dismissal of the ethical/political institutions in favor of an unspecified future emancipation. The work of Fredric Jameson exemplifies this well: "The proposition that in our time politics and political questions have superseded ethical or moral ones implies a complete transformation of society" (124).

26. In the next chapter, I will discuss Habermas's new version of this argument through language and the ideal speech situation.

27. Calvin Schrag phrases this well: "Understanding is geared principally to a reading of human thought and action in their configurative shapes and contextual wholes. Explanation fixes its attention on the constitutive elements. Interpretation is the ongoing play between the holistic and elemental as illustrated in the interrelated progression of understanding and explanation" (78).

28. For Bakhtin, the drive to theory is a drive for a theory without a speaker— that is, "thoughts, assertions, propositions that can by themselves be true or untrue, depending on their relationship to the subject and independent of the carrier to whom they belong" (1984, 93).

29. Ricoeur says of psychoanalysis, "The economic model . . . preserves something essential. . . , namely, that man's alienation from himself is such that mental functioning does actually resemble the functioning of a thing. This simulation keeps psychoanalysis from constituting itself as a province of the exegetical disciplines applied to texts—as a hermeneutics, in other words— and requires that psychoanalysis include in the process of self-understanding operations that were originally reserved for the natural sciences" (1981, 261).

30. Roy Schaefer says that "psychoanalysts may be described as persons who listen to the narratives of analysands and help them to transform these narrations into others that are more complete, coherent, convincing, and adaptively useful than the ones they have been accustomed to constructing" (240).

31. Taylor discusses the role of strong evaluations in the constitutive dimension of language in *Human Agency and Language*.

Chapter 3:
The Poststructuralist Critiques of Interpretation

1. The difference between Heidegger and Sartre emerged publicly in Heidegger's "Letter on Humanism," a response to Sartre's *Existentialism Is a Humanism*. See Fell, *Heidegger and Sartre*, for a full discussion.

2. For example, in 1953 Heidegger says, "This Europe, in its ruinous blindness forever on the point of cutting its own throat, lies today in a great pincers,

squeezed between Russia on the one side and America on the other. From a metaphysical point of view, Russia and America are the same; the same dreary technological frenzy, the same unrestricted organization of the average man" (1961, 35). For an interesting attempt to bring Heideggerian perspectives, particularly his idea of practical understanding, into politics, see the work of Hannah Arendt, especially "Understanding and Politics," in which she draws out the similarities between liberalism and totalitarianism. For Heidegger's critique of Western philosophy's understanding of being as production, see *The Basic Problems of Phenomenology*, 106–112, and *The Question Concerning Technology and Other Essays*.

3. See "Différance" and "Ousia and Gramme: Note on a Note from *Being and Time*" in *Margins of Philosophy* as well the book-length study *De l'esprit*.

4. In "Différance," Derrida links the term of his title to Heidegger's ontic-ontological distinction: "In a certain aspect of itself, *différance* is certainly but the historical and epochal unfolding of Being or the ontological difference" (1982, 22).

5. Richard Rorty says, "One of the most intriguing features of Heidegger's later thought is his claim that if you begin with Plato's motives and assumptions you will end up with some form of pragmatism. I think that this claim is, when suitably interpreted, right. But, unlike Heidegger, I think pragmatism is a *good* place to end up" (1991, 27).

6. It is important to note that Gadamer rejects Heidegger's view, in which, in Gadamer's words, "science has expanded into a total technocracy, and thus brings on the 'cosmic night' of the 'forgetfulness of Being'" (1975, xxv). Gadamer is interested in revivifying practical philosophy, not going beyond it. See Richard Bernstein's *Beyond Objectivism and Relativism* for a good discussion of this dimension of Gadamer's work.

7. The language of laughter, dance, and affirmation beyond hope is reminiscent of Nietzsche, who also influenced Derrida.

8. Derrida later abandons the term "freeplay" and talks about "différance" as the "site" that produces both logocentrism and its other.

9. Derrida sometimes uses the phrase "transcendental signified" (Positions, 190) to designate the place in Saussure where there is a signified that "would refer to no signifier, would exceed the chain of signs, and would no longer itself function as a signifier" (19–20).

10. "Différance" reworks Saussure's notion of "différence," and it means both to differ and to defer. The "a" instead of "e" is not discernable in speech, only in writing. Derrida defines différance later in his career as follows: "Différance 'is' a difference (discontinuity, alterity, heterogeneity) and also the possibility and the necessity of an economy (relay, delegation, signification, mediation, 'supplement,' reappropriation) of the other *as such*: difference and in-difference without dialectics. Economy of the other, economy of the same" (1987, 258–59). "As such" indicates the transcendental dimension of the argument.

11. See Eve Tavor Bannet's *Structuralism and the Logic of Dissent*, 202–27, for an analysis of Derridean moves.

12. In his exchange with Derrida in Paris in 1981, Gadamer picks up on the difference between Derrida's ontology of the sign (word) and his own idea of dialogue but misses Derrida's point about why deconstructive critique is not reducible to dialogue: "It seems to me I go beyond Derrida's deconstruction, since a word exists only in conversation and never exists there as an isolated word but as the totality of a way of accounting by means of speaking and answering" (1989, 112). For an interesting comparison of Derrida and hermeneutics, see James Lawlor's *Imagination and Chance: The Difference Between the Thought of Ricoeur and Derrida*. Lawlor contrasts Derrida's disclosure of the contingency of our being with Ricoeur's hermeneutic focus on expanding philosophical imagination.

13. Derrida clarifies the difference between "understanding" and his account of how language functions in daily life: "The fact that a 'break'" with the notion of understanding "is always possible" means "the mark still does not cease functioning, that a minimum of legibility and intelligibility remains, constitutes the point of departure of SEC's argumentation" (1977, 202).

14. Habermas discusses the "performative contradiction" in *Moral Consciousness and Communicative Action*.

15. See Charles Taylor's "What's Wrong with Negative Liberty?" in *Philosophy and the Human Sciences*, where he gives a preliminary definition of negative freedom as a view that defines "freedom exclusively in terms of the independence of the individual from interference by others, be these governments, corporations or private persons" (1985, 211).

16. Derrida says in response to a question about whether his work leads to noncommitment, "Not at all. But the difficulty is to gesture in opposite directions at the same time: on the one hand, to preserve a distance and suspicion with regard to the official political codes governing reality; on the other, to intervene here and now in practical and engaged manner whenever the necessity arises" (1984, 120). In *The Ethics of Deconstruction: Derrida and Lévinas*, Simon Critchley recuperates the ethical moment of deconstruction at the same time that he points out its political weakness: "The move that deconstruction is unable to make . . . concerns the passage from undecidablity to decision . . . from deconstruction to critique, from ethics to politics" (236). This chapter does not address Derrida's most recent reflections on justice in *Du droit à la philosophie* (Paris: Galilée, 1990).

17. Habermas never discusses Lyotard, preferring to focus on Foucault and Derrida. Lyotard does refer to Habermas in several places.

18. Habermas notes that Hegel had the opportunity to develop a notion of communicative reason rather than subject-centered reason but took the wrong turn: "In Hegel's youthful writing the option of explicating the ethical totality as a communicative reason embodied in intersubjective contexts is still open" (1987, 40).

19. Robert Holub's defense of Habermas against Lyotard repeats Habermas's mistake of making the "everyday" the metatype that grounds language. As Holub says, "Lyotard fails to grasp that Habermas conceives of consensus, discourse, validity claims and the ideal speech situation as notions derived from reflection on everyday language. The common denominator for Habermas does not reside in some metaphysical principle, but in normal linguistic competence" (1991, 149).

20. I translate "phrase" as "sentence," not "phrase." In the English translation of this work, Georges Van den Abbeele uses "phrase" for reasons I do not find convincing. (See *The Différend: Phrases in Dispute* [Minneapolis: University of Minnesota Press, 1988], 194.) All translations are my own. Even though Lyotard's use of the term is sometimes eccentric, "phrase" does not capture this eccentricity any better than "sentence." Moreover, as Geoff Bennington points out, "sentence" shows the relationship of the text to the Anglo-Saxon philosophical tradition (123–24).

21. Donald Davidson's "On the Very Idea of a Conceptual Scheme" in *Inquiries into Truth and Interpretation* is perhaps the best-known argument against radically different worldviews. Davidson maintains that the idea of various conceptual schemes that organize the world differently is unintelligible since no language that is radically different from our own would be understandable. As Hilary Putnam says in his update of Davidson's argument, "However different our images of knowledge and conceptions of rationality, we share a huge fund of assumptions and beliefs about what is reasonable with even the most bizarre culture we can succeed in interpreting at all" (1981, 119). Lyotard and I would also reject the scheme/world distinction and accept the necessity of some shared concepts; however, this sharing is not sufficient to mediate all incommensurabilities or to make linguistic differences unimportant.

22. Lyotard criticizes his earlier discussion of narrative in *Le Postmoderne expliqué aux enfants:* "It is not right to give the narrative genre an absolute privilege over other genres of discourse in the analysis of human or in particular 'language' (ideological) phenomena, and even less in a philosophical approach. Certain of my previous reflections perhaps succumbed to this 'transcendental spectre' ('Présentations,' *Instructions païennes*, even *La condition postmoderne*)" (1986, 45).

23. In the assertive mode, the sentence seeks to locate truth and particular reference: "The intimation had the next thing, in a flash, taken on a name—a name on which our friend seized as he asked himself if he weren't perhaps really dealing with an irreducible young Pagan. This description—he quite jumped at it—had a sound that gratified his mental ear, so that of a sudden he had adopted it" (James 1964, 99). In the ethical mode, the subject looks for consistency in moral norms, for virtues as well as rules, and the language is frequently argumentative: "He must approach Chad, he must wait for him,

deal with him, master, but he mustn't dispossess himself of the faculty of seeing things as they were" (79). In the aesthetic mode, the subject spins out and plays with possibilities, and this play is informed by a search for harmony of meaning rather than truth. "He [Strether] was in fact quite able to cherish his vision of it, play with it in idle hours, only speaking of it to no one and quite aware he couldn't have spoken of it without appearing to talk nonsense" (120–21). I develop this analysis at length in "Value and Subjectivity: The Dynamics of the Sentence in James's *The Ambassadors*."

24. James's "The Beast in the Jungle," which is the tragic pendant to Strether's comic tale, illustrates more directly the cost of such hiding, for in this story the protagonist uses the prospective narrative about the leap of the beast in order to avoid contact with his affective life and the world.

25. In his afterword to the English translation of *Au juste*, Samuel Weber formulates two parts of this objection. First, "does not the concept of absolute, intact singularity remain tributary to the same logic of identity that sustains any and all ideas of totality?" (103). Second, "by prescribing that no game, especially not that of prescription, should dominate the others, one is doing what is simultaneously claimed is being avoided: one is dominating the other games in order to protect them from domination" (105). Weber's first point raises what could be called the Derridean objection. Lyotard's understanding of language is situated at the level of the sentence, not the sign, like Derrida's. Lyotard tries to overcome totalizing not by double writing but by emphasizing the continuous reconfiguration of the map of discourse. In the second, Weber points out that Lyotard's project is not just descriptive but evaluative. I return to this at the end of this section.

26. Lyotard characterizes his own philosophical discourse as follows: "The rule for philosophical discourse is to discover a rule. Its a priori is its stake [*enjeu*]" (1983, 95). This genre is not all-encompassing discourse that trumps others: "The examination of sentences is a genre that cannot take the place of politics. . . . The philosophical genre, which has the appearance of a metalanguage, remains in this genre only if it knows that there is no metalanguage. Thus, it remains popular and humorous" (227).

27. In "Capitalist Culture and the Circulatory System," Stephen Greenblatt discusses Jameson's and Lyotard's reduction of the complexities of capitalism. If for Lyotard capitalism reduces differends, for Jameson it is "the perpetuator of separate discursive domans, the agent of privacy, psychology, and the individual." Hence, for both critics, "history functions as a convenient anecdotal ornament upon a theoretical structure, and capitalism appears not as a complex social and economic development in the West but as a malign philosophical principle" (262).

28. I will not address late works or the change in Foucault's thought from his "archaeological" period (e.g., in *The Order of Things*), during which he examines anonymous systems of discourse, to his genealogical period, during which he is concerned with disciplinary practices and power. My focus is on the ge-

nealogical. See Hubert Dreyfus and Paul Rabinow's *Beyond Structuralism and Hermeneutics* for a discussion of this shift. David Hoy phrases Foucault's critique of Derrida well: "His critique of Derrida is that Derrida's insistence on the plurality of truth is a merely negative point, and does not raise the more interesting question about why specific statements get uttered" (1991, 279). In "Cogito and the History of Madness," Derrida offers a critique of Foucault's early work *Madness and Civilization*. See François Dosse's *Histoire du structuralisme* for a good account of Foucault and Derrida in the context of French life from 1954 to the present.

29. Nietzsche says, "To make an animal entitled to make promises"—i.e., able to guarantee the constancy of his future conduct—he needs to be made "up to a certain point regular, uniform, equal among equals, calculable" (1956, 190).

30. "Various concepts have been constructed and domains of analysis carved out: psyche, subjectivity, personality, consciousness, etc; on it have been built scientific techniques and discourse. . . . The man described for us whom we are invited to free, is already in himself the effect of a subjection much more profound than himself" (Foucault, *Discipline and Punish*, 30).

31. Dews pursues this point. He says that Foucault "dissolves the philosophical link—inherited by the Marxist tradition from German Idealism—between consciousness, self-reflection, and freedom" and denies that there "remains any progressive political potential in the ideal of an autonomous subject" (160). Habermas voices a similar objection: "His [Foucault's] theory tries to rise above . . . pseudo-sciences to a more rigorous objectivity, and in doing so gets caught all the more hopelessly in the trap of a presentist historiography, which sees itself compelled to a relativist self-denial and can give no account of the normative foundations of its own rhetoric" (1987, 294).

32. In *Contingency, Irony, and Solidarity* (65) Richard Rorty uses this phrase to characterize Foucault's work. The phrase comes from Bernard Yack's *The Longing for Total Revolution: Philosophical Sources of Social Discontent*.

33. See James Miller, *The Passion of Michel Foucault*, especially 137–44.

34. In his earlier work *Les Mots et les choses*, Foucault gives a hint of his later formulation: "This is why transcendental reflection in its modern form does not, as in Kant, find its fundamental necessity in the existence of a science of nature . . . but in the existence, mute, yet ready to speak, and secretly impregnated with potential discourse—of that not-known from which man is endlessly called toward knowledge of the self" (cited in James Miller, 143).

Later, in "What Is Enlightenent?," Foucault rewrites Kant's transcendental investigation of the conditions of the possibility of the practice of science, ethics, and aesthetics as follows: "The point, in brief, is to transform the critique conducted in the form of necessary limitation into a critique that takes the form of a possible transgression" (1984, 45). This permits us to "separate out, from the contingency that made us what we are, the possibility of no longer being, doing, or thinking what we are, do or think. . . . It [this kind of critique] is seeking to give new impetus, as far and wide as possible, to the undefined work of freedom" (1984, 45).

Chapter 4:
Feminist Theories

1. For feminist revisions of liberalism, see Nancy Rosenblum, *Another Liberalism: Romanticism and the Reconstruction of Liberal Thought*; Susan Moller Okin, *Justice, Gender, and the Family*; and Amy Gutman, *Democratic Education*.

2. On the question of Gilligan's research, see Linda Kerber et al., "On *In a Different Voice*: An Interdisciplinary Form," *Signs* (1986): 304–33; and Seyla Benhabib's "The Generalized and the Concrete Other: The Kohlberg-Gilligan Controversy and Moral Theory" in *Situating the Self*, 148–77.

3. I will come back to Gilligan later, since Jessica Benjamin recuperates her work in *The Bonds of Love*.

4. Catherine MacKinnon says of Gilligan's book, "What is infuriating about it . . . is that it neglects the explanatory level. She also has found the voice of the victim—yes, women are a victimized group. The articulation of the voice of the victim is crucial because laws about victimization are typically made by people with power. . . . But I am troubled by the possibility of women identifying with what is a positively valued feminine stereotype. It is the 'feminine'" (cited in Benhabib 1992, 195).

5. The early Kristeva, most notably in *Revolution in Poetic Language*, uses Lacanian vocabulary.

6. Kristeva says, "Let us know that an ostensibly masculine, paternal identification . . . is necessary in order to have a voice in the chapter of politics and history. . . . [But] let us right away be wary of the premium on narcissism that such an integration can carry . . . and let us rather act on the socio-politico-historical stage as her negative: that is, act first with all those who refuse and 'swim against the tide'—all who rebel against the existing relations of production. But let us not take the role of Revolutionary either, whether male or female: let us on the contrary refuse all roles to summon truth outside of time" (1986, 156).

7. Butler is contrasting her idea of "constituted" with Benhabib's idea of "situated" because Benhabib's "situated self" leaves the self intact as it places it in situations. Butler's constituted subject gets rid of the ontological borders between self and situation.

8. In her review of Gordon's *The Heroes of Their Own Lives: The Politics and History of Family Violence*, Scott accuses Gordon of idealizing the agency of the women she studies. Scott thinks Gordon could have avoided this problem through the adoption of a "conceptualization [that] would see agency not as an attribute or trait inhering in the will of autonomous individual subjects, but as a discursive effect" (1990, 853). For Gordon, such a way of understanding agency "drains that notion of any meaning" (853). What concerns me in this dispute is not the empirical question about these particular historical subjects; rather, my point is that Scott must recuperate the agency of some of her predecessors in order to make her analysis possible. Such an account breaks down the incommensurability between her stance and Gordon's. I discuss the negotiation

between agency and constructivism at greater length in my book *Theorizing Textual Subjects: Agency and Oppression* (Cambridge University Press, 1997).

9. See Gayatri Spivak's *In Other Worlds* for a discussion of strategic essentialism.

10. Hooks asks, "How do we create an oppositional worldview, a consciousness, an identity, a standpoint that exists not only as that struggle which also opposes dehumanization but as that movement which enables creative, expansive self-actualization?" (15).

11. There is a curious connection with Sartre here. In his view, humans are free. This is their ontological condition independent of their empirical (or ontic) conditions. Because this condition is terrifying, humans try to give themselves an essence. Poststructuralists abandon this subject-centered view and yet keep the obsession with essence.

12. Fraser's question to Foucault, cited in chapter 3, is "Why is struggle preferable to submission? Why ought domination to be resisted? Only with the introduction of normative notions of some kind could Foucault begin to answer questions . . . to tell us what is wrong with the modern knowledge/power regime and why we ought to oppose it" (1989, 29).

13. See Bardes and Gosset's *Declarations of Independence: Women and Political Power in Nineteenth Century American Fiction* and Ellen Messer-Davidow's "Acting Otherwise" in *Provoking Agents*, in which she discusses how women "were able to reconstitute themselves" (34).

14. For a wholesale critique of the Enlightenment that does not acknowledge the complicity of its own ideals with this project, see Jane Flax's "Is Enlightenment Emancipatory?" in *Disputed Subjects*, 75–91.

15. See Nina Baym's "Melodramas of Beset Manhood," 1146–57.

16. See Claire Kahane's "Object-Relations Theory" in *Feminism and Psychoanalysis*, 284–90, and Teresa Brennan's *Between Feminism and Psychoanalysis* for a critique of object-relations theory from an intrapsychic (constructivist) point of view. Brennan phrases this critique as follows: "Object-relations theory makes sexual difference the result of the social order rather than the result of the foundation of the symbolic order. . . . Sexual difference is not only the result of social actions but its foundation" (8).

17. The conception of the liberal moral subject to which Benjamin alludes is that of John Rawls, which he elaborates in *A Theory of Justice* and later in *Political Liberalism*. Rawls develops the notion of an "original position" as a regulative ideal for reflecting on justice. In this position, the subject is deprived of a knowledge of his/her identity in order to insure fairness (1971, 137; 1993, 22–28). The problem is that Rawls's formulation evaporates both the self and the other. For important critiques of Rawls's view, see Michael Sandel's *Liberalism and the Limits of Justice* and Seyla Benhabib's "The Generalized and the Concrete Other: The Kohlberg-Gilligan Controversy and Moral Theory" in *Situating the Self*, 148–77.

18. Benjamin says, "I believe that those critics who see only this element [reversal] and thus claim that she [Gilligan] espouses a 'feminine ethos' have over-

looked her critique of feminine self-sacrifice. . . . This misinterpretation has arisen, as Seyla Benhabib suggests, because Gilligan's book contained no explicit discussion of the historical constitution of these gender differences . . . in light of woman's oppression" (194).

19. Cardinal frequently moves between the first-person and third-person voices.

20. Although the text has an autobiographical dimension, Cardinal insists that her book is not a document of her psychoanalytic treatment: "I had no desire to speak of psychoanalysis. . . . I wrote the story of woman, a story in which psychoanalysis has a large role" (1977, 27).

21. This passage—and indeed the entire paragraph in which it is contained—does not appear in the English translation.

22. The resolution to her illness includes an unexamined reconciliation with her husband. She wants to start with her husband and family: "A family, a microcosm, the ferment of society" (1983, 268). She realizes that there are other ways to go about returning to life but that "one alone was right" for her (268). We do not see what this new relationship with her family will look like. Her husband somehow comes to appreciate her new self, which it took her seven years to work out (and comes to make the necessary changes in himself), in the time it takes him to read her manuscript. Another woman's story—such as Cardinal's own subsequent text *Une Vie pour deux*—might bring out what the narrator's desire for home covers over.

23. In *The Contexture of Feminism*, Carolyn Durham discusses this transference on the husband but is silent about the feminist implications of this reconciliation.

24. Durham makes a similar move when she reads the analysand's negative transference as evidence of Cardinal's critique of the patriarchy. Durham is forced to go to such length to attack psychoanalysis because Cardinal has spoken openly of what she owes to therapy. The dedication of *The Words to Say It* reads, "To the doctor who helped me be born." Durham makes some good points about Bruno Bettelheim's silence on gender in his preface and afterword to the English translation of Cardinal's novel.

25. Lorde's lesbianism has clearly kept her out of mainstream feminist theory and criticism and African American feminist theory and criticism. An exception is Beverley Guy-Shefthall's *Words of Fire: An Anthology of African-American Feminist Thought*.

26. For a discussion of the Algerian theme, see Françoise Lionnet's chapter "Privileged Difference and the Possibility of Emancipation: *The Words to Say It* and *A l'autre bout de moi*" in *Autobiographical Voices: Race, Gender, Self-Portraiture*.

Chapter 5:
Exile or Rootedness

1. In *Culture and Imperialism*, Said distances himself from Western theorists from Foucault to the Frankfurt School because they ignore non-Western culture (278–79).

2. Said expresses the hermeneutic dimension succinctly: "Are there ways we can reconceive imperial experience in other than compartmentalized terms, so as to transform our understanding of both the past and the present and our attitude toward the future?" (1993, 17).

3. For Said, Foucault's pursuit of the "unthought" is not like Derrida's project. Whereas Derrida's goal is to attack "a lazy understanding of signs, language, and textuality," Foucault's aim, as Said sees it, is to expose "what at a specific time and in a specific way cannot be thought because certain other things have been imposed upon thought instead" (1983, 214).

4. Spivak's essay "Can the Subaltern Speak?" in *Marxism and the Interpretation of Culture* is the classic statement of the view that the "subaltern" is completely colonized by the discourse of colonization.

5. In *The World, the Text, and the Critic* Said asks of Auerbach, "How did exile become converted from a challenge or a risk, or even from an active impingement on his European selfhold, into a positive mission. . . ? (7). To justify his own politics of exile, Said cites Auerbach's remark that "the most priceless and indispensable part of a philologist's heritage is still his own nation's culture and heritage. Only when he is first separated from this heritage, however, and then transcends it, does it become truly effective" (cited in Said 1983, 7). McGowan says that Said wants distance and intimacy to be compatible so that "universalism and localism coexist in critical consciousness" (170).

6. Foucault and Chomsky met for a program aired on Dutch television in 1971. See James Miller's account of their exchange in *The Passion of Michel Foucault*, 201–202.

7. For McGowan, this emphasis leads to individualism: "Said posits a version of the postmodern monolith insofar as he finds that worldliness and interest delegitimate all existing forms and that all cultures have enormous powers of 'identity-reinforcement,' but he also claims a heroic disentanglement from such determinants for the critic" (173).

8. Said notes Terence Ranger and Eric Hobsbawm's collection *The Invention of Tradition*, which considers tradition only as a patchwork of rationalization, a factitious product of power, not a resource.

9. Said cites James's chapter "From Toussaint L'Ouverture to Fidel Castro" in *Black Jacobins*. In this chapter, James places the Santo Domingo slave revolt "as a process unfolding within the same history as that of the French Revolution" (Said 1993, 279). James then move to Aimé Césaire and T. S. Eliot. The problem with all this is that Said's praise for James is merely for his metaphilosophical agility, for his ability to juxtapose discrepant experiences without saying how we are to cash out these juxtapositions.

10. Catherine Gallagher raised questions about Said's political location after the publication of *The World, the Text, and the Critic*: "Complete unspecifiability is the most striking feature of [Said's] politics, the feature that emerges most strikingly from the rootlessness, the disengagement, inherent in critical affiliation" (cited in McGowan, 170).

11. West praises Derrida because he "focuses on the political power of rhetorical operations—of tropes and metaphors in binary oppositions like white/black, good/bad . . . showing how these operations sustain hierarchal worldviews by devaluing the second term as something subsumed under the first" (1993, 21–22). However, Derrida's work, in West's view, "puts a premium on sophistical ironic consciousness that tends to preclude and foreclose analyses that guide action and purpose" (22).

12. See Steven Lukes, *Marxism and Morality*, chapters 1–3.

13. See *The Return of the Political* and *Radical Democracy*, in the latter of which Mouffe says, "If the Left is to learn from the tragic experiences of totalitarianism it has to adopt a different attitude towards liberal democracy, and recognize its strengths as well as reveal its shortcomings. In other words, the objective of the Left should be the extension and deepening of the democratic revolution initiated two hundred years ago" (1).

14. West uses the word "prophetic" because he "harks back to the Jewish and Christian tradition of prophets who brought urgent and compassionate critique to bear on the evils of their day. The mark of the prophet is to speak the truth in love and courage—come what may. Prophetic pragmatism proceeds from this impulse. It neither requires a religious foundation nor entails a religious perspective, yet prophetic pragmatism is compatible with certain religious outlooks" (1989, 233).

15. Gooding-Williams says, "The paradox here is that Nietzsche and Foucault deliberately intend the conception of genealogy they advocate as a critique of organic models" (519).

16. We find this tension in West's own revisions to pragmatism, which suggest the need to appropriate Hegel and Marx: "Unlike Dewey, prophetic pragmatism promotes a more direct encounter with the Marxist tradition of social analysis" (1989, 213).

17. For a discussion of the differences between pragmatism and other contemporary theories of language, see my essay "How Philosophy of Language Informs Ethics and Politics: Richard Rorty and Contemporary Theory." For a good sampling of the controversy surrounding Rorty's pragmatism, see *Reading Rorty*, ed. Alan Malachowski.

18. West points out that in Malcolm's second conversion (1964), he abandoned the Nation of Islam for "orthodox Islam that rejected any form of racial supremacy" (Malcolm, 52).

19. Rorty argues for distinguishing between the vocabulary of self-creation and the vocabulary of justice: "The vocabulary of self-creation is necessarily private, unshared, unsuited to argument," whereas "the vocabulary of justice is necessarily public and shared, a medium for argumentative exchange" (1989, xiv).

20. See Georgia Warnke's *Justice and Interpretation* for the role of hermeneutics in political theory.

Conclusion

1. I develop my own views and my difference from pragmatism in *Theorizing Textual Subjects: Agency and Oppression*.

2. See Benjamin Barber's *McWorld Versus Jihad* for a discussion of the corrosive effects of global commercialization on culture and civil society and *Public Education in a Multicultural Society*, edited by Robert Fullinwider, for an analysis of the conflicts surrounding the teaching of U.S. history.

Bibliography

Arendt, Hannah. "Understanding and Politics (The Difficulties of Understanding)." In *Essays in Understanding: 1930–1954*. Ed. Jerome Kohn. New York: Harcourt Brace and Company, 1994. 307–27.

Avi-Ram, Amittai. *Telling Rhythm*. Ann Arbor: University of Michigan Press, 1994.

Bakhtin, Mikhail. *The Dialogic Imagination*. Trans. Caryl Emerson and Michael Holquist. Austin: University of Texas Press, 1981.

———. *Problems in Dostoevsky's Poetics*. Ed. and trans. Caryl Emerson. Minneapolis: University of Minnesota Press, 1984.

———. *Speech Genres and Other Late Essays*. Trans. Vern W. McGee. Austin: University of Texas Press, 1986.

Bannet, Eve Tavor. *Structuralism and the Logic of Dissent: Barthes, Derrida, Foucault, and Lacan*. Urbana: University of Illinois Press, 1989.

Barber, Benjamin. *Jihad vs. McWorld*. New York: Random House, 1995.

Barthes, Roland. *The Rustle of Language*. Trans. Richard Howard. Berkeley: University of California Press, 1989.

———. *S/Z*. Trans. Richard Miller. New York: Hill and Wang, 1974.

Baym, Nina. "Melodramas of Beset Manhood: How Theories of American Fiction Exclude Women Authors." In *The Critical Tradition: Classic Texts and Contemporary Trends*. Ed. David H. Richter. New York: St. Martin's, 1989. 1146–57.

Benhabib, Seyla. *Critique, Norm, and Utopia*. New York: Columbia University Press, 1986.

———. "Introduction: Beyond the Politics of Gender." *Feminism as Critique: On the Politics of Gender*. Minneapolis: University of Minnesota Press, 1987. 1–15.

———. *Situating the Self: Gender, Community and Postmodernism in Contemporary Ethics*. New York: Routledge, 1992.

Benjamin, Jessica. *The Bonds of Love: Psychoanalysis, Feminism, and the Problem of Domination*. New York: Pantheon, 1998.

Bennington, Geoff. *Lyotard: Writing the Event*. Manchester: Manchester University Press, 1988.

Benveniste, Emile. "La forme et les sens dans le langage." In *Problémes de linguistique générale*. Paris: Gallimard, 1974. 215–40.

Bernstein, Michael André. "Poetics of Ressentiment." *Rethinking Bakhtin: Extensions and Challenges*. Eds. Gary Saul Morson and Caryl Emerson. Evanston: Northwestern University Press, 1989. 197–224.

Bernstein, Richard. *Beyond Objectivism and Relativism*. Philadelphia: University of Pennsylvania Press, 1983.

———. *The New Constellation: The Ethical-Political Horizons of Modernity and Postmodernity*. Cambridge: MIT Press, 1992.

Blumenberg, Hans. *The Legitimacy of the Modern Age*. Trans. Robert M. Wallace. Cambridge: MIT Press, 1983.

Braxton, Joanne M. *Black Women Writing Autobiography: A Tradition Within a Tradition*. Philadelphia: Temple University Press, 1989.

Brennan, Teresa. Introduction. *Between Psychoanalysis and Feminism*. New York: Routledge, 1989. 1–24.

Brooks, Cleanth. "Literary Criticism: Poet, Poem, and Reader." In *Varieties of Literary Experience: Eighteen Essays in World Literature*. Ed. Stanley Burnshaw. New York: New York University Press, 1962.

——— and Robert Penn Warren. *Understanding Poetry*. New York: Holt, 1939.

———. *The Well-Wrought Urn: Studies in the Structure of Poetry*. New York: Harcourt, Brace, and World, 1947.

Butler, Judith. *Bodies That Matter: On the Discursive Limits of "Sex."* New York: Routledge, 1993.

———. "Contingent Foundations." *Feminist Contentions*. New York: Routledge, 1995. 35–38.

Cardinal, Marie. *Autrement dit*. Paris: Grasset, 1977.

———. *Les mots pour le dire*. Paris: Grasset, 1975.

———. *The Words to Say It*. Trans. Pat Goodheart. Preface and afterword by Bruno Bettelheim. Cambridge: VanVactor and Goodheart, 1983.

Connolly, William. *Identity and Difference: Democratic Negotiations of Political Paradox*. Ithaca: Cornell University Press, 1991.

Critchley, Simon. *The Ethics of Deconstruction: Derrida and Levinas*. Cambridge: Blackwell, 1992.

Culler, Jonathan. "Beyond Interpretation." In *The Pursuit of Signs*. Ithaca: Cornell University Press, 1981. 3–17.

———. "Communicative Competence and Normative Force." *New German Critique* 35 (1985): 133–44.

———. *Ferdinand de Saussure*. Rev. ed. Ithaca: Cornell University Press, 1986.

———. Review of Terry Eagleton, *Literary Theory. Poetics Today* 5 (1984): 149–55.

———. *Roland Barthes*. New York: Oxford University Press, 1983.

———. *Structuralist Poetics*. Ithaca: Cornell University Press, 1975.

Davidson, Donald. *Inquiries into Truth and Interpretation*. New York: Oxford University Press, 1984.

Derrida, Jacques. "Afterword: Toward an Ethic of Discussion." In *Limited Inc*. Evanston: Northwestern University Press, 1988. 111–60.

―――. "But, beyond . . . (Open letter to Anne McClintock and Rob Nixon)." Trans. Peggy Kamuf. In *Race, Writing, and Difference*. Ed. Henry Louis Gates, Jr. Chicago: University of Chicago Press, 1986. 354–69.

―――. "Choreographies." *Diacritics* 12 (1982): 66–76.

―――. *De l'esprit*. Paris: Galilée, 1987.

―――. "Deconstruction and the Other." Interview with Richard Kearney. In *Dialogues with Contemporary Continental Thinkers*. Ed. Kearney. Manchester: Manchester University Press, 1984. 105–26.

―――. *Dissemination*. Trans. Barbara Johnson. Chicago: University of Chicago Press, 1981.

―――. *Du droit à la philosphie*. Paris: Galilée, 1990.

―――. "Limited Inc." *Glyph* 2 (1977): 162–254.

―――. *Margins of Philosophy*. Trans. Alan Bass. Chicago: University of Chicago Press, 1982.

―――. *Of Grammatology*. Trans. Gayatri Chakravorty Spivak. Baltimore: Johns Hopkins University Press, 1976.

―――. *Points . . .: Interviews, 1974–1994*. Trans. Peggy Kamuf et al. Stanford: Stanford University Press, 1995.

―――. *Positions*. Trans. Alan Bass. Chicago: University of Chicago Press, 1981.

―――. "Some Questions and Responses." In *The Linguistics of Writing: Arguments Between Language and Literature*. Eds. Nigel Fabb et al. New York: Methuen, 1987. 252–64

―――. *Writing and Difference*. Trans. Alan Bass. Chicago: University of Chicago Press, 1978.

Dews, Peter. *Logics of Disintegration: Post-Structuralist Thought and the Claims of Critical Theory*. London: Verso, 1987.

Dosse, François. *Histoire du structuralism*. 2 vols. Paris: Editions La Decouverte, 1992.

Dostal, Robert. "Philosophical Discourse and the ethics of Hermeneutics." In *Festivals of Interpretation*. Ed. Kathleen Wright. Albany: State University of New York Press, 1990. 63–88.

―――. "Time and Phenomenology in Husserl and Heidegger." *Cambridge Companion to Heidegger*. Ed. Charles Guignon. Cambridge: Cambridge University Press, 1993. 141–69.

Dreyfus, Hubert. "Beyond Hermeneutics: Interpretation in Late Heidegger and Recent Foucault." In *Hermeneutics: Questions and Prospects*. Eds. Gary Shapiro and Alan Sica. Amherst: University of Massachusetts Press, 1984. 66–83.

――― and Paul Rabinow. *Michel Foucault: Beyond Structuralism and Hermeneutics*. 2d. ed. Chicago: University of Chicago Press, 1983.

Du Bois, W. E. B. *The Souls of Black Folks*. New York: Signet, 1969.

Eagleton, Terry. *Literary Theory*. Minneapolis: University of Minnesota Press, 1983.

Ellison, Ralph. "Flying Home." *Flying Home and Other Stories*. Ed. John F. Callahan. New York: Random House, 1996. 147–74.

Farias, Victor. *Heidegger and Nazism.* Trans. Paul Burrell and Gabriel R. Ricci. Philadelphia: Temple University Press, 1989.

Fell, Joseph. *Heidegger and Sartre: An Essay on Being and Place.* New York: Columbia University Press, 1979.

Ferry, Luc, and Alain Renaut. *La Pensée 68: essai sur l'anti-humanisme contemporain.* Paris: Gallimard, 1988.

Fetterley, Judith. "Reading about Reading: 'A Jury of Her Peers,' 'The Murders in the Rue Morgue,' and 'The Yellow Wallpaper.'" In *Gender and Reading: Essays on Readers, Texts, and Contexts.* Eds. Elizabeth Flynn and Patracino P. Schweickart. Baltimore: Johns Hopkins University Press, 1986. 147–64.

————. *The Resisting Reader: A Feminist Approach to American Fiction.* Bloomington: Indiana University Press, 1977.

Flax, Jane. *Disputed Subjects: Essays on Psychoanalysis, Politics and Philosophy.* New York: Routledge, 1993.

Flynn, Elizabeth, and Patricino Schweickart, eds. *Gender and Reading: Essays on Readers, Texts, and Contexts.* Baltimore: Johns Hopkins University Press, 1986.

Foucault, Michel. *Discipline and Punish: The Birth of the Prison.* Trans. Alan Sheridan. New York: Pantheon, 1977.

————. *The Foucault Reader.* Ed. Paul Rabinow. New York: Pantheon, 1984.

————. *The History of Sexuality.* Trans. Robert Hurley. 3 vols. New York: Pantheon, 1978–87. Vol. 1: *Introduction* (1978); vol. 2: *The Uses of Pleasure* (1985); vol. 3: *The Care of the Self* (1987).

————. *Language, Counter-Memory, Practice: Selected Essays and Interviews.* Trans. Donald F. Bouchard and Sherry Simon. Ithaca: Cornell University Press, 1977.

————. *The Order of Things.* Trans. Alan Sheridan. New York: Random House, 1970.

————. *Politics, Philosophy, Culture: Interviews and Other Writings, 1972–77.* Trans. Alan Sheridan et al. Ed. Lawrence D. Kritzman. New York: Routledge, 1988.

————. *Power/Knowledge: Selected Interviews and Other Writings, 1972–77.* Trans. Colin Gordon et al. Ed. Colin Gordon. New York: Pantheon, 1981.

Frank, Manfred. *What Is Neostructuralism?* Trans. Sabine Wilke and Richard T. Gray. Minneapolis: University of Minnesota Press, 1988.

Fraser, Nancy. "False Antitheses: A Response to Seyla Benhabib and Judith Butler." *Feminist Contentions: A Philosophical Exchange.* New York: Routledge, 1995. 59–74.

————. Introduction. *Revaluing French Feminism: Critical Essays on Difference, Agency, and Culture.* Bloomington: Indiana University Press, 1992. 1–24.

————. "Rethinking the Public Sphere." *Habermas and the Public Sphere.* Ed. Craig Calhoun. Cambridge: MIT Press, 1992. 109–42.

————. "Toward a Discourse Ethic of Solidarity." *Praxis International* 5 (1986): 425–29.

————. *Unruly Practices*. Minneapolis: University of Minnesota Press, 1989.

Freud, Sigmund. *New Introductory Lectures on Psychoanalysis*. Trans. James Strachey. New York: Norton, 1965.

Fullinwider, Robert, ed. *Public Education in a Multicultural Society: Policy, Theory, Critique*. Cambridge: Cambridge University Press, 1996.

Fuss, Diana. *Essentially Speaking: Feminism, Nature, and Difference*. New York: Routledge, 1989.

Gadamer, Hans-Georg. "Destruktion and Deconstruction." In *Dialogue and Deconstruction*. Eds. Dianne P. Michelfelder and Richard Palmer. Albany: SUNY Press, 1989. 102–13.

————. *Dialogue and Dialectic*. Trans. P. Christopher Smith. New Haven: Yale University Press, 1976.

————. "Hermeneutics and Logocentrism." In *Dialogue and Deconstruction*. 114–25.

————. *Philosophical Hermeneutics*. Trans. David E. Linge. Berkeley: University of California Press, 1977.

————. "The Problem of Historical Consciousness." *Interpretive Social Science: A Second Look*. Eds. Paul Rabinow and William Sullivan. Berkeley: University of California Press, 1987. 103–62.

————. *Reason in the Age of Science*. Trans. Frederick G. Lawrence. Cambridge: MIT Press, 1981.

————. *The Relevance of the Beautiful and Other Essays*. Trans. Nicholas Walker. Ed. Robert Bernasconi. Cambridge: Cambridge University Press, 1986.

————. "Reply to Jacques Derrida." In *Dialogue and Deconstruction*. 55–57.

————. "Text and Interpretation." In *Dialogue and Deconstruction*. 21–51.

————. *Truth and Method*. 2d. rev. ed. Trans. Garrett Barden and John Cumming. Translation revised by Joel Weinsheimer and Donald G. Marshall. New York: Continuum, 1994.

Gardiner, Judith Kegan, ed. *Provoking Agents: Gender and Agency in Theory and Practice*. Urbana: University of Illinois, 1995.

Gardiner, Michael. *The Dialogics of Critique: M. M. Bakhtin and the Theory of Ideology*. New York: Routledge, 1992.

Gasché, Rodolphe. *The Tain of the Mirror: Derrida and the Philosophy of Reflection*. Cambridge: Harvard University Press, 1986.

Gates, Henry Louis, Jr. "Canon-Formation, Literary History, and the Afro-American Tradition." In *Afro-American Literary Study in the 1990s*. Eds. Houston A. Baker, Jr., and Patricia Redmond. Chicago: University of Chicago Press, 1990. 14–39.

————. "Criticism in the Jungle." In *Black Literature and Literary Theory*. New York: Methuen, 1984. 1–24.

————. "The Master's Pieces." In *Politics of Liberal Education*. Durham: Duke University Press, 1992. 95–118.

————. *The Signifying Monkey*. New York: Oxford University Press, 1988.

Genette, Gérard. *Figures III*. Paris: Seuil, 1972.

Gilbert, Sandra, and Susan Gubar. *No Man's Land: The Place of the Woman Writer in the Twentieth Century*. New Haven: Yale University Press, 1988.

Gilligan, Carol. *In a Different Voice*. Cambridge: Harvard University Press, 1982.

———. "Moral Orientation and Moral Development." In *Women and Moral Theory*. Eds. Eva Kittay and Diana Meyers. Totowa, N.J.: Rowman and Littlefield, 1987. 19–33.

Glaspell, Susan. "A Jury of Her Peers." In *Best Short Stories of 1917*. Ed. Edward J. O'Brien. Boston: Small, Maynard, 1918. 265–80.

Gooding-Williams, Robert. "Evading Narrative Myth, Evading Prophetic Pragmatism: Cornel West's *The American Evasion of Philosophy*." *Massachusetts Review* (1991–1992): 517–42.

Gordon, Linda. "Response to Joan Scott." *Signs* 15 (1990): 852–53.

Graff, Gerald. *Beyond the Culture Wars: How Teaching the Conflicts Can Revitalize American Education*. New York: Norton, 1992.

———. *Professing Literature: An Institutional History*. Chicago: University of Chicago Press, 1987.

Greimas, Algirdas Julien. *Structural Semantics: An Attempt at a Method*. Trans. Danielle McDowell, Ronald Schliefer, and Alan Velie. Lincoln: University of Nebraska Press, 1983.

Greenblatt, Stephen. "Capitalist Culture and the Circulatory System." In *The Aims of Representation*. Ed. Murray Krieger. New York: Columbia University Press, 1987.

Grosz, Elizabeth. "Julia Kristeva." In *Feminism and Psychoanalysis: A Critical Dictionary*. Ed. Elizabeth Wright. Cambridge: Blackwell, 1992. 194–200.

Guignon, Charles, ed. *The Cambridge Companion to Heidegger*. Cambridge: Cambridge University Press, 1993.

Gunn, Giles. *Culture of Criticism and the Criticism of Culture*. New York: Oxford University Press, 1987.

Gusdorf, Georges. *Les Origines de l'herméneutique*. Paris: Payot, 1988.

Guy-Shefthall, Beverly. *Words of Fire: An Anthology of African-American Feminist Thought*. New York: The New Press, 1995.

Habermas, Jürgen. *Autonomy and Solidarity: Interviews*. Ed. Peter Dews. New York: Verso, 1986.

———. *Communication and the Evolution of Society*. Trans. Thomas McCarthy. Boston: Beacon Press, 1979.

———. "The Hermeneutic Claim to Universality." In *The Hermeneutic Tradition*. Eds. Gayle Ormiston and Allan Schrift. Albany: SUNY Press, 1990. 245–72.

———. *Knowledge and Human Interests*. Trans. Jeremy Shapiro. Boston: Beacon Press, 1971.

———. *The Philosophical Discourse of Modernity*. Trans. Frederick Lawrence. Cambridge: MIT Press, 1987.

———. "Philosophy as Stand-In and Interpretation." In *After Philosophy: End or Transformation*. Cambridge: MIT Press, 1987. 296–315.

————. "A Postscript to Knowledge and Human Interests." *Philosophy and the Social Sciences* 3 (1973): 157–85.

————. "Reply to My Critics." In *Habermas: Critical Debates*. Eds. David Held and John Thompson. Cambridge: MIT Press, 1982. 219–83.

————. "A Review of Gadamer's *Truth and Method*. In *The Hermeneutic Tradition*. Eds. Gayle Ormiston and Allan Schrift. Albany: SUNY Press, 1990. 213–44.

————. "Questions and Counter-Questions." In *Habermas and Modernity*. Ed. Richard Bernstein. Cambridge: MIT Press, 1985. 192–216.

————. *The Theory of Communicative Action*. Trans. Thomas McCarthy. 2 vols. Boston: Beacon Press, 1983.

Heidegger, Martin. *The Basic Problems of Phenomenology*. Trans. Albert Hofstader. Bloomington: Indiana University Press, 1982.

————. *Being and Time*. Trans. John Macquarrie and Edward Robinson. New York: Harper and Row, 1962.

————. *An Introduction to Metaphysics*. Trans. Ralph Manheim. New York: Doubleday-Anchor, 1961.

————. "Letter on Humanism." In *Basic Writings*. Trans. David Krell. New York: Harper Row, 1977. 193–242.

————. *Nietzsche: The Will to Power as Art*. Trans. James S. Churchill. Bloomington: Indiana University Press, 1979.

————. *The Question Concerning Technology and Other Essays*. Trans. William Lovitt. New York: Harper and Row, 1977.

Henderson, Mae Gwendolyn. "Speaking in Tongues: Dialogics, Dialectics, and Black Woman Writer's Literary Tradition." In *Reading Black, Reading Feminist*. Ed. Henry Louis Gates, Jr. New York: Meridian, 1990. 116–42.

Hiley, David R., et al., eds. *The Interpretive Turn: Philosophy, Science, Culture*. Ithaca: Cornell University Press, 1991.

Hirsch, E. D., Jr. *The Aims of Interpretation*. Chicago: University of Chicago Press, 1976.

————. "Meaning and Significance Re-interpreted." Critical Inquiry 11 (1984): 202–25

————. *Validity in Interpretation*. New Haven: Yale University Press, 1967.

Hirschkop, Ken. Introduction. *Bakhtin and Cultural Theory*. Eds. Ken Hirschkop and David Shepherd. Manchester: Manchester University Press, 1989. 1–38.

Holub, Robert. *Jürgen Habermas: Critic in the Public Sphere*. New York: Routledge, 1991.

————. *Reception Theory: A Critical Introduction*. New York: Methuen, 1984.

hooks, bell. *Yearning: Race, Gender, and Cultural Politics*. Boston: South End Press, 1990.

Horkheimer, Max, and Theodor Adorno. *The Dialectic of Enlightenment*. Trans. John Cumming. New York: Seabury Press, 1972.

Hoy, David. *The Critical Circle: Literature, History, and Philosophical Hermeneutics*. Berkeley: University of California Press, 1978.

————. "Heidegger and the Hermeneutic Turn." In *The Cambridge Companion to Heidegger.* Ed. Charles Guignon. New York: Cambridge University Press, 1993. 170–94.

———. "A History of Consciousness: From Kant and Hegel to Derrida and Foucault." *History of the Human Sciences* 4 (1991): 261–81.

———. "Splitting the Difference: Habermas's Critique of Derrida." *Praxis International* 8 (1989): 447–64.

Iser, Wolfgang. *The Act of Reading: A Theory of Aesthetic Response.* Baltimore: Johns Hopkins University Press, 1978.

Jakobson, Roman. "Concluding Statement: Linguistics and Poetics." In *Style in Language.* Ed. Thomas Sebeok. Cambridge: MIT Press, 1960. 50–77.

James, Henry. *The Ambassadors.* New York: Norton, 1964.

———. *The Golden Bowl.* New York: Scribners, 1909.

Jameson, Fredric. *Ideologies of Theory.* Vol. 1. Minneapolis: University of Minnesota Press, 1988.

Jauss, Hans Robert. *Aesthetic Experience and Literary Hermeneutics.* Trans. Michael Shaw. Minneapolis: University of Minnesota Press, 1982.

———. *Toward an Aesthetic of Reception.* Trans. Timothy Bahti. Minneapolis: University of Minnesota Press, 1982.

Johnson, Barbara. *A World of Difference.* Baltimore: Johns Hopkins University Press, 1987.

———. "Thresholds of Difference: Structures of Address in Zora Neale Hurston." *"Race," Writing, and Difference.* Ed. Henry Louis Gates. Chicago: University of Chicago Press, 1986.

Kaelin, E. F. *Heidegger's Being and Time: A Reading for Readers.* Tallahassee, 1988.

Kahane, Claire. "Object-Relations Theory." In *Feminism and Psychoanalysis: A Critical Dictionary.* Ed. Elizabeth Wright. Cambridge: Basil Blackwell, 1992. 280–90.

Kant, Immanuel. *The Critique of Judgment.* Trans. Werner S. Pluhar. Indianapolis: Hackett, 1987.

———. *The Critique of Practical Reason.* Trans. Lewis White Beck. Indianapolis: Bobbs-Merrill, 1956.

———. *The Critique of Pure Reason.* Trans. Norman Kemp Smith. New York: St. Martin's Press, 1965.

———. *Groundwork of the Metaphysics of Morals.* Trans. H. J. Paton. New York: Harper and Row, 1964.

Kerber, Linda, et al. "On *In a Different Voice:* An Interdisciplinary Forum." *Signs* 11 (1986): 304–33.

Kermode, Frank. *An Appetite for Poetry.* Cambridge: Harvard University Press 1989.

———. *Forms of Attention.* Chicago: University of Chicago Press, 1985.

———. *History and Value.* New York: Oxford University Press, 1987.

Kolodny, Annette. "A Map for Misreading: Gender and the Interpretation of Literary Texts." In *The New Feminist Criticism.* Ed. Elaine Showalter. New York: Pantheon, 1985. 46–62.

Kristeva, Julia. *The Kristeva Reader.* Ed. Toril Moi. Oxford: Blackwell, 1986.

――――. "Psychoanalysis and the Polis." In *The Politics of Interpretation*. Ed. W. J. T. Mitchell. Chicago: University of Chicago Press, 1983. 83–98.

――――. *Revolution in Poetic Language*. Trans. Margaret Walker. New York: Columbia University Press, 1984.

――――. *Tales of Love*. Trans. Leon S. Roudiez. New York: Columbia University Press, 1987.

Kuykendall, Eleanor H. "Questions for Julia Kristeva's Ethics of Linguistics." In *Thinking Muse*. Eds. Jeffner Allen and Iris Marion Young. Bloomington: Indiana University Press, 1989. 180–94.

Lacan, Jacques. *The Four Fundamental Concepts of Psychoanalysis*. Trans. Alan Sheridan. New York: Norton, 1978.

――――. *Le Seminaire II, le moi dans la théorie de Freud*. Paris: Seuil, 1978.

Lauter, Paul. *Canons and Contexts*. New York: Oxford University Press, 1991.

Lawlor, James. *Imagination and Chance: The Difference between the Thought of Ricoeur and Derrida*. Albany: SUNY, 1992.

Leland, Dorothy. "Lacanian Psychoanalysis and French Feminism: Toward an Adequate Political Psychology." In *Revaluing French Feminism*. Ed. Nancy Fraser. Bloomington: Indiana University Press, 1992. 113–35.

Lionnet, Françoise. *Autobiographical Voices: Race, Gender, and Self-Portraiture*. Ithaca: Cornell University, 1985.

Lukes, Steven. *Marxism and Morality*. New York: Oxford University Press, 1985.

Lynn, Steven. *Texts and Contexts: Writing about Literature with Critical Theory*. New York: HarperCollins, 1994.

Lyotard, Jean François. "Answering the Question: What Is Postmodernism?" In *The Postmodern Condition*. 71–82.

――――. *Au juste*. Paris: Christian Bourgeois, 1979.

――――. *Le Différend*. Paris: Minuit, 1983.

――――. *The Différend: Phrases in Dispute*. Trans. Georges Van Den Abbeele. Minneapolis: University of Minnesota Press, 1988.

――――. *L'Enthousiasme: La critique kantienne de l'histoire*. Paris: Galilée, 1986.

――――. "Histoire universelle et différences culturelles." *Critique* 456 (1985): 559–68.

――――. "Interview." *Diacritics* 14 (1984a): 16–18.

――――. "Judiciousness in Dispute, or Kant after Marx." In *The Aims of Representation: Subject/Text/History*. Ed. Murray Krieger. New York: Columbia University Press, 1987.

――――. *The Postmodern Condition*. Trans. Geoff Bennington and Brian Massumi. Minneapolis: University of Minnesota Press, 1984b.

――――. *Le Postmoderne expliqué aux enfants*. Paris: Galilee, 1986.

MacIntyre, Aladair. *Three Rival Versions of Moral Enquiry: Encyclopedia, Genealogy, and Tradition*. Notre Dame: University of Notre Dame Press, 1990.

Marshall, Donald. *Contemporary Critical Theory: A Selective Bibliography*. New York: Modern Language Association, 1993.

McCarthy, Thomas. *Ideals and Illusions: On Reconstruction and Deconstruction in Contemporary Critical Theory*. Cambridge: MIT Press, 1991.

——— and David Hoy. *Critical Theory*. Cambridge: Blackwell, 1994.

McGowan, John. *Postmodernism and Its Critics*. Ithaca: Cornell University Press, 1990.

Meyers, Diana. "The Subversion of Women's Agency in Psychoanalytic Feminism: Chodorow, Flax, Kristeva." In *Revaluing French Feminism*. Ed. Nancy Fraser. 136–61.

Michelfelder, Dianne, and Richard Palmer, eds. *Dialogue and Deconstruction*. Albany: SUNY Press, 1989.

Miller J. Hillis. "But Are Things as We Think They Are?" (Review of *Time and Narrative*). *The Times Literary Supplement*, 9–15 October 1987: 1104–6

Miller, James. *The Passion of Michel Foucault*. New York: Anchor, 1993.

———. *Ethics of Reading*. New York: Columbia University Press, 1988.

Mohanty, S. P. "Us and Them: On the Philosophical Bases of Political Criticism." *Yale Journal of Criticism* 2 (1989): 1–31.

Morrison, Toni. *Playing in the Dark*. New York: Vintage, 1993.

Morson, Gary, and Caryl Emerson. *Mikhail Bakhtin: Creation of a Prosaics*. Stanford: Stanford University Press, 1990.

Mouffe, Chantal. *Radical Democracy*. New York: Verso, 1992.

———. *The Return of the Political*. New York: Verso, 1993.

Mueller-Vollmer, Kurt, ed. *The Hermeneutics Reader*. New York: Continuum, 1985.

Nehamus, Alexander. *Nietzsche: Life as Literature*. Cambridge: Harvard University Press, 1985.

Nietzsche, Friedrich. *Beyond Good and Evil*. Trans. Walter Kauffman. New York: Vintage, 1966.

———. *The Birth of Tragedy and The Genealogy of Morals*. Trans. Francis Golffing. Garden City, N.Y.: Doubleday, 1956.

———. *The Will to Power*. Trans. Walter Kaufmann and R. J. Hollingdale. New York: Vintage, 1968.

Okin, Susan. *Justice, Gender, and the Family*. New York: Basic Books, 1989.

Ormiston, Gayle L., and Alan D. Schrift, eds. *The Hermeneutic Tradition: From Ast to Ricoeur*. Albany: SUNY Press, 1990.

———. *Transforming the Hermeneutic Context: From Nietzsche to Nancy*. Albany: SUNY Press, 1990.

Palmer, Richard. *Hermeneutics: Interpretation Theory in Schleiermacher, Dilthey, Heidegger, and Gadamer*. Evanston: Northwestern University Press, 1969.

Parry, Benita. "Overlapping Territories and Intertwined Histories: Edward Said's Postcolonial Cosmopolitanism." In *Edward Said: A Critical Reader*. Ed. Michael Sprinker. Cambridge: Blackwell, 1992. 19–47.

———. "Problems in Current Theories of Colonial Discourse." *Oxford Literary Review* 9 (1987): 27–58

Pratt, Mary Louise. "Arts of the Contact Zone." *Profession* (1991): 33–40.

———. "Ideology and Speech-Act Theory." *Poetics Today* 7 (1986): 59–72.

———. "Linguistic Utopias." In *The Linguistics of Writing: Arguments Between Language and Literature*. Eds. Nigel Fabb et al. Manchester: University of Manchester Press, 1987. 48–66.

Prince, Gerald. *Narratology: The Form and Functioning of Narrative*. Berlin: Walter de Gruyter, 1982.

Rajchman, John. *Michel Foucault: The Freedom of Philosophy*. New York: Columbia University Press, 1985.

Rasmussen, David. *Reading Habermas*. Oxford: Basil Blackwell, 1990.

Ricoeur, Paul. *The Conflict of Interpretations: Essays in Hermeneutics*. Trans. Don Ihde et al. Evanston: Northwestern University Press, 1974.

———. *Du texte à l'action*. Paris: Seuil, 1986.

———. *Freud and Philosophy: An Essay on Interpretation*. Trans. Denis Savage. New Haven: Yale University Press, 1970.

———. *Interpretation Theory: Discourse and the Surplus of Meaning*. Fort Worth: Texas Christian University Press, 1976.

———. "On Interpretation." In *Philosophy in France Today*. Ed. Alan Montefiore. Cambridge: Cambridge University Press, 1983. 175–97.

———. "Psychoanalysis and the Movement of Contemporary Culture." In *Interpretive Social Science*. Eds. Paul Rabinow and William Sullivan. Berkeley: University of California Press, 1979.

———. *Hermeneutics and the Human Sciences*. New York: Cambridge University Press, 1981.

———. *The Rule of Metaphor*. Trans. Robert Czerny. Toronto: University of Toronto Press, 1977.

———. "The Teleological and Deontological Structures of Action: Aristotle and/or Kant." In *Contemporary French Philosophy*. Ed. A. Phillips Griffiths. Cambridge: Cambridge University Press, 1987. 99–112.

———. *Time and Narrative*. Trans. Kathleen Blarney and David Pellauer. 3 vols. Chicago: University of Chicago Press, 1984–88.

Rorty, Richard. *Contingency, Irony, and Solidarity*. Cambridge: Cambridge University Press, 1989.

———. *Essays on Heidegger and Others*. Cambridge: Cambridge University Press, 1991.

———. *Philosophy and the Mirror of Nature*. Princeton: Princeton University Press, 1979.

Rosenblum, Nancy. *Another Liberalism: Romanticism and the Reconstruction of Liberal Thought*. Cambridge: Harvard University Press, 1979.

Said, Edward. *Culture and Imperialism*. New York: Knopf, 1993.

———. *Orientalism*. New York: Pantheon, 1978.

———. *The World, the Text, and the Critic*. Cambridge: Harvard University Press, 1983.

"Interview with Edward Said." In *Edward Said: A Critical Reader*. Ed. Michael Sprinker. Cambridge: Blackwell, 1992. 221–64.

Salusinszky, Imre. "Interview with Edward Said." In *Criticism in Society*. Ed. Imre Salusinszky. New York: Methuen, 1987. 122–49.

Saussure, Ferdinand. *Course in General Linguistics*. Eds. Charles Bally and Albert Sechehaye. Trans. Wade Baskin. New York: McGraw-Hill, 1966.

Schaefer, Roy. *The Analytic Attitude*. New York: Basic Books, 1983.

Scholes, Robert. *Semiotics and Interpretation*. New Haven: Yale University Press, 1982.

Schott, Robin. "Whose Home Is It Anyway? A Feminist Response to Gadamer's Hermeneutics." In *Gadamer and Hermeneutics*. Ed. Hugh Silverman. New York: Routledge, 1991. 202–9.

Schrag, Calvin. *Communicative Praxis and the Space of Subjectivity*. Bloomington: Indiana University Press, 1985.

Scott, Joan. Review of Linda Gordon, *Heroes of Their Own Lives: The Politics and History of Family Violence*. *Signs* 15 (1990): 848–52.

Sedgwick, Eve. *The Epistemology of the Closet*. Berkeley: University of California Press, 1990.

Selden, Raman. *Practicing Theory and Reading Literature*. Lexington: University Press of Kentucky, 1989.

———. *A Reader's Guide to Contemporary Literary Theory*. 3d. ed. Lexington: University Press of Kentucky, 1993.

Shapiro, Gary, and Alan Sica, eds. *Hermeneutics: Questions and Prospects*. Amherst: University of Massachusetts Press, 1984.

Shlovsky, Victor. "Art as Device." In *Russian Formalist Criticism: Four Essays*. Eds. and trans. Lee T. Lemon and Marion J. Reis. Lincoln: University of Nebraska Press, 1965.

Sluga, Hans. *Heidegger's Crisis: Philosophy and Politics in Nazi Germany*. Cambridge: Harvard University Press, 1993.

Spivak, Gayatri. "Can the Subaltern Speak?" *Marxism and the Interpretation of Culture*. Urbana: University of Illinois, 1988. 271–313.

———. *In Other Worlds: Essays in Cultural Politics*. New York: Routledge, 1988.

Staton, Shirley. *Literary Theories in Praxis*. Philadelphia: University of Pennsylvania Press, 1987.

Steele, Meili. "The Dangers of Structuralist Narratology: Genette's Misinterpretation of Proust." *Romance Notes* 26 (1986): 1–7.

———. "Explanation, Understanding, and Incommensurability in Psychoanalysis." *Analecta Husserliana* 41 (1994): 367–76.

———. "How Philosophy of Language Informs Ethics and Politics: Richard Rorty and Contemporary Theory." *boundary 2* 20 (1993): 140–72.

———. "Language and African American Culture: The Need for Meta-Philosophical Reflection." *Philosophy Today* 40 (1996): 179–87

———. "Lyotard's Politics of the Sentence." *Cultural Critique* 16 (1990): 193–214.

———. "The Ontological Turn and Its Ethical Consequences: Habermas and the Poststructuralists." *Praxis International* 11 (1992): 428–46.

———. "Ontologie linguistique et dialogue politique chez Bakhtine." In *Mikhail Bakhtine et la pensée dialogique*. Eds. André Collinot et Clive Thomson. Ontario: Mestengo Press, forthcoming.

———. Review of Barbara Herrnstein Smith, *Contingencies of Value: Alternative Perspectives for Critical Theory*. *Comparative Literature* 44 (1992): 105–8.

———. *Theorizing Textual Subjects: Agency and Oppression*. Cambridge: Cambridge University Press, 1997.

Steiner, Peter. *Russian Formalism: A Metapoetics*. Ithaca: Cornell University Press, 1984.

Taylor, Charles. *Human Agency and Language*. Cambridge: Cambridge University Press, 1985.

———. *Multiculturalism and the Politics of Recognition*. Princeton: Princeton University Press, 1992.

———. *Sources of the Self*. Cambridge: Harvard University Press, 1989.

———. "Understanding and Explanation in the *Geisteswissenschaften*." In *Wittgenstein: To Follow a Rule*. Ed. S. Holtzman and C. Leich. 198–210.

———. "The Validity of Transcendental Arguments." *Proceedings of the Aristotlean Society* 79 (1978–79): 151–65.

———. "What's Wrong with Negative Freedom?" In *Philosophical Papers*. Vol. 2. Cambridge: Cambridge University Press, 1985. 211–29.

Todorov, Tzvetan. *Grammaire du Decameron*. The Hague: Mouton, 1969.

———. *The Poetics of Prose*. Trans. Richard Howard. Ithaca: Cornell University Press, 1977.

Wachterhauser, Brice R., ed. *Hermeneutics and Modern Philosophy*. Albany: SUNY Press, 1986.

Warnke, Georgia. *Gadamer: Hermeneutics, Tradition, and Reason*. Cambridge: MIT Press, 1987.

Weinsheimer, Joel. *Gadamer's Hermeneutics: A Reading of Truth and Method*. New Haven: Yale University Press, 1985.

———. *Philosophical Hermeneutics and Literary Theory*. New Haven: Yale University Press, 1991.

Wellek, René, and Austin Warren. *Theory of Literature*. New York: Harcourt Brace, 1949.

Wellmer, Albrecht. "Models of Freedom in the Modern World." *Philosophical Forum* 21 (1989–90): 227–52.

West, Cornel. *The American Evasion of Philosophy*. Madison: University of Wisconsin Press, 1989.

———. "Black Leadership and the Pitfalls of Racial Reasoning." In *Race-ing Justice, En-Gendering Power*. Ed. Toni Morrison. New York: Pantheon, 1992. 390–401.

———. *The Ethical Dimensions of Marxist Thought*. New York: Monthly Review Press, 1991.

———. "Ethics and Action in Jameson's Marxist Hermeneutics." In *Postmodern and Politics*. Ed. Jonathan Arac. Minneapolis: University of Minnesota Press, 1986. 123–44.

———. *Keeping Faith: Philosophy and Race in America*. New York: Routledge, 1993.

———. "Malcolm X and Black Rage." In *Malcolm X: In Our Own Image*. Ed. Joe Wood. New York: St. Martin's, 1992. 48–58.

———. "The Politics of American Neo-Pragmatism." In *Post-Analytic Philosophy*. 259–75.

———. *Prophesy Deliverance: An Afro-American Revolutionary Christianity*. Philadelphia: Westminster, 1982.

Wimsatt, William K., Jr. *The Verbal Icon: Studies in the Meaning of Poetry*. Lexington: University Press of Kentucky, 1954.

Wolin, Richard. *The Politics of Being: The Political Thought of Martin Heidegger*. New York: Columbia University Press, 1990.

Wood, Allen. "Habermas's Defense of Rationalism." *New German Critique* 35 (1985): 145–64.

Yack, Bernard. *The Longing for Total Revolution: Philosophic Sources of Discontent from Rousseau to Marx and Nietzsche*. Princeton: Princeton University Press, 1986.

Young, Iris Marion. "Humanism, Gynocentricism, and Feminist Politics." In *Hypatia Reborn: Essays in Feminist Philosophy*. Eds. Azizah Y. Al-Hibriand and Margaret Simons. Bloomington: Indiana University Press, 1990. 231–48.

———. *Justice and the Politics of Difference*. Princeton: Princeton University Press, 1990.

Index